PIPELINE POPULISM

PIPELINE
Grassroots Environmentalism
POPULISM
in the Twenty-First Century

KAI BOSWORTH

University of Minnesota Press | Minneapolis | London

Portions of chapter 1 were originally published as "'They're Treating Us like Indians!' Political Ecologies of Property and Race in North American Pipeline Populism," *Antipode* 53, no. 3 (2021): 665–85. Portions of chapter 4 were originally published as "The People Know Best: Situating the Counterexpertise of Populist Pipeline Opposition Movements," *Annals of the American Association of Geographers* 109, no. 2 (2019): 581–92; reprinted by permission of the publisher, Taylor and Francis Ltd., http://www.tandfonline.com.

Published by the University of Minnesota Press
111 Third Avenue South, Suite 290
Minneapolis, MN 55401-2520
http://www.upress.umn.edu

ISBN 978-1-5179-1105-8 (hc)
ISBN 978-1-5179-1106-5 (pb)

A Cataloging-in-Publication record for this book is available from the Library of Congress.

Printed in the United States of America on acid-free paper

The University of Minnesota is an equal-opportunity educator and employer.

CONTENTS

PREFACE AND ACKNOWLEDGMENTS

HOW SHOULD WE UNDERSTAND the changing—and frequently ambivalent—role of environmentalism in shaping political responses to fossil fuel infrastructure? It is easy to conceive of the current situation through a political and moral opposition: on the one hand, we have bad forces like oil companies, and on the other hand, we have an embattled righteous collective protagonist. It is the people versus the pipelines, a classically populist setup. Such narrative structures can be helpful in sharpening the divide between friend and foe, which some theorists take to be the heart of political activity and group identity. However, the contention of this book is that such narratives are too crude, as the story is more complicated and dynamic. Understandings of friend and foe change over time; collectives must be forged and can be rather unstable. Historical, economic, and material contexts shape who might become enrolled in such political activity, for what reasons, and with what baggage. The political stakes of opposition can paper over deep contradictions in the visions and demands of any given group. Attending to populist environmentalism as one orientation in a dynamic, processual field of stylistic conventions and differential forms of opposition helps us understand how it has reshaped climate politics, with aspirational consequences as well as missteps and limitations. I will unpack this argument throughout the rest of this book, hoping to convince that populist environmentalism is an adequate descriptor of one tendency of pipeline resistance and contemporary climate politics, a helpful analytic for diagnosing the shortcomings of the cycle of climate justice struggles from 2009 to 2016. In this short preface, I reflectively situate this argument within my own political, economic, historical, and intellectual context.

I first learned of the Keystone pipeline system in 2007 or 2008 when a group of students from the University of South Dakota in Vermillion visited Minnesota and shared an account of their battle against the Keystone I system. As a student at Macalester College in Saint Paul, I was involved in political organizing with other youth around the country interested in halting new fossil fuel infrastructure while affirming a vision of an environmentally just future. We had delayed and ultimately canceled the construction of the Big Stone II coal plant just over the border in my home state of South Dakota, a huge regional victory. We were also working with several national groups in the Youth Climate Movement—such as Power Shift, the Energy Action Coalition, and the Sierra Student Coalition—to try to push federal climate legislation and to constitute a left environmental justice edge to older, more inertial green groups. We thought (perhaps with youthful naivete) that we were pushing these organizations—and the movement more broadly—toward better recognition of the necessity of working-class, Black, and Indigenous leadership in the climate struggle and the inextricability of addressing inequality in any framework addressing climate change.

Despite some crucial victories, however, many of us increasingly became disaffected with the nonprofit-influenced orientation toward lobbying and legislation. Our fears seemed to bear out in experience, as the Obama administration's weak push for bipartisan climate legislation failed and the Copenhagen Accord of 2009 included no mandatory targets. Meanwhile, organizing within the Youth Climate Movement was thornier than expected. The second Power Shift conference in 2009 brought over ten thousand youth to Washington, D.C., to plan and strategize how to exert our power. But despite the increased focus on environmental justice issues led by groups like Van Jones's Green for All and the intertribal Black Mesa Water Coalition, Power Shift was a different experience for some Indigenous activists. One session meant to create space for Indigenous participants alone was resisted by schedulers, resulting in several hundred non-Indigenous people packing the room. An emotional and tense talkback ensued, in which Indigenous youth described to the diverse young audience the persistent ignorance of the broader climate movement toward the horizons of Indigenous struggle. By contrast, the multifaceted movements present at the 2010 U.S. Social Forum in Detroit shimmered with possibilities.

Together these experiences prompted me to turn toward research to try to understand the persistent racial structures of environmentalism in popular movements, on the one hand, and the history of environmental injustice in South Dakota, on the other. I held a brief summer internship at the Minneapolis office of Honor the Earth, a tribal environmental justice advocacy organization, where I contributed to a project to uncover the debilitating effects of the U.S. military on Indigenous lands (see LaDuke and Cruz 2013). At the same time, I increasingly heard of resistance to new oil pipelines and uranium mining in the Dakotas, along with a push for wind power by Indigenous leaders. This led me to conceive of an academic research project that might further uncover the history and present of western South Dakota as an energy landscape "sacrifice zone" (LaDuke and Churchill 1985). Over the years, the meandering project transformed several times as the resistance to Keystone XL (KXL) grew: Was it a study of liberal strategies of environmental governance, of the biopolitics of environmental racism in settler colonialism, of the limits of pluralistic multiculturalism, of the nexus of state violence and oil economics? I was overwhelmed by the thought of becoming "the pipeline guy," so I was thankful to find at conferences more and more scholars studying aspects of these pipeline resistance movements (McCreary and Milligan 2014; Grant 2014; Holmes 2017; Kojola 2017; Pasternak and Dafnos 2018; Spice 2018; Estes 2019; LeQuesne 2019; Benton-Connell and Cochrane 2020; Simpson and Le Billon 2021). The emergence of this network of scholarship allowed me to focus on what I finally remembered was the initial object of study: environmentalism. This focus means that less attention is given in this book to conservatives and the political right, the state, the oil industry, and Indigenous-led resistance as some readers might expect. This is certainly not because these do not need attention, and I do address some of these aspects elsewhere (Bosworth, forthcoming; Bosworth and Chua 2021).

The economic context of this research also shaped my approach. I was grateful to receive predissertation research from the Social Science Research Council, and the University of Minnesota Department of Geography also supported summer research at strategic points. Nonetheless, I did not benefit from the kind of yearlong research support that most scholars usually seek. Frustratingly, in the summer of 2015, I found that it was easier to secure funding to travel to South Africa and Palestine than funding that would support living and traveling around the Upper Midwest. It was crucial for me to learn from comrades in these places—each of which I learned had somewhat analogous settler colonial pasts and presents to that of South Dakota. Nonetheless, I was troubled by this pattern in research funding. Finally in 2016, I decided to self-fund my research, channeling money from my teaching assistant position, a second job with a catering company, and a third job as a researcher with the Natural History Museum to support extended research in the Dakotas and Iowa from May to November.

I point this out not to elicit sympathy or excuses for my position but rather because some scholars seem unaware of the shifting political economy of academic research and the effects this has on where—and what kind—of geographical knowledge is produced. As I write this preface in 2021, universities around the country have instituted hiring freezes. Many remain increasingly dependent on graduate students and adjunct faculty to fill teaching gaps while refusing to raise salaries to match changes in cost of living or even inflation. Graduate students and precarious faculty are increasingly put at risk of losing their jobs when advocating for better work conditions via unionization, attenuation of campus policing, or combating university roles in urban gentrification, to name but a few. In 2020, the National Science Foundation Human-Environment and Geographical Sciences Program announced that it would no longer fund research that used "predominantly humanistic, non-scientific framings and methods" and suggested that "research that is predominantly post-modern, post-structural, humanistic etc., is not a good fit for NSF," incurring significant pushback from our discipline (National Science Foundation 2020). These and other conditions are shaping the stories we tell and recognize as legitimate, influencing who is understood as a knowledge producer. They demand wide-ranging changes to our discipline and the conditions of our labor.

Nonetheless, despite some adverse conditions, I remain singularly responsible for this research and writing. I was driven to do this research by three commitments. First, I understand myself as in some ways constituted by the historic arc of environmentalism and climate justice activism that I describe. Second, because my life has been shaped by the settler colonial landscape and political economy of western South Dakota, I feel responsible to that place as well. The inheritance and responsibility that such a position demands should not be borne by an individual, though I am certain that it constitutes blind spots and stylistic as well as political constraints on this narrative. The book cannot help but be a kind of immanent critique of aspects of my context. Though such introspection could come off as navel gazing, I hope that instead it is read as a set of responsibilities to my interlocutors, positioning ideology critique not as a moral chiding from an exterior vantage but instead as a careful sussing out of elements that make up the affective infrastructure of politics, in all its excitement and constraints.

Still, a third commitment also exists somewhat adjacent to the work: the methodologies of Marxist political theory and, consequently, a desire to make revolutionary socialist and communist struggle conditions of this thought. *Pipeline Populism* is not a work of scholar-activism but what I hope to be a sympathetic critique from a vantage point conditioned by revolutionary strategies and tactics, frustrations and joys, organizations and ideologies. I expect young people of all kinds might see aspects of themselves and their movements in this book, and in that way it might provoke introspection concerning our strategies. Ideology critique here functions as an immanent practice of understanding the material and ideological conditions of possibility for political struggle, reflecting in an interregnum on what we might change in the future.

Every Spinozist introduction must begin by noting that by definition "common notions" emerge from webs of relationships, which I trace here for intellectual genealogy and gratitude alike. For advising this project, Arun Saldanha has my unending appreciation. Arun guided my research through its messiest phases, pushing me to hone and distill it to the sharpest end possible by producing my own concepts. Bruce Braun, Vinay Gidwani, and Ajay Skaria funneled my unending and frequently disjointed enthusiasm for reading theory into a more precise research project. Their kindness and generosity in attending to my wayward thought and practice has been remarkable, and they will find many of their initial questions expanded on below. The broader University of Minnesota intellectual community, now or soon far-flung, formed the condition of possibility for laughter and survival alike: I think in particular of Morgan Adamson, Ateeb Ahmed, Nikhil Anand, Tony Brown, Valentine Cadieux, Cesare Casarino, Charmaine Chua, Jacqui Daigneault, Kate Derickson, Stacy Douglas, Joshua Eichen, Sinan Erensü, Anjali Ganapathy, Joe Getzoff, George Henderson, Chase Hobbs-Morgen, Mingwei Huang, Jen Hughes, David Hugill, Simi Kang, Laura Matson, Stuart McLean, Devika Narayan, Sara Nelson, Julie Santella, Lisa Santosa, Stephen Savignano, and Mike Simpson. A special mention must go to Lalit Batra, Laura Cesafsky, Julia Corwin, Spencer Cox, Jessi Lehman, and Bill Lindeke. I would have happily continued my PhD for another eight years if you all had not left. Many of us met in classrooms, as well as two particularly important collectives for this project: the Spinoza Scholarship Group and the Theoretical Humanities Collective.

At the Institute at Brown for Environment and Society, conversations with Brian Lander, Myles Lennon, Elizabeth Lord, and Timmons Roberts helped me clarify the stakes of this project; I am deeply saddened that Elizabeth is not here with us to share it. In Providence, Rhode Island, more generally, Mary Tuti Baker, Kylie Benton-Connell, Kylie King, Thea Riofrancos, Damian White, and Brett Zehner helped me chew through difficult concepts and contexts. A whole host of comrades too long to list invited me to organize and agitate in a new and unfamiliar context—especially at the George Wiley Center. At Virginia Commonwealth University, Mark Wood and Jesse Goldstein have each been crucial sounding boards for shaping the ultimate argument of this work. Jesse advocated for its importance at critical moments. Our conversations and coteaching sharpened how I write about emotion and affect in climate politics. Rohan Kalyan and Aspen Brinton further helped me understand how "populism" would be read, serving as important sounding boards at crucial moments.

I am further humbled by the incredible generosity of Nic Beuret, Jesse Goldstein, Rohan Kalyan, Ben Rubin, Levi Van Sant, and Brett Zehner for reading chapters in the midst of the debilitating pandemic. Aspects of this book's main argument were presented at the Royal Geographical Society in 2017. I tested some of the arguments at the Pipeline Safety Trust Conference in New Orleans; Jeffrey Insko graciously introduced me to this industry-advocacy angle. Chapter 1 benefits from a presentation at the University of Richmond Unsettling Ecologies speaker series, and I thank Nathan Snaza and Julietta Singh for fostering conversation. Earlier versions of these arguments were read by Levi Van Sant, Richard Milligan, and Katherine McKittrick upon their publication in *Antipode* and much later by a group of brilliant political ecologists led by Jared Margulies and Sophie Sapp Moore at Dimensions of Political Ecology. In particular, I thank Carrie Mott for generous and generative facilitation. Aspects of chapter 2 were first presented at a 2016 University of California, Berkeley workshop, "Fossil Fuels and Radical Sovereignties: Boardrooms, Blockades, and Jurisdictional Struggles over Oil and Gas Development in 'North America.'" Tyler McCreary and Philippe Le Billon organized, and conversations with Nick Estes and Shiri Pasternak also changed my thinking in important ways. Aspects of chapter 3 were presented at a 2020 American Association of Geographers panel skillfully taken online after the beginning of the pandemic by Gabe Schwartzman and Gretchen Sneegas.

Pipeline Populism simply would not have happened without the encouragement and guidance of Jason Weidemann at the University of Minnesota Press. It took a while for me to gain the confidence that this was a book, and Jason's belief in the project helped steer it to a readable end. Lida Maxwell generously read the entire book, perceptively noting where it ought to be strengthened. Unending thanks for this work. Finally, Zenyse Miller patiently guided me through the production process.

For transforming my thought and politics, I must especially thank comrades from Out of the Woods, Antipode Geographies of Justice, Anthropocene Campus, and World of Matter. The Natural History Museum, especially Beka Economopoulos, Jason Jones, and Steve Lyons, reshaped my understanding of politics and aesthetics. Intellectual passion emerged from a series of conversations with an itinerant and patchwork community of thinkers: not already mentioned, I must acknowledge Patrick Bigger, Angie Carter, Nigel Clark, Nicole Fabricant, Carrie Freshour, Omar Jabary Salamanca, Elizabeth Johnson, AM Kanngieser, Angela Last, Sophie Lewis, Christopher Lizotte, Nerve Mapascap, Annabelle Marcovici, Daniela Marini, Harlan Morehouse,

Isobel Plowright, Rory Rowan, Sara Smith, and Kathryn Yusoff. Finally, I would not even be thinking at all without having had the guidance of Roopali Phadke and Stephanie Rutherford at Macalester College.

Extremely special thanks to my parents, from whom my dedication to this world emerged. I could not have conducted this research without various waylays at their house in Spearfish. My mom deserves further credit for finding, saving, and mailing hundreds of local news articles to me, wherever in the world I was at the time.

This research was conducted on the traditional and occupied lands of the Oceti Sakowin Oyate, the Ponca, and the Ojibwe people, and was written on the lands of the Narragansett, Wampanoag, and Powhatan people—without consent. This book's existence (and my own) emerges within settler colonialism as an enduring structure. I hope aspects of this work are responsible to this inheritance.

This project is dedicated to the friends, interlocutors, and comrades here, there, and around the world. You know who you are, and I hope this contributes to our solidarity.

ABBREVIATIONS

DAPL	Dakota Access Pipeline
DRA	Dakota Rural Action
EIS	environmental impact statement
ERM	Environmental Resources Management
ETP	Energy Transfer Partners
I&R	initiative and referendum
KXL	Keystone XL pipeline
NEPA	National Environmental Policy Act
PUC	public utilities commission

INTRODUCTION
AFFECTIVE INFRASTRUCTURES OF POPULIST ENVIRONMENTALISM

A LIVELY POLITICAL GENRE of ecological and climate politics has grown in recent years: populist environmentalism. Rather than advocating individualistic behavioral changes, incremental national or international policy shifts, or radical cells fostering direct action or sabotage, we have seen desires for a mass movement of the people to confront the climate crisis. Consider the student climate strikes of September 2019, inspired by Greta Thunberg but led by a bevy of the youth of the world. Or the push for a transformative Green New Deal, sparked by the savvy politics of the Sunrise Movement and Alexandria Ocasio-Cortez, who says she "first started considering running for Congress, actually, at Standing Rock in North Dakota" (Solnit 2019). Maybe you attended an iteration of the People's Climate March in New York City or elsewhere in 2014 and 2015, or perhaps earlier cycles of struggle that inspired these, such as the 2010 World People's Conference on Climate Change and the Rights of Mother Earth, held in Cochabamba, Bolivia. Indigenous peoples led these marches, youth from small islands and coastal environmental justice communities spoke of the extermination of their places and languages, migrants diagnosed the connections between rising waters and rising border walls. At these events, you might have heard "righteous Left-populist rage about the havoc that corporations and the wealthy have wreaked on our lives" (Aronoff et al. 2019, 178). You might have learned about "people power," about reclaiming our institutions, about the theft of our future by corporations, politicians, and the rich (Prakash 2020). At these events, what was at stake was not so much a new definition of nature. It is even possible, as Naomi Klein suggests, that such actions "shouldn't be referred to as an environmental movement at all, since [they are] primarily driven by a desire for a deeper form of democracy" (2014, 295). You might have even heard Klein speak these words at one of the above events.

These scenes of climate uprisings take part in a populist genre of politics, more so than other sorts of so-called environmentalism; public figures like Klein acknowledge this when they hope for a "sustained and populist climate movement" (2014, 157). By *populist environmentalism,* I wish to indicate a generalized antielitism or antiestablishment character of these movements that sought change not through technoscientific policy but through a multiracial coalitional politics of grassroots mass democracy: a politics of "the people." This book seeks to understand one of the key events through which the populist genre of environmental politics emerged: the struggle against the Keystone XL (KXL) and Dakota Access (DAPL) oil pipelines on the Great Plains. You may already know that contestation of these pipelines gathered in resistance a coalition of progressives, farmers and ranchers, environmentalists, and Native Nations, though not necessarily always with the same objectives in mind. These two pipelines were proposed, respectively, to bring bitumen from the Alberta tar sands and fracked light crude from North Dakota to refineries on the Gulf Coast and in Illinois. But in planning routes across the sparsely populated, politically conservative Upper Midwest region (North Dakota, South Dakota, Nebraska, and Iowa), infrastructure corporations might not have expected organized political opposition. Between 2009 and 2016, the grievances against these pipelines were organized into a series of moments and then movements that pitted the people against the pipelines. Though aspects of this story are undeniably true, it is a partial and at times uncomplicated portrait. This book argues that there were and remain difficulties in successfully constructing such a left-populist environmentalism. Reflecting in detail on the complexity of these struggles is crucial for climate activists, especially since the broader politics of populist environmentalism often ties their theories of change to lessons learned from this movement (e.g., Prakash 2020). It is further critical, of course, because we cannot adequately address the root causes of the climate crisis that underpin such pipeline build-outs without reflecting on political strategy.

Below, I will argue that there are sufficient reasons to evaluate one tendency of the movement as populist based on its rhetoric and action (including that some individuals and organizations called themselves "populists"). First, however, I want to be clear upfront: not all pipeline opposition draws upon the generic scenes of populist environmentalism. The field of political-ideological struggle over pipelines and climate politics alike is dynamic and fractured; even within the Global North there are, as Guha and Martinez-Alier (1997) influentially argue, numerous "varieties of environmentalism." For example, most of the so-called Big Greens approached pipeline struggles with their old tools: petitions, litigation, membership drives. On another hand, anarchists and other radical environmentalists, anticapitalists, and co-conspirators in decolonization sought to prevent pipeline construction through direct action. Native Nations opposed the pipelines on the grounds of tribal sovereignty, land-based modes of life, anticolonial and socialist traditions, and opposition to colonial sexual violence. There are good reasons to account for each of these elements in ways that do not flatten their different orientations. Indigenous and non-Indigenous scholars have rightly centered what Nick Estes (Kul Wicasa) calls "the long tradition of Indigenous resistance" in the wake of the massive and inspiring blockade of DAPL (Estes 2019; see also Estes and Dhillon 2019; Gilio-Whitaker 2019; Grossman 2017; Whyte 2017). Indigenous struggles augur the broader transformations needed for addressing the roots of ecological crisis, which entail not a separate ecological new social movement but an increasingly concatenated radical dismantling of the interlinking and differentiating world systems of racial capitalism and settler colonialism.

Although the orientations of Big Greens, Native Nations, and radical anarchists and anticapitalists are not populist, they sometimes overlapped with—and sometimes contradicted—more populist political genres. So, attending to the populist tendency of pipeline resistance enriches our understanding of the stakes and struggles of contemporary climate politics. In the Midwest, pipeline populism emerged from and mobilized desires to defend private property from eminent domain, to relocate political power in grassroots participation, to demonize the involvement of Canadian oil corporations and Chinese finance, and to develop practices of intervention in scientific review. *Pipeline Populism* argues that these politics were shaped by "affective infrastructures"— underlying emotions emerging from spaces and situations—that produced a collective sense of "the people." My analysis of populist environmentalisms examines the promise and pitfalls of such a political genre composed by scenes in which a mass movement of "the people" reclaims democracy from elites, corporations, and the political establishment: Rural landowners do not always possess the same understandings of land and stewardship as Native Nations. Individuals and groups across the political spectrum approach institutional processes like public participation meetings and evidentiary hearings with different levels of enthusiasm and forms of political organization. And the enemy of the opposition groups was sometimes located in a foreign outsider. If it is a desire for deeper democracy that increasingly orients populist environmentalisms, then this book asks: Out of what relationships did such desires and grievances that form pipeline populism emerge? What do these affective infrastructures tell us about populism and environmentalism, respectively? And with what consequences not only for environmentalism but also for building a strategy for a "popular" international socialist revolution desperately needed for adequate climate justice?

Answering such questions helps explain how a populist environmentalism can concurrently transform regressive aspects of ecological politics and defend aspects of the status quo of settler colonialism. Environmentalism has long had a sordid relationship with Indigenous movements for emancipation and decolonization. Settler environmentalists have turned toward Native Nations for spiritual, political, and ethical guidance, seeking alternative modes of relation with the earth and its nonhuman inhabitants, but they have not frequently done so with adequate respect. As Dina Gilio-Whitaker (Colville Confederated Tribes) explains, settler environmentalists of the 1970s "unconsciously brought with them worldviews and behavior patterns that were inconsistent with Indigenous paradigms and tried to fit Indigenous worldviews and practices into their own cognitive frameworks" (2019, 104). Geographer Andrew Curley (Diné) shows how dominant settler interpretations of Indigenous political struggle as environmentalism displace the centrality of anticolonial political sovereignty to Indigenous resistance to pipelines and related movements (Curley 2019; see also Harkin and Lewis 2007). This is important because the framing of such struggle contributes to perceived or real solidarity with Indigenous movements—or lack thereof (Mott 2016; Curnow and Helferty 2018). Commenting on KXL resistance in a 2015 interview, political theorist Glen Coulthard (Yellowknives Dene) said this struggle should "not be framed as simply an environmental issue but one of decolonization and framed through the lens of indigenous sovereignty. It's too easy for environmentalists to play their ally card in a very instrumental way" (Coulthard and Epstein 2015). By separating environmentalism and even environmental justice from broader spheres of Indigenous, anticapitalist political struggle, settlers can produce reductive, limited, and harmful engagements with the normative relational grounds that Indigenous struggles uphold. This does not mean that collaboration between Indigenous nations and settlers is impossible. Rather, the political and ontological frameworks through which that collaboration is understood need to be broached in a conscious and nuanced manner (Larsen and Johnson 2017).

To say *Pipeline Populism* is a study of only environmentalism is thus a partial description, especially since many pipeline opponents understood themselves as populists rather than as environmentalists. Instead, this book is a study of populism as one of several dynamic varieties of settler environmental politics. Although populist environmentalisms frequently criticize the elite, white, settler environmentalisms of the past, they do not inherit a blank slate or innocent subject, easily claiming the "ally card," as Coulthard puts it. By posing the solution to climate injustice in mass movements of "we the people" reclaiming democracy, populist environmentalism risks renewing a different format of whiteness. In this situation, it is not (white) elitism but the popular "we" that, though aspirationally coalitional, still allows white settlers to think of themselves as transcending history. Demonstrating the failures of settler politics might seem all too easy from an external position, reinforcing critical distance, melancholia, or even racial nihilisms that I do not espouse. Furthermore, academic language and modes of analysis can reinforce charges of elitism that populists decry. Consequently, I attend to populist aspects of the movement by showing how the genre's openness and flexibility sometimes presaged internal contradictions, such as grappling with the limitations of democracy in the context of ongoing settler colonialism. As described in the preface, I have no liberty for critical distance anyway, given my involvement with climate politics and background in South Dakota.

But why analyze this tendency of environmental rhetoric and activism as populism? *Populism* is a contemporary buzzword. Liberal pundits and political theorists use populism to describe, diagnose, and dismiss all manner of demagogic politicians, left and right, who seek to represent the will or interests of "the people" as corrupt or out-of-touch elitists. Raised in South Dakota, I understood populism to instead hearken back to the subjugated history of grassroots, progressive struggles beginning with the Farmers' Alliance of the late 1800s, which was particularly potent in the prairie states of the Upper Midwest. When describing populist environmentalism, I am interested instead in the principled reaction against the elite, institution-driven discourse on science and policy by an aspirationally multicultural, grassroots, transnational struggle for climate justice using the language of "the people." Populist environmentalism can be understood as a kind of left populism, described by Chantal Mouffe (2018) as a "strategy" for radicalizing democracy, a flexible, open-ended, but realistic movement to reclaim popular sovereignty in a time of global reaction. Left populism has a fundamentally different understanding of "the people," democracy, and political leadership than the right, which always mobilizes "the people" against not only the elites but some outside group.

Inverting a pundit's negative ascription of populism, the journalist Thomas Frank retorts that "populism isn't the name for this disease; it's the cure" (2018; see also 2020, 6). Though many reasons to critique liberal antipopulism exist, I argue populism is more complicated than either disease or cure: its power to transform the subjects it produces depends on the contextual situation in which it emerges. Advocates of left populism desire to be popular, but in doing so they explicitly create disciplinary mechanisms that hinder the creation of anticapitalist and revolutionary socialist struggles—which they take to be self-evidently unpopular (Mouffe 2018, 50). While such left populists understand the central role of affect to politics, they posit desires as relatively unchangeable. Thus, they orient their politics to an imagined "regular person" or "common man": invariably nationalist in some way, skeptical of the left, uninterested in radical tactics. Left populists argue that radicals would rather be right than win.

Though some populists think of themselves as socialists, political Marxists today are skeptical that "the people" is the subject capable of producing transformative political culture and material redistribution that is desperately needed. By refusing to name a particular, properly political subject like the proletariat, populism is argued to be too vague to enact an exact justice (Swyngedouw 2010, 224). Defenders of left populism today also largely agree they are not Marxists. Thomas Frank says of U.S. populism that "it is *our* radical tradition, a homegrown Left that spoke our American vernacular and worshipped at the shrines of Jefferson and Paine rather than Marx" (2020, 33). Though this book will defend Marxist ideology critique, I admit that Marxists can move quickly to denunciation, forgoing analysis that would explain how and why populism might emerge rather than (or alongside) a working-class movement for socialism. Rather than positing a simplistic class struggle, we should aspire to the classic analysis of populism in Marx's *The Eighteenth Brumaire of Louis Napoleon.* In this text, we do not find a simplistic bifurcation of class interests, but as Stuart Hall (2016, 96) reminds us, a series of dynamic "social movements, social groupings, alliances, and blocs." Marx offers a complex (and not entirely optimistic!) portrait of the class influences on political struggle. Yet the Marxist framework remains, in my mind, the crucial analytic for pinpointing the structural source of ecological destruction in rapacious colonial and racist exploitation of land and labor (J. Moore 2015; Barca 2020).

Given the latter is apparent to many around the world, why do we not have a more popular mass mobilization against fossil fuels and the governments that entrench their use? As with populism, Marxist scholarly and popular assessments of environmentalism and ecosocialism—and why they are not more popular—have not always been convincing. Marxist theories of ideology sometimes posit that the masses have been hoodwinked, and thus all we have to do is unmask the villain in a Scooby-Doo cartoon to see—a ha!—it was capitalism all along. This book resuscitates a different version of ideology critique by elaborating upon Lauren Berlant's provocative suggestion that "affect theory is another phase in the history of ideology theory" (2011, 53). Accounting for the entanglement of emotion and politics forms one of the oldest political quandaries. In the seventeenth century, the philosopher Baruch Spinoza grappled with understanding why it seems that people fight for their servitude as much as their freedom. His immediate answer was superstition (a form of ideology) misleads or distorts the truth. This argument has made his thought appealing to rationalists and liberals, enduring in our era where distrust of the masses prevails. But behind this shorthand explanation, Spinoza gives a far more complex account of the interplay of bodies, ideas, and emotions. Though we desire collective emancipation, we also are condemned to fight for what we think will make us free or provide us joy. We are torn asunder by the inconstancy of the relationship between thought (ideas, imaginaries, concepts) and extension (collectively composed bodies, social and more-than-human). Consequently, our imagination is always fluctuating because it is never fully adequate to the dynamic world, frequently allowing obscure and confused causes to appear real. The latter beget sad passions, like fear of doubt, failure, or death.

If this is the case, scholars of emotion and affect ought to benefit from an engagement with historical materialism, and vice versa. Ideology critique untangles the affective infrastructures of populist politics, allowing us to become more conscious and aware of the many determinations that compose our thoughts, actions, and, ultimately, our world. Rational reflection and collective communication are still important methods for attenuating sad affects for Spinoza, who devoted scathing criticism of the ignorance produced by carelessly following (only) emotion, imagination, or ideology—making his work the "matrix of every possible theory of ideology" (Althusser 1997, 7). We must struggle for what Spinoza called "common notions"—collective ideas more adequate to explaining the world around us and how its dynamic components compose our emotions. Ideology critique thus entails a "search for a strategy of collective liberation, whose guiding motto would be *as many as possible, thinking as much as possible*" (Balibar 1998, 98). This is a collective critical-reflective project by which we ought to investigate and modify the material causes of our imaginary states, creating—hopefully—more adequate common notions that could stave off ignorance and ideological servitude and instead produce concatenated empathies and solidarities. Such struggle is never simply accomplished; fluctuations always persist because no one (other than God, who, for

Spinoza, is Nature) can understand the full concatenations of the universe. Translating this problem into the language of Marxist ideology critique, theory is not as a set of guarantees but a test of "the net of constraints, the 'conditions of existence' for practical thought and calculation about society" (Hall [1983] 2021a, 115). As the adage goes, the point is to change it.

As infrastructures, affects condition political collectivity, but they do not determine its outcomes. So, the description of these affects contributes to such practical thought and calculation about society, which I argue requires a socialist and anticolonial future on this planet. *Pipeline Populism* poses a question to political movements: How could we reflect on these affects, which emerge from material situations, so they might be institutionalized otherwise? I return to posit some answers in the conclusion of this book. The rest of this introduction outlines two contributions that ground the following four substantive chapters. The first section examines the historical roots of populist environmentalism in the 1960s and 1970s, before describing how it became reinvigorated in climate justice politics from 2009 to 2016. The second part of the introduction develops a conceptual framework for understanding populism as formed by affective infrastructures, as a genre, and as a transition. My research methods and the description of the rest of the book follow. Rather than exemplifying affective infrastructure in general, each of the chapters of *Pipeline Populism* names and develops a precise affect: territorialized resentment, resigned pragmatism, heartland melodrama, and jaded confidence. These descriptions are tools for thinking with populist environmentalism's possibilities and diagnosing its shortcomings.

Elitism and Populism in U.S. Environmentalism

The first contribution this book makes concerns the relevance of a concept of populist environmentalism, which stands in contrast to the frequently critiqued history of U.S. environmentalism as provincially elitist. In this section, I seek to elucidate the historical meaning of *populist environmentalism* by tracing its emergence in a dialectic oscillation with North American elitist environmentalism since the 1960s. I conclude this section by making a secondary argument that the period from 2009 to 2016 saw an upsurge in populist environmentalism in reaction to the failures of global climate politics in 2008–2009. Historicizing populist environmentalism helps reveal that the struggles of our contemporary moment are not unique but an inherited legacy.

From its earliest inceptions in the conservation movement, U.S. environmentalism sought to consolidate power in particular visions of nature that both stemmed from and benefited settlers. Historians of early environmental movements of the 1920s frequently contrast conservation and preservation, with the former elaborating an enlightened management of natural resources for human use and the latter rooted in the idea that unspoiled nature should be maintained separate from the areas of civilization and humankind. Yet both orientations rested on an erroneous idea that although cities were important sites of commerce, statecraft, and culture, man must regularly travel to the wilderness to reinvigorate his blood and prevent the white race from degeneration. Teddy Roosevelt, Madison Grant, Henry Fairfield Osborn, and Carl Akeley (among others) built this eugenic vision through many of the primary institutions of early conservation: the Forest Service, the U.S. National Park System, natural history museums, and zoos. The writings of John Muir and the photographs of Ansel Adams rested on visions of natural landscapes depopulated of Indigenous peoples. These visions did not just preserve or conserve natural spaces for white settler men; such actions also required that poor people, Native Nations, women, Black people, and immigrants be differentially restricted, subjugated, or exterminated (Day 2016; Gilio-Whitaker 2019; D. Taylor 2016). Scientific and political authority were central to the attempts to produce this ideology, while desires for racial purity and fears of outsiders were only shallowly beneath the surface, if at all.

It is sometimes assumed that the eugenic and xenophobic elements of this movement were rendered taboo by the postwar transformation of conservation and preservation toward planetary concerns with pollution. Numerous scholars have demonstrated that this was not the case: both the elitism and racial supremacy of early movements transformed into new (and demonstrably fictional) concerns that "overpopulation" was resulting in planetary resource scarcity (Hartmann 1999; Hultgren 2015; Murphy 2017). Much like earlier discourses of conservation, overpopulationists like Paul Ehrlich, Garrett Hardin, and John Tanton relied on scientific authority to couch thinly veiled fears of Black and brown people—especially women. Their policy recommendations reinforced the consolidation of elite power, as in Hardin's proposal for a triage or "lifeboat ethics" in which he recommends that "rich countries" should solidify their borders while allowing the global poor to die of hunger without aid (Hardin 1974). Though Hardin, of "tragedy of the commons" fame, has come to bear sustained criticism for the overlooked racism and nativism that played into his foundational role alongside Tanton in the U.S. nativist/anti-immigrant movement (Denvir 2020, 29), it is less frequently noted that Hardin's theories were explicitly anti-Indigenous. He ends the lifeboat ethics essay with a claim that a restoration of Indigenous land sovereignty would be a form of reductio ad absurdum, arguing that "we Americans of non-Indian ancestry" should not be obligated to "give back the land" because "the logical consequence would be absurd." The conclusion of such a line of thinking would be that "since all our other wealth has also been derived from the land, wouldn't we be morally obliged to give that back to the Indians too?" (Hardin 1974). That Hardin finds such a claim unthinkable provides one window into settler colonialism's role in elitist environmentalism.

Elite environmentalisms thus were premised upon a defense and consolidation of settler power at home at the same time as they emphasized the imperialist subjugation of populations abroad. The existence of social movements like Zero Population Growth and the decades-long debates about overpopulation and sterilization within the Sierra Club demonstrate that such fears and the desires they authorized were not confined to scientists (Park and Pellow 2013). The legacy of settler colonialism was an explicit pillar of elite environmentalism.

THE NEW ENVIRONMENTALISM

Consolidated environmental elitism was certainly not the only environmental ideology of the twentieth century. Like today, these periods were characterized by a messy field of varieties of environmentalism. Throughout the twentieth century, grassroots movements emerged against toxins and waste as working-class movements struggled for better collective living conditions, frequently led by Indigenous, Black, and migrant workers. The twentieth century—and especially the last half century of Black-, Indigenous-, Asian American–, and Latinx-led resistance to racial capitalism, colonialism, and ecological crisis—could be read as a "long" environmental justice movement, provided that environmental justice is understood critically and expansively rather than as a narrow "interest" (Nishime and Williams 2018; Pellow 2017; Sze 2020).

Alongside environmental justice struggles and elitist environmentalisms, populist groups formed another aspect of the muddled field of environmental ideologies and political formations in the 1960s and 1970s. Galvanizing events like the Santa Barbara oil spill, the revelation by Rachel Carson that the pesticide DDT was endangering the American eagle (among other species, including humans), and the first Earth Day resulted in an increasingly popular ecological movement, rather than simply an elite-driven edifice. While the old conservationist organizations like the Sierra Club and Wilderness Society looked on with feelings ranging from wariness to shock, a novel form of what became known as "the new environmentalism" began to emerge, coalescing around opposition to industrial pollution, resource consumption, and the destruction of urban green space (Gottlieb 2005; Rome 2013; Sale 1993). The new environmentalism was not necessarily coherent in political orientation, organized initially as community-based and local responses to toxins, waste, consumerism, resource extraction, and endangered species. Nonetheless, its rhetorical form—emphasizing the grassroots and localized environmental impacts—applied populist conventions.

Historians describe the environmental movements of the post-1970s period as primarily divided in their strategies and their visions of nature (e.g., Sale 1993; Bevington 2009; Woodhouse 2018). But populist environmentalism can also be seen in several aspects of the intensive space of this new environmentalism. The language of "the people" bled in from antiwar, counterculture, Black Power, and New Left organizations. The contemporary emergence of the Public Interest Research Group network in the early 1970s, led by Ralph Nader, coalesced an anticorporate message with the idea that people ought to be active participants in governance. By the late 1970s and early 1980s, the massive antinuclear and peace movement sought to break out of siloed issues by bringing together antiwar, environmental, rural farmer and rancher, and Red Power and Indigenous activists across the world, including in the Upper Midwest (Grossman 2017; LaDuke and Churchill 1985; Stock 2017). And while it was somewhat ignored and marginalized by the Big Greens, the 1970s saw an explosion of grassroots environmental groups operating at local and regional scales, many of which we would today recognize as oriented toward environmental justice.

Critics saw in the new environmentalism a lingering antipolitics (Gottlieb 2005, 139). Elements of the new environmentalism were also implicated in the countercultural politics of the hippies, the back-to-the-land and New Age movements, and the appropriate technologies and Whole Earth movements. As Gilio-Whitaker argues (2019, 105), aspects of the new environmentalism took an appropriative and reductive stance toward Indigenous cultures, one of Native Nations' bases for skepticism toward environmental coalitions. In any case, in the wake of Earth Day, legislation passed by the Nixon administration seemed aimed to dispel this energy (Dryzek et al. 2003, 59), as new environmentalist organizations reoriented citizens and activists toward litigation, lobbying and legislative advocacy, watchdog activities, and electoral work. Though such professionalization would come to be absorbed into a new kind of "mainstream environmentalism" by the 1980s, these social struggles and their resultant political gains should be understood as complex and contradictory rather than as simply part of one undifferentiated history of elite, white environmentalism (Purdy 2019).

Organizing against coal and uranium mining, nuclear weapons, and militarization in the Dakotas in the 1970s and 1980s exemplifies how populism stretched beyond the confines of typical environmental ideologies. The North Central Power Study of 1971 suggested a massive build-out of coal and uranium mines in the Black Hills region. Minuteman missile silos peppered the plains with hidden nuclear weapons. Farming and ranching economies were both busting in the late 1970s and early 1980s, as a drought combined with low commodity prices to shave already thin profits. In 1979, the Black Hills Alliance was formed as a coalition of "Lakota, grassroots environmentalists, Black Hills residents, and about twenty to thirty off-reservation ranchers and farmers opposed to corporate plans for the region" (Grossman 2017, 154). It was one of several progressive organizations in the region formed to fight resource extraction and militarism in the Great Plains, including the Western Organization of Resource Councils, *High Country News,* and the South Dakota Peace and Justice Center (Ferguson 2015; Heefner 2012). Later in the 1980s, the Cowboy and Indian Alliance first formed to oppose munitions testing in western South Dakota.

The popularity of this opposition movement peaked in the early 1980s. In 1979, the Black Hills National Gathering of the People drew several thousand activists to western South Dakota. Just a year later, at the height of fears of nuclear meltdown, the Black Hills Alliance and Women of All Red Nations (WARN) organized the Black Hills International Survival Gathering, which brought an estimated twelve thousand people to camp on the private Black Hills land of Marvin Kammerer, oft-described "cowboy populist." The basic issue of the Survival Gathering, one attendee told me, was "land and the control of land." But the event was multi-issue, featuring the full array of antiwar, environmental, feminist, punk, queer, Native, back-to-the-land, and renewable energy activists. These events sometimes drew on the language of "the people" to try to create a united-front coalitional radical politics. Though we might see the foregrounding of treaty rights and extraction as environmental justice issues, these were stitched to economic and geopolitical relations, broadening the coalitions. This led to a cross-pollination with the inheritors of the rural progressive populist movements of the earlier part of the century, such as PrairieFire, the North American Farm Alliance, United Family Farmers, and Farm Aid. I was always chuffed to find that a pipeline opponent would reveal in an interview that they had attended the Survival Gathering thirty years prior.

Aspects of this political collective drew on populist histories, rhetoric, language, and organizing tactics "to publicize that farmers had protested before, and that those protests had helped" (Pratt 1996, 33). A *New York Times* article from the time suggested that "virtually all" of these farmer groups "describe[d] themselves as 'populist'" (quoted in Pratt 1996, 25). Likewise, the "environmental political culture" of South Dakota foregrounded a "populist anti-corporatism, which shunned large-scale development by external entities that disrupted the community's interactions with the land" (Husmann 2011, 241–42). As one activist put it, "Isn't it also a question of selling a natural resource, a birthright if you will, to a private company, rather than using this scarce resource for the benefit of the people?" (quoted in Husmann 2011, 256). Such assessments also could be found in grassroots environmentalism across the country. The Citizens Clearinghouse for Hazardous Waste described itself in 1986 as "an old-fashioned Movement that addresses old-fashioned American values of neighbor helping neighbor, of grassroots democracy where the people lead and the leaders follow" (quoted in Szasz 1994, 82). The director of the Big Green organization Natural Resources Defense Council described such organizing somewhat fearfully as "a real populist grassroots movement" in the face of which the Big Greens were "in real danger of becoming obsolete" (quoted in Dowie 1995, 147).

Though principles of environmental justice were upheld by these grassroots organizations, their somewhat race-neutral language did not always work to construct the mass movement they imagined it would. The *New York Times* covered a 1996 meeting on populism that spawned the Alliance for Democracy, attended by such figures as self-described populist humorist Jim Hightower and historian of populism Lawrence Goodwyn. The paper of record described that "many in attendance fretted over the minuscule number of African-Americans, Hispanic people and other minorities at the event" (Verhovek 1996). Emergent populist environmentalisms further resonated with the "new populism" or "neo-populism" of the era (e.g., Boyte 1986), though similar problems connecting race and class bedeviled them. These situations also mirrored another, sometimes-forgotten line of academic theorizing associated with the *Telos* journal, which rejected globalization and Marxism alike from a self-described "populist" perspective that merged aspects of the left and the right in a manner inspiring to some environmental thinkers (e.g., Luke 1995; Klein 2014, 117; see also Frankel 1997). These contradictory legacies continued to influence "left populism" in ensuing years.

CLIMATE CHANGE AND THE RISE OF NEOLIBERAL ENVIRONMENTALISM

Populist environmentalism was somewhat quelled by the dark period of the late 1990s and early 2000s, in which complex environmental problems like climate change loomed large simultaneously as neoliberal politics became dominant. A depoliticized and paternalistic ecological politics contributed to this impasse. For the neoliberal technocrats of the 1990s, regular people were not important environmental actors; grassroots organizing was "at best helpful, at worst an embarrassing sideshow" (Dowie 1995, 5). Instead, neoliberal environmental governance asked: How can policy produce positive environmental outcomes given the economic self-interest of individuals and corporations in a marketplace? Within this ideological framework, compromise among corporations and policymakers was more impactful than creating a popular environmentalism. Such an environmental politics is sometimes described as "postpolitical" because it emphasizes the transcendence of political disagreement concerning socioenvironmental values through building consensus toward administering regulative changes (Swyngedouw 2010; Wetts 2020). Knowledgeable elites would be responsible for steering the masses toward proper environmental outcomes, mediating any dissent or disagreement between industry and people. To the extent that people should act, it would only be by voting or making personal consumption choices. This form of neoliberal environmentalism sometimes explicitly framed itself as antipopulist, contributing to the long-standing and ongoing liberal project to define populism as a threat to democracy.

A prototypical example of the antipopulism of neoliberal environmentalism is the now infamous essay "The Death of Environmentalism: Global Warming Politics in a Post-Environmental World" by Ted Nordhaus and Michael Shellenberger in 2005, an argument they expanded into the book *Break Through* published in 2007. The authors offer a scathing indictment of the transformation of environmentalism into a place-based, small-scale, moralistic movement with little chance at achieving meaningful political change. Their political end is not primarily a world of radical equality and justice but rather to demonstrate that U.S. environmentalism's focus on capital-*N* Nature diverts focus from policies such as emissions standards. These policies would not fundamentally require change in regular peoples' interests in consumption and economic growth, but they would result in better environmental outcomes and supposedly be in the economic interests of U.S. firms and workers alike. Rarely addressed in many critiques of the essay is the key division for Nordhaus and Shellenberger between such smart policy approaches, on the one hand, and populist anger, on the other (though see Meyer 2008). Comparing contemporary environmentalism to 1890s agrarian populism, Nordhaus and Shellenberger note that both decried the inequalities of their eras. But populists rhetorically emphasized that producers were victims of forces beyond their control and thus were unable to construct an affirmative social vision. This narrative of "the fall," the authors argue, bears a structural similarity with that of environmentalism's tragic (or apocalyptic) tale. Contra those who would be inspired by radical agrarian organizing of the 1890s, Nordhaus and Shellenberger find populists to be "insecure, desperate, and often quite mean and prejudiced" (2007, 159). Though the authors frame their argument as a departure from the norms of U.S. environmentalism, their position actually exemplifies the antipopulist trend in dominant climate politics of the period (Wetts 2020).

If prior to the mid-2000s, addressing climate change seemed to be the province of the Big Greens (Ciplet, Khan, and Roberts 2015, 169), then this began to change in the mid-2000s as global justice organizations took the United Nations as a site of struggle. Organizing surrounding these meetings facilitated important political and tactical cross-pollination from leading Global South organizations such as La Via Campesina, a transnational peasant and farmer movement, that resulted in a more robust climate justice movement (Featherstone 2012; Tokar 2014). Organizing at the transnational level also led activists to pressure national organizations, as some of the more amenable Big Greens such as the Sierra Club were finally persuaded to foreground climate change and the impacts of fossil fuels. Working within, against, and beyond the Big Greens, the goal of many in the Youth Climate Movement at the time—including myself, as a young organizer—was to popularize environmental justice along with more radical, confrontational tactics. Regulatory compromise with fossil fuel industries was not possible in a climate justice framework.

The Copenhagen Summit's weak results and the failure of the Obama administration to pass a comprehensive climate change bill caused self-reflection within international climate justice politics. These failures were not solely due to the missteps of the Youth Climate Movement: increasing fossil fuel political lobbying and the global shakiness of neoliberal political consensus after the financial crisis contributed. Yet, the movement against climate change became even more split at the activist level between policy- and lobbyist-oriented strategies and those of grassroots climate justice organizing. Despite the foregrounding of climate justice, many environmental justice organizers were frustrated by the persistent whiteness of the climate movement, its focus on national policy mechanics, and its tendency to neutralize transformative political critiques emerging from Black- and Indigenous-led organizations. The latter also included more radical actions emerging from the Global South, notably a refusal to compromise at Copenhagen led by the left-leaning delegates from Bolivia, Nicaragua, Cuba, Ecuador, and Venezuela. At the Copenhagen meeting, Bolivian president Evo Morales invited delegates and activists to Cochabamba, Bolivia, the following year to create a different kind of agreement outside the strictures of the U.N. process. Some thirty thousand activists, peasants, and Indigenous people gathered for the World People's Conference on Climate Change and the Rights of Mother Earth, hashing out what would become a People's Agreement rooted in principles of anticapitalism and anti-imperialism (Featherstone 2012, 236–38; Tokar 2014, 66). In this context, youth organizers Russell et al. describe the North American climate movement during this period as "flailing and fractured," having failed to "unif[y] around common opponents" (2014, 167). Goodrich, another organizer, also describes the situation as an impasse, assessing this moment in retrospect: "By failing to commit to the agonism of politics, which attempts to unite a diverse cross-section of the electorate against an identifiable enemy, the climate movement opted for marginality" (2019).

THE POPULIST GENRE AND THE MOVEMENT AGAINST THE PIPELINES

By 2010, the climate movement in the United States was at a crossroads. Focusing on climate policy at a national level seemed like a losing battle, while the United Nations stage also seemed a dead end. But at the same time, on the Great Plains of the Upper Midwest, a new and different movement was forming. Antipipeline sentiment had been bubbling in the Dakotas and Nebraska, where farmers, ranchers, Native Nations, and conservationists, among others, were increasingly disgruntled by the sudden appearance of TransCanada in their communities. Emerging antipipeline sentiments coalesced into organized opposition to KXL. These groups' strategy of coalition building populist alliances across difference appealed to many of us who had organized in the Youth Climate Movement. While media exposure and financial support were funneled from the Big Greens to some of the antipipeline groups, the strategy of coalitional left-populist opposition stands out as transforming U.S. environmentalism from a postpolitical orientation back toward mass political struggle. Rural populist organizing, scholars and organizers hoped, could serve as an alternative to burgeoning movements of the far right (e.g., Campbell and Linzey 2016; Cadieux et al. 2019; Koenig and Scaralia 2019; Roman-Alcalá, Graddy-Lovelace, and Edelman 2021; Patel and Goodman 2020). The KXL and DAPL struggles exemplify these complex tendencies.

The Keystone pipeline system is a series of proposed and partially completed pipelines that would bring diluted bitumen over two thousand miles from the Canadian tar sands near Hardisty, Alberta, across the continental United States to refineries near Port Arthur, Texas, and Patoka and Wood River, Illinois. The route of its first phase, Keystone I, was proposed from Hardisty to Illinois via Steele City, Nebraska, in 2007 and completed in 2010 with minimal local opposition. Another leg, the Cushing Extension, traveled from Steele City to storage facilities in Cushing, Oklahoma, and was completed in 2011. The KXL phase of the system was formally proposed in 2008 and included another route from Hardisty to Steele City, but instead traversing a shorter route through Montana, South Dakota, and Nebraska in order to connect to the Bakken field in Montana and North Dakota. (A second part of the Keystone system, from Cushing to Port Arthur, Texas, was originally part of the XL project but later cleaved into a different project after the heightened controversy surrounding the northern, international portion of the pipeline. This rebranded Gulf Coast Extension was completed in 2014 despite significant opposition in Oklahoma and Texas.) The so-called tar sands transported by the Keystone system are named as such for their mixture of bitumen (a heavy crude oil) with sand and/or clay. Because of this state, tar sands surface and in situ mining uses more energy and water than conventional oil extraction techniques, produces more by-products (like petcoke) when refined, and produces more carbon dioxide when burned. Such unconventional oil only becomes profitable when the price of oil is high. It is speculated that oil pipelines transporting bitumen—which must be diluted with a mixture of light petrochemicals in order to flow—might be subject to more corrosion and thus cause more frequent leaks.

As the name suggests, Keystone XL was a larger pipeline, at thirty-six inches in diameter, designed to transport around 830,000 barrels per day of oil (of which up to 100,000 barrels per day of light crude would be from the Bakken Formation). While oil, natural gas, and other pipelines crisscross most parts of North America, KXL would be the first to cross stretches of western South Dakota. Its route deftly avoided the administrative boundaries of South Dakota's nine Native American reservations. As TransCanada would quickly discover, however, the Lakota, Dakota, and Nakota—collectively known as the Oceti Sakowin Oyate—have legally contested the entire portion of western South Dakota stretching back to the Treaties of Fort Laramie signed in 1851 and 1868. In 1980, the U.S. Supreme Court ruled that the appropriation of this land was unjustly compensated, but the Oceti Sakowin have refused to accept the financial settlement, instead pursuing return of the land (Ostler 2011).

The groundwork for KXL began in 2008, as TransCanada's contracted land agents worked their way from Montana to Nebraska collecting easements. Residents recall that TransCanada quickly and quietly conducted business, seemingly to prevent communication and organization among property owners. As I discuss in chapter 1, some landowners first heard of the pipeline from the appearance of contractors surveying their land from public roadsides. It seemed to landowners that there was little choice in signing easements, and most did not object to the financial compensation package. TransCanada reportedly presented those signing voluntary easements with bonuses, while holdouts were promised a legal challenge through condemnation of property by eminent domain. In South Dakota, many landowners had signed easements in 2008 and 2009.

However, there were some holdouts. A group of landowners formed Protect South Dakota Resources and successfully negotiated more beneficial easement agreements for its members who settled by 2014. In Nebraska, by contrast, rumors of the pipeline's arrival preceded the land agents who were traveling the route of the pipeline from the north to the south. This, some organizers suggested to me, allowed Nebraska landowners extra time to prepare. In Nebraska, 16 percent of property

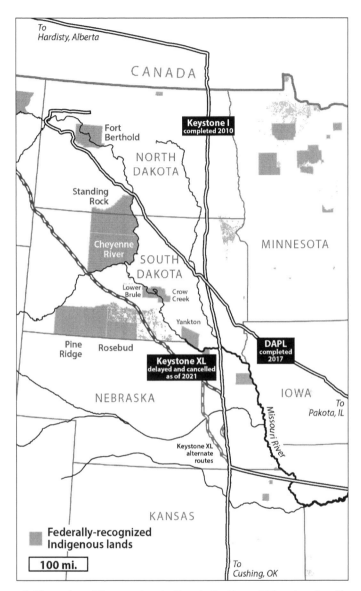

Figure 1. The routes of three major pipelines in the Upper Midwest region. The administrative boundaries of federally recognized Native American reservations are included here in part to demonstrate the attempt to skirt their edges, but the contestation of land by these and other Native Nations does not end at these state-drawn borders, especially given the Fort Laramie treaties of 1851 and 1868, among others. Map by Timothy Stallmann; Keystone XL pipeline data courtesy of Thomas Bachand; DAPL and Keystone data via Energy Information Administration.

owners along the pipeline's route refused to sign easements and many engaged in litigation with TransCanada. Prior to a 2012 rerouting, a portion of KXL passed through the Sandhills region, a sensitive and unique ecological region characterized by grassy sand dunes, a high water table that flows through permeable soil, and unique wetland flora and fauna. The Sandhills are also the northernmost portion of the massive Ogallala Aquifer, which stretches geographically south to Texas and provides drinking and irrigation water to millions of people.

Following the official announcement of the pipeline proposal, TransCanada filed for state-level permits with the South Dakota Public Utilities Commission (PUC) and the Nebraska Department of Environmental Quality, while filing with the U.S. State Department for an environmental impact statement (EIS). Numerous rounds of public comment sessions and evidentiary hearings ensued (see chapters 2 and 4) as the pipeline became increasingly mired in a series of controversies. By 2010, organizing against the pipeline began to accelerate on the Great Plains. Dakota Rural Action, a member-based progressive advocacy organization, had initially advocated for better easements for landowners whose property was crossed by the pipeline. But driven by increasing membership disapproval, the group increasingly began to veer toward full opposition to Keystone. It joined with Native-led organizations to form the NoKXL Dakota coalition. Bold Nebraska began to organize an antipipeline campaign in their state based on contesting the use of eminent domain for private gain. Bold Nebraska also organized coalitions with Oceti Sakowin and Ponca people. Chapters of national conservation organizations such as the Audubon Society and Sierra Club also began to take harder stances against the pipeline, especially its threat to the Nebraskan Sandhills. Environmental justice groups like Plains Justice, Honor the Earth, and the Indigenous Environmental Network had been organizing against Keystone I and continued legal, financial, and administrative support against KXL.

This organizing against the pipeline was only later (and somewhat reluctantly) picked up on by national environmental groups. A vanguard was James Hansen, the head of the NASA Goddard Institute for Space Studies, who began to prominently and repeatedly suggest that any infrastructure that would facilitate the combustion of the tar sands would be "game over" for the global climate (Hansen 2012; Romm

2011). Hansen would, in intervening years, occasionally describe his favored third-party approach and cap and dividend program as populist. He also sought to lend his testimony to the South Dakota PUC (this, and all other climate discussion, was denied by this institution). The leadership of Native Nations against the pipeline was initially somewhat ignored by national environmental organizations and the mainstream press; the latter would continually reframe KXL as another "jobs versus the environment" issue despite obviously visible Indigenous leadership (e.g., Johnson and Frosch 2011). Though opponents of the pipeline sometimes clashed with individual supporters and some construction unions in Nebraska, the character of pipeline support in South Dakota at the time was mostly passive and led by politicians and the media.

By 2012, the antipipeline campaign had become the highest profile environmental struggle in the United States. Pipeline opposition represented a fundamental change in model and strategy for organizations focused on climate change. As mentioned above, many within the climate movement felt that focusing on climate policy at a national and international level was responsible for alienation and failure, as such policies were overly technical and did not connect to people's experiences or values. However, direct action models derived from environmental justice coalitions "seemed more capable of keeping carbon in the ground than lobbying efforts" (Russell et al. 2014, 168). Climate organizers correctly saw that what was inspiring about such coalitional organizations, especially led by First Nations in Canada and Native Nations in the United States, was that they catalyzed mobilization through action rather than bickering over complete agreement concerning principles or tactics. In the Midwest, this led pipeline opponents to at times follow the St. Paul Principles, an outline of mutual respect for a diversity of tactics developed in the context of opposition to the 2008 Republican National Convention.

The broad-based "unlikely alliances" model served as a framework for the Reject and Protect protest that brought the Cowboy and Indian Alliance to Washington, D.C., and the People's Climate March in New York City, both in 2014. The peripheries of the latter event featured radical offshoots, including the ecosocialist coalition System Change Not Climate Change and an action called Flood Wall Street, which referenced Occupy Wall Street and the global movement of the squares. Despite a diversity in their political orientations, both supporters and critics of the march frequently drew on populist generic forms in assessing its success, or lack thereof (Bosworth 2020). Naomi Klein's *This Changes Everything: Capitalism vs. the Climate,* released the same month as the march, lauded "a rich populist history of winning big victories for social and economic justice in the midst of large scale crises" (2014, 10). The book described the opposition to KXL as "a movement so large it revived (and reinvented) US environmentalism" (303).

The strategies of the left edge of the Big Greens were partially shaped by the actions, rhetoric, and concrete relationships with antipipeline organizers in the Great Plains. But the choices made by organizations such as 350.org—now understood as a new Big Green—were not always received kindly by political organizing on the front line of the pipeline's route. It seemed odd that such large organizations were now claiming grassroots political organizing as their own. The financial benefits of this shift in focus were unequally distributed to different organizations who were on the ground in the Great Plains. Political and financial connections empowered the supposedly grassroot organiza-

Figure 2. Protesters hold signs reading "People Power" and "People over Profit" at the 2015 People's Climate March in Saint Paul, Minnesota. Photograph by the author.

tions that were most legible to outsiders—those that were least radical, most online, and most amenable to a nonprofit campaign strategy. This led to an uneven geography of visibility and political orientations. For example, some I spoke to in South Dakota were annoyed that Bold Nebraska received all the fame (and financial support) from the now-repopularized Cowboy and Indian Alliance, which had historic roots not in Omaha but in western South Dakota. Rumors frequently swirled about from whom and to whom foundation and nonprofit money was traveling. The most cynical analysis I heard claimed that Bold Nebraska was being funded by Warren Buffett via the Tides Foundation to manipulate pipeline opposition to consolidate oil transportation via his railways.

But most folks, in a classically Midwestern manner, made a more roundabout critique of Bold Nebraska for the glitz and glamour of their well-branded campaigns. An organizer named Sheila told me that the fame gained by others ultimately did not bother her, because "we did the real, tough work of organizing." When asked about national environmental organizations, Rick, a rancher, told me that he read almost all of the materials that they put out online. But he told me that "a lot of it's garbage." The major benefit of their involvement, which Rick joked was completely self-interested, was that he might get to meet Daryl Hannah. Regardless of any individual's or group's reasons for participating, the coalition held through 2014, and KXL seemed tantalizingly close to being canceled. The success of the movement also led to further popularity of its strategies and messaging. In South Dakota, Rick Weiland unsuccessfully ran for the U.S. Senate on a campaign that projected a folksy "prairie populism" alongside "aggressive opposition" to KXL. Weiland would argue that outsiders "just don't get our state. . . . It's more of a populist state than a red state" (Sargent 2014). Bold Nebraska leader Jane Kleeb would reflect in an article titled "Let's Get Rural: Middle America Wants Less Establishment, More Populism" that "a movement of We the People, in the Heartland of America, still exists and is one of the big reasons we stopped a pipeline" (Kleeb 2016).

In the fall of 2015, the northern portion of KXL was ultimately rejected by the Obama administration. In a statement, President Obama lamented that the pipeline had become "a symbol too often used as a campaign cudgel by both parties rather than a serious policy matter"

(Obama 2015). As with so many of his administration's policies, this seemed to be a cry for a return to the mythic depoliticization of neoliberalism, a rationally adjudicated process in which the pipeline was not supposed to represent the nation's commitment to oil, the climate crisis, or Indigenous dispossession. But as the KXL victory seemed more and more likely, similar issues would bedevil another pipeline, the Dakota Access Pipeline. Proposed by Houston-based Energy Transfer Partners (ETP), DAPL is a 1,172-mile-long pipeline designed to bring Bakken crude from western North Dakota across South Dakota and Iowa to southern Illinois. Because DAPL did not cross any international borders and its environmental impact was deemed to be lesser (a decision since challenged in the courts), its permitting process was much less stringent. Whether for financial or national reasons, ETP also took a different strategy than TransCanada with regard to permitting and public relations. TransCanada adhered to the global industry standards of corporate social responsibility, which try to give the appearance of transparency, responsible infrastructure governance, community relations, Indigenous and community consultation, and democratic decision-making. ETP, by contrast, did not seem to care much about community relations or social responsibility. Its goal was to get the pipeline in the ground as quickly as possible.

The arrival of a rapacious petro-PR machine on the scene around 2015 and 2016 intensified, at times, disagreement about the direction that populist strategy might take, for appearing unified in message and strategy appeared tantamount. This was most visible in Iowa, where pipeline populism was more intensely split between, on the one hand, top-down community organizations and, on the other hand, small-scale grassroots organizers, many of whom were younger, more attuned to social justice, and had worked on the Bernie Sanders campaign. Both groups were loosely organized into the No Bakken Coalition, which included some twenty organizations with varying levels of involvement in organizing pipeline opposition. In an interview, one organizer further described the split as coinciding with gender as well. "It just seems like the men really like giving stump speeches behind the mic without actually listening to what people are saying on the ground." The Midwest Alliance for Infrastructure Now, an oil industry coalition, attempted to discredit grassroots organizers as fraudulent and antidemocratic. This context made it difficult to resolve the real and important political disagreements in the group, which in part stemmed from the populist paradox itself.

In contrast to Iowa, in South Dakota I found less collective organizing against DAPL than I expected. Although some of the same organizations and individuals from the KXL battle opposed DAPL in South Dakota, the organizational infrastructure of non-Indigenous groups was not quite as strong due to lack of funding and some discord within some of these organizations. Consequently, when talking to many landowners, I was astonished by the extent that their opposition had been individualized. For example, one landowner said she spent over ten hours a week for the last six months conducting research and had "a whole room full" of boxes of printed documents and news articles. She was aware of, but had not organized with, any structured opposition group. Although the Indigenous Environmental Network and several Native Nations strongly opposed DAPL, its path through the eastern part of the state (along with neglect of consultation processes by ETP) seemed to make their popular involvement more difficult. In the summer of 2016, I speculated that the lack of opposition might be, in part, because the pipeline crossed through farmland instead of ranchland and thus engaged a slightly different political landscape than the more fiercely independent and libertarian western part of the state. I expected to write a postmortem about the failure of pipeline opposition to sustain itself, flaming out in opposing KXL and building little capacity for the future.

This thesis could not have been more wrong. In April 2016, a DAPL opposition camp popped up on the corner of the Standing Rock Reservation in North Dakota, within a mile or so of the pipeline's Missouri River crossing near the South Dakota border. Over the next few months, organizing would expand and then explode. Thousands of individuals and groups from around the world—among them, representatives from hundreds of Native Nations—streamed into North Dakota. The philosophy of *mni wiconi* (water is life) and the reframing of protestors as water protectors marked the rise to prominence of anticolonial environmental justice movements and antiextraction movements within the global climate justice movement. The events and impact of the DAPL blockades have been told in books, movies, and blog posts that center Indigenous history, politics, land, language, and experiences (Estes 2019; Estes and Dhillon 2019; Gilio-Whitaker 2019; Keeler 2021; LaDuke 2020; Sze 2020; Whyte 2017). And as Winona LaDuke (Anishinaabe) poetically writes, as much as "social scientists and historians can always identify the conditions that made it possible," the blockade evidenced a "mysterious spark that eludes all attempts at analysis" (2020, 95).

Despite such a mysterious spark, the movement's peak during the fall of 2016 and Obama's final months in office did not offer a saving grace. Though the Obama administration flirted with a DAPL reroute or even a rejection, they ultimately only turned against the pipeline's shoddy permitting process. Subsequently, both DAPL and KXL were revived by President Trump, who, more amenable to taking advantage of the symbolic importance of oil pipeline struggles, made their approval his first act as executive officer in January 2017. Shifts in the oil market alongside litigation have prevented KXL construction, and DAPL has been further challenged in courts. As of 2021, four years later, KXL's construction has been halted as President Joe Biden revoked the pipeline's presidential permit yet again, and it appears that the Trudeau administration of Canada will not seek a challenge in free trade courts associated with the North American Free Trade Agreement. TC Energy (née TransCanada) has finally terminated KXL, citing permitting risks.

With this historical context in mind, should we identify some pipeline opponents as populists? First, they broadly used the language of "the people" pitted against a corrupt elite, corporations, or the state. Public discourse, from protest signs to testimony, frequently displayed slogans such as "People Power," "People > Pipelines," and "We the People . . ." as grounds for opposition. Second, due to the political culture of the Upper Midwest, their political formation sometimes drew on the history of progressive populism in the region. Bold Nebraska, for example, cited Nebraskan populist William Jennings Bryan as a predecessor, while South Dakotans drew on a long tradition of land-based struggles associated with populism (Fite 1985). Finally, as I document in the chapters below, some explicitly and affirmatively called themselves populists. In fact, many would be more amenable to being called populist than environmentalist! Though "populist environmentalism" is still more of an exogenous than endogenous ascription, I believe it is an appropriate and clarifying lens of analysis.

Is the rejection of KXL a victory for pipeline populists? Much of the media and scholarship would point instead (correctly, in my mind) to Indigenous leadership. Nonetheless, a conventional narrative summary of pipeline opposition sometimes goes like this: progressive populism helped groups come together across different identities and social positions to defeat a common enemy. Through gathering their diverse—sometimes contradictory—grievances against the pipeline, people were able to break out of the social isolation of U.S. individualism and begin to reactivate collective forms of social struggle. The name of "the people" helped affirmatively stitch together these social demands into a shared commitment, while "the pipeline" symbolically stood not just for oil but also for corruption, elitism, and the shortcomings of contemporary democracy.

There is truth to this story, and I do not begrudge the grievances or strategy at face value. But in taking a critical approach, I also examine how the scenes that populate the populist genre tend to produce some key roadblocks for achieving transformative justice through social revolution. Reclaiming popular sovereignty (the "power of the people") presumes a form of politics that risks erasing historical difference by accepting that although settler colonialism must be critiqued, it can be superseded by a state that lives up to its ideals. Civic nationalism (tolerant and inclusive in the interest of the people) must still accept transnational difference, whether via geopolitical competition or global economic leadership. In composing a normative subject, populism was liable to reproduce generic conventions of whiteness. The emphasis on building unlikely alliances—including among Native and non-Native, rural and urban, left and right—was strategic in scope. But this strategy also created an inertia of demands in which a pluralistic lowest-common-denominator consensus was seen to be crucial to build the broadest movement possible. This level playing field of demands and grievances meant that critiques of the settler colonial state and capitalism, for example, were seen to risk the unity of the movement for being too radical. Such contradictions are too frequently ignored in shorthand histories.

The chapters in this book examine how such negotiations take place in desires for land, scientific expertise, political participation, and energy independence. In tracing these processes, this book challenges the supposition that left populism—because it has progressive aims or values—is especially well-suited to transforming the political trajectory of North American environmentalism away from its history of white elitism. But there are also wider implications for theories of populism. If movements participating in a populist tendency face similar problems, this can and should inform the strategies and tactics we choose in producing an adequate response to the climate crisis as an expression of racial capitalism and settler colonialism. The next section explores what conceptual tools we need to assess populist environmentalism and left populism more generally.

Theorizing Populism as Genre and Transition

The second contribution this book makes is to describe populism as a genre and transition, using the concept of affective infrastructures to elucidate the oscillations of populist movements. The concept of populism emerged in the late nineteenth century to describe progressive "people's movements" in the United States and Russia. In an era of extreme class inequality and gilded democracy, the U.S. People's Party sought to (re)claim from wealthy landowners, corrupt politicians, and parasitical corporations what they imagined to be a democratic power for the people. This power was political insofar as it sought to reorient decision-making power from elites to the common people. It was also economic, as it saw the uneven distribution of wealth as a pillar through which ensconced elites retained decision-making over poorer people. Finally, it was actively constructed: "the people" as an identity did not preexist its assembly. Historians have developed detailed studies of the character of populism as an agrarian movement whose power centers were in the South and the Upper Midwest, including South Dakota, Nebraska, and Minnesota.[1] The Farmers' Alliance and, later, the People's (or Populist) Party was strong in Dakota Territory and the newly minted state of South Dakota, absorbing the Democratic Party and even electing a governor. Many nineteenth-century populists, including in South Dakota, were or became socialists after populism's demise.[2] Yet this radical edge did not prevent populism from historically extending settler empire by "justifying a particularly intense commitment to Indian expropriation" (Rana 2011, 130). This section first describes how critical scholars have explained the ambivalences of the history and concept of populism. I examine how both Marxist and radical democratic approaches paradoxically fall into similar problems understanding the internal complexity of this political formation. I then describe how Spinozist-inspired affect theory and Marxist ideology critique, when taken together, provide important conceptual toolboxes for evaluating the role of emotion and affect in populist politics.

POPULISM IN CRITICAL THEORY

Despite massive definitional debates, to me the populist genre is rather simple to outline: populism is a genre of political performance that stages a fundamental difference between the people and the elites, diagnosing social ills as stemming from the power imbalance between these two groups that ought to be rectified. Yet liberals, radical democratic theorists, and Marxists have differed in interpreting the implications of this political genre.

Liberal scholars take populism as necessarily entailing antipluralism or illiberalism, seeing the attack on elites as unjust. They commonly suggest that populist movements, including its nineteenth-century originators, are defined by demagogic authoritarian leaders using anti-immigrant rhetoric to sway ignorant, overly emotional masses in an explicitly antidemocratic manner.[3] While these thinkers could admit that the rise of populism might require introspection about the representational challenges of liberal democracy, instead they propose a rigorous defense of liberal parties and the depoliticized, rational institutions they supposedly protect. Suffice to say, the liberal position is not particularly relevant to the analysis of the movements this book examines. Since its emergence in the mid-twentieth century, the liberal discourse has been countered by what Laura Grattan calls a "persistent counter-refrain" (2016, 19). In this reading, the populist movement of the 1890s, and populism more generally, evidences the possibility of a radical "democratic culture" (Goodwyn 1978). Populism could be democratic if it aims to seize and redistribute the universal promises of equality and freedom—promises that liberalism supposedly grants to all but in fact uses to reinforce racial and class strata. Some political theorists suggest that populism might have an experimental democratic spirit or an aspirational praxis, insofar as populist rhetoric seeks a redistribution of political power in an egalitarian fashion (Grattan 2016; J. Frank 2017).

Marxist scholars throughout the twentieth century also saw in populist politics some inchoate class struggle, although some assessments retain an amount of skepticism. The historian Norman Pollack argues that in the nineteenth-century U.S. Midwest, "Populism described the results of ideology, and Marx the causation" (1976, 92). Similarly, the Jamaican British cultural theorist Stuart Hall describes the 1960s New Left in the United Kingdom as "populist in the [Russian] 'Narodnik' sense of 'going to the people' and in terms of what they/we might become" ([1990] 2017, 139). Despite writing strongly against what he famously termed "authoritarian populism"—a "deliberately contradictory term" ([1985] 2021b, 285)—Hall emphasizes throughout his writing that "the discourses of 'populism' and of 'democracy' . . . do not belong intrinsically to any single class. They can, as the outcome of particular ideological struggles, be differently articulated in different conditions" (1980, 174–75). But many Marxists since have practiced a principled opposition to populism as a strategy. As Jodi Dean puts it, populism elides class politics by overly relying on a flexible identity, thus "effacing the fundamental antagonism at the heart of capitalism" (2017, S43). The rhetorical split between the people and the elites, however useful it might be to historical or contemporary proletarian movements, is not the same as the material antagonism between workers and capital that Marx diagnosed as the "capital relation" (1976, 763).

Despite their different aims and methods, Marxist and radical democratic analyses frequently understand left populism as fundamentally ambivalent or split between a potentially more hopeful and more reactionary side. The best of the Marxist accounts of populism tend to come from readers of Antonio Gramsci, like the aforementioned Hall and geographer Gillian Hart (2014, 2019).[4] The Gramscian approach emphasizes that the political struggle for hegemony also takes place within popular cultural forms and the "common sense" that inheres in everyday social existence. This includes the languages of everyday resignation and the works of literature, media, and religion that interpret social and class formations. As a communist, Gramsci's analysis is aimed at understanding this terrain in order to transform it. His work is further important for providing a pathway for critical intellectual activity to be seen as both emerging from and transforming heterogeneous and confused "common sense" by drawing out the elements of "good sense" that lie jumbled within it (Crehan 2016, 57). Gramscians thus understand populism as a form of emergent mass politics that engages in a counterhegemonic struggle for political power with the historical bloc that currently rules. As argued above, the hegemony of technocratic and antipolitical neoliberalism at least partially explains the appeal of a populist environmentalism explicitly emphasizing the divide between elites and people. Rather than conforming to a preexisting theory, populism could be taken to be one of those "most bizarre combinations" that defines the reality of political struggles (Gramsci 1971, 200).

Though sometimes influenced by Gramsci, radical democracy approaches emphasize populist desires to enact democracy as popular sovereignty—the rule of the people—through grassroots movements. Sometimes these approaches also draw some amount of inspiration from the pathbreaking—though not always Marxist—work of Ernesto Laclau (1979, 2005) and Chantal Mouffe (2000, 2018), alongside other traditions of democratic theory (e.g., Canovan 1999). Within grassroots movements for radical democracy, Grattan sees a split between "rebellious" and "democratic" populist aspirations and those more "reactionary" and "cruel." Rebellious aspirations are not so much organized left resistance but "incipient" and "frustrated desires" that critically indict undemocratic structures of social life (2016, 41). Reactionary and cruel aspirations are those critiques that "distort people's aspirations for power" (40), blame minorities and outsiders, place faith in a strong leader, and suggest individualism and ethnonationalism will liberate the people. The best of radical democratic theory refuses to divide everyday life from moments of hotter resistance; the approach in *Pipeline Populism* similarly sees frustrated desires emerging from structures embedded in everyday life. These readings of contemporary populism are again crucial for helping us understand why populist politics might emerge in the wake of—and against—neoliberal political cultures that have individualized and depoliticized democracy. The material conditions of everyday austerity and both individual and global debt leveraged during the last forty years have further created feelings of

resentment and woundedness that are mobilized in left and right populisms alike.

Yet even when contradictions among its aspirational elements are
acknowledged, both Gramscian and radical democratic approaches
sometimes seem to suggest the rebellious and reactionary elements of
populism are historically or structurally distinct. We might be left with
the sense that reactionary populisms are simply distortions of authentic
rebellious aspirations. The problem with such an argument is that democratic aspirations of a populist movement might emerge from material
conditions like landed private property, which maintain the status quo
of white supremacy and dispossession. The subject instituted by populism might imagine themselves to innocently escape their conditions
(Grattan 2021). Such a gesture toward a liberatory "transparency"
would entail the counterposition of racial subjects who are still "affectable" in their determinations (Silva 2007). Popular sovereignty in action
could entail a practice built through a version of erasing prior, ongoing,
and unextinguished Indigenous sovereignty (Tuck and Yang 2012). The
antagonistic play of forces on the stage of politics, it could be argued,
rests on political-economic and libidinal economies of anti-Blackness
(Bledsoe and Wright 2019; Wilderson 2003). So long as these structural
elements are disavowed, populism's democratic aspirations would therefore be cruel aspirations, without formal or analytic separation. The
failure to fully critique such populisms except as exclusionary seems
symptomatic, to me, of liberal theory and method that overemphasizes
discourse as an autonomous sphere of politics rather than one that becomes efficacious only recursively through the material and spatial arrangements of political-economic flows. A populist environmentalism
would thus remain an ambivalent political program even if (and perhaps because) it states a desire for multiracial or multicultural coalitions, which would emerge primarily through a liberal politics of inclusion (Melamed 2006).

None of this is to suggest left analyses of actually existing populism
fall into the form of ethnonationalist equivocation that liberal critics
take. Nor do I wish to be mistaken for producing a nihilistically critical
or mean-spirited account of the shortcomings of movement building,
which is extraordinarily difficult. As I explain in the following section,
the point of ideology critique is to understand from what conditions

such shortcomings emerge rather than simply judge and hastily dismiss them as inadequate. The goal is to understand "the rich totality of many determinations and relations" (Marx 1973, 100) or "the problematic field" (Deleuze 1994, 165) that begets the emergence of a populist environmentalism rather than another kind of movement solution. *Pipeline Populism* shows how the supposedly progressive elements of populism—such as democratic imaginaries, territorial belonging, and antielitism—expose major fault lines in U.S. environmentalism and everyday political life precisely through the affective infrastructure through which they emerge. Populists do not solve or exhaust the problematic field (of left or socialist organizing in a reactionary context) because the problem "insists and persists in these solutions" (Deleuze 1994, 163). Ultimately, "radical democratic" populist strategy will not be able to adequately address and redress the structural issues outlined above if they reject class analysis (as a theory) and class struggle (as a practice) in favor of liberal constructions of "the people." Marxist analysis leads us to believe that populism must be superseded by a movement that rearranges the material and thus affective infrastructures that maintain settler colonialism and racial capitalism by mediating our collective understandings of these as our conditions of existence. The next section develops the Spinozist-Marxist conceptual architecture that I see as a crucial (though not exhaustive) contribution to that project.

AFFECTIVE INFRASTRUCTURES OF GRASSROOTS POPULISM

Though I remain influenced by the Gramscian and radical democratic theoretical schemas for understanding left populism, without a theory of desire they struggle to fully explain why populist movements either wax or wane. We must instead examine how and which affects emerge in material relations and are channeled into different political formations so that we can reflect on and transform them. It is axiomatic to Spinoza that "desire is man's very essence" (1985, 531 [EIIIDI]). The composition of social life through the passions helps us develop an answer to Spinoza's political question posed earlier in this introduction: Why is it that people sometimes fight as much for our servitude as our freedom?[5] In the context of this project, we might reshape this question: Why is it that the aspirations of populist environmentalisms seem to resecure aspects of liberal, racial capitalism when many involved in such

movements wish to surpass these? And why did populist pipeline opposition emerge alongside but separate from revolutionary socialism or
anticolonialism?

Traditional Marxist emphasis on economic and class interests in
maintaining the status quo can partially explain people's investment
in the mythos of U.S. liberal democracy. The U.S. American emphasis
on "We, the People" was, as Ellen Meiksins Wood argues (1995, 219),
an attempt by Federalists to appropriate a veneer of popular sovereignty
to shore up federal power and imperial government. Subsequently, this
ruling class has since invested everyday meanings of democracy with an
atomizing individualism to the point they become "common sense," as
if they were timeless reality or human nature rather than historically
constructed social formations.

Yet people frequently betray their collective interests and common
sense and fight against them instead. Pipeline construction unions fight
on behalf of their jobs and employers rather than a livable future for all.
Or, conversely, white settler farmers and ranchers betray their accumulated inheritance by returning their land back to Native Nations. So too
do subjects frequently act against our class interests even with the
knowledge—rational or common sense—that it is against our interest
to do so. As W. E. B. Du Bois argues, class interests do not suffice to
explain the cruelty of white supremacy or the lack of solidarity among
poor white and Black workers either prior to or in the wake of the U.S.
Civil War (1935, 27). In addition to their actual wages, Du Bois famously theorizes that white workers also receive a "psychological wage"
in the form of preferential treatment over Black workers in both industrial and social spaces (1935, 700). The problem Du Bois sought to
highlight with this concept was eminently Spinozist: why did poor
whites in the south not immediately see formerly enslaved Black people
as members of the working class? Interest or knowledge, as formed by
history and ideology, could only provide a partial understanding of the
complex determinations that can lead to either political antagonism or
quiescence. "But what on earth is whiteness that one should so desire
it?" Du Bois asks. "Whiteness is the ownership of the earth forever and
ever, Amen!" ([1920] 1999, 18; see Myers 2019). Spinoza, Du Bois,
and others suggest that ownership or dominion not only imparts self-
interest or collective interests but also is formed through an infrastructure of desire that constructs political subjectivities.[6]

Desire, emergent from the material arrangements of violent racial capitalism and settler empire, produces subjects who are invested in upholding these systems—sometimes economically, sometimes ideologically. Desire helps explain populism's power expressed in the people's collective imaginations of their own self-identity, their ascriptions of the systemic failures of capitalism to demonized individuals, and their utopian dreams of a better or different world. In short, produced by people's life histories and everyday engagements with an uneven landscape shaped by inequality, desire forms the matrix through which populist ideology comes to make sense. When combined with Marxism's materialist analysis of political economy and method of ideology critique, such an account of affect can offer meaningful explanations for why cruel aspirations persist among populist environmentalism and how they might be reconstructed otherwise.

Though populism is sometimes definitionally described by critics as an overly emotional form of politics, Spinoza helps us see that collective affects shape every political subject. Affect comes to shape our more or less conscious political decision-making in a nondeterministic fashion, but such "forces of encounter" (Gregg and Seigworth 2010, 2) still produce tendencies.[7] For the purposes of writing political affect, *Pipeline Populism* allows *affect* to capaciously designate perceived and felt states that can be named and described (Chen 2012, 11–12). In contrast to more measured yet apolitical investigations of affect, I follow Berlant (2011, 53) in taking "affect theory [as] another phase in the history of ideology theory. . . . It enables us to formulate, without closing down, the investments and incoherence of political subjectivity and subjectification in relation to the world's disheveled but predictable dynamics." Consequently, heterodox Marxist political theory can be reevaluated as crucial to dissembling the affectability of white subjects who would otherwise be posed as free and transparent. In an expansive study of theories of race and subjectivity, Denise Ferreira da Silva argues that in those moments "when writing consciousness as an effect of material production" of "actual conditions," Marx and Engels "opened up the possibility of a critical analysis of the social in which spatiality—where 'being and meaning' emerge in exteriority-affectability—became the privileged moment of signification" (2007, 192). Though Silva's arguments concerning the stakes and sites of "exteriority" are too complex to explore here, I interpret this statement as indicating a materialist analysis that sees emancipation in affectability rather than as a transcendence of it. Affectability, in this reading, would be akin to what Ajay Skaria (2016, 26) proposes as "a will and freedom without autonomy" as a potential mode of exiting from European imperialism, rendering European thought a (self-destructive) gift. These thinkers, in my mind, demonstrate the importance of an analysis of affect for critical, Marxist scholarship and revolutionary socialist, anticolonial political struggle.

The concept of affective infrastructures pries open the significance of affect as one of many determinations that undergirds political struggle.[8] Affective infrastructure, for me, highlights how emotion emerges from political-economic contexts and material landscapes, nondeterministically conditioning political struggles. The infrastructural relation in affective infrastructure denotes not so much a strong determination, as if given affects determine a politics. Instead, the infrastructural relation ought to be understood as a topology of desire, a recursive spatial relationship that offers a certain amount of plasticity within a fuzzy range (P. Harvey 2012; Saldanha 2017, 136). And while one might worry that such a concept ungrounds us from "real" infrastructures, the genealogy of "infrastructure" unveils that accusations of vagueness and metaphoricity accompanied the concept's emergence and use (Carse 2016). As affective infrastructures generate social opposition, the latter modes of dissent recursively work to reinterpret those very affects. Naming affects can help us become conscious of how they might be channeled otherwise. A caution: while affective infrastructures help explain how populist environmentalism emerges in a space and time, they do not explain the totality of many determinations of the political situation. The affective infrastructures described in this book need not result in populist environmentalism. Many of these—such as territorial resentment or heartland melodramas—could be rerouted through either reactionary or liberal politics (or antipolitics, for that matter).

Affect theory can benefit from engaging the sharp tools of Spinozist-Marxist ideology critique concerned with understanding the complex determinations among a material, economic infrastructure and assemblages of political ideologies. By *ideology*, I understand "the (overdetermined) unity of the real relation and the imaginary relation between [people] and their real conditions of existence" (Althusser 1969, 233–34).[9] The Marxist use of the concept of ideology has often been understood as a denunciation of people's seemingly contradictory political stances as false consciousness, as if ideology tricked or duped ignorant people into holding incorrect and hurtful political stances. Certainly, this seems to have been Spinoza's stance when he appears to denounce the superstitions of the masses. However, the point of the concept of ideology is not a rebuke of the falsity of superstition from the position of reason. Given the contradictory way affects shape all collective life, we are all subject to various ratio of affective forces.[10] The imaginary relation at stake is not transparently representational; it also includes, in Spinoza's words, "only a confused and mutilated knowledge of itself, of its own Body, and of external bodies" (1985, 471 [EIIP29Cor]). This confusion is an effect of desire, as the spatial arrangements of bodies produce combinations of joyful and sad affective resonances in one's imagination that escape our full knowledge. Nonetheless, the affective realm continues to constitute every attempt at rationality, the development of adequate ideas. It does not distort, because it contributes to adequate ideas "with the same necessity" as it determines inadequate ideas (1985, 473 [EIIP36]). There is no form of thought that does not emerge from this play of forces, no free thinker who escapes the world. Thought emerges not from the subject but from the interrelation of bodies and the interrelation of ideas.

From a poststructuralist perspective, ideology critique is sometimes said to rely on a nonrelative or absolute truth hiding behind ideology, grounding it in the materiality of the political economy in the last instance. Thus, ideology critique is understood to be foundationalist or essentialist (Foucault 1980, 118), especially if positing a theory of false consciousness. Furthermore, it can seem like all critique does in or to the world is destroy. Ideology critique is said to be mean-spirited in its approach to social worlds, and thus primarily reproduces sad affects such as paranoia, suspicion, or the seeking of personal glory (Latour 2004; Braun 2015). Ideology seems to describe the social as too airtight, too structural, too deterministic, a world with no wiggle room or agency for its subjects.

Such critiques of critique are important to acknowledge for pointing out the limits of an ideology critique without humility or self-reflection. But Spinozist and Marxist critical practice exists not to destroy worlds but to reconstruct the genesis of their representation. "The point of critique is not justification but a different way of feeling: another sensibility" (Deleuze 1983, 94) such that critique can be "relocated . . . immanent to the experiment itself" (Braun 2015, 110). For Spinozists, critique exists not just to demonstrate the inadequacy of certain ideas but as an ongoing project of building alternative modes of attention to those determinations that compose us. As Antonio Negri puts it, the Spinozist critique relies on the articulation of the destructive "internal critique of the ideology" with an ethical-constructive "identification of the critical threshold of the system in the emergence of the irreducible ethicality of the world" (1991, 84). In short, Spinoza finds politics in the relations that seek to comprehend and compose a common world in that very world. This is how Spinozists analyze political orientations via a resolutely and complexly "materialist" method even as they investigate ideas, forbidding, in Hasana Sharp's assessment, "any kind of exit from thought to matter, insisting upon the irreducibility of one to the other" (2011, 62).

Though the focus of affect theory is sometimes on affect-as-such, Spinoza also offers us a rich yet nonexhaustive inventorial practice of naming affects, which I rely on throughout this book. Spinoza's tack is to, as best we can, rationally investigate what certain affects do to bodies and their powers and name the particular forms that these take in order to better understand how bodies and powers can be ordered differently. If inventory can help us understand the material arrangement, and if the material arrangement can help us change the affects that are produced, then through conscious reflection and collective action, we can better augment what sorts of activities increase or decrease our collective powers. This is to say again, as Jason Read argues, "critique cannot be separated from construction" of a new ontology and politics (2016, 21). A critical method attending to affective infrastructure compels us to examine the composition of political subjects not only by knowledge and common sense (without downplaying their importance) but also by prepersonal and unconscious forces that underlie and condition them.

Here, I am riffing on the practice developed by contemporary feminist and queer theorists examining the work that affective performances in intimate and social spaces accomplish in congealing or disrupting complex social subjectivities. Sara Ahmed, for example, points us to how affects can "align individuals with communities—or bodily space with social space—through the very intensity of their attachments" (2004, 119). Ahmed shows how bodily-affective relationships are understood to be more complex in mediating the relationship between individual and collective in specific historical-political contexts. Even more germane to this study, Mel Chen (2012), Shiloh Krupar (2013), and Nicole Seymour (2018) each seek to dislodge what Spinozists would call the "sad affects" of environmentalism, such as anxiety, fear, and moral righteousness. Instead, these scholars see more open-ended environmental justice possibilities in critical performances of absurdity, toxicity, humor, and irony. Such analyses help demonstrate that in its genre conventions "environmentalism is itself a performance, one with very strict codes" (Seymour 2018, 36). To say that environmentalism is a performance does not mean that it is "fake," of course, but actually that it is open to being recomposed through performances of all sorts (Vasudevan 2012).

If the codes and conventions of climate action sometimes subsume emotion to instrumental political or scientific projects, awareness and reflection of this work can create spaces for reconstructing what Lida Maxwell (2017) calls an "environmental politics of desire." This would be emergent from a variety of potential place-based and multispecies social relations and affectations. In describing such a politics, Maxwell further allows us to see that desire need not be an unconscious restraint to our politics but also, as Eve Tuck (Unangax̂) puts it, that "desire constitutes our expertise" (2010, 646). Environmentalism, beyond its populist form, is surely produced through a repertoire of scenes and zones that collectively constitute a generic affective infrastructure. In reflecting on the constitution of our desires as a pedagogical project, feminists and queer theorists argue that we can augment these to make environmentalism into a more just project of flourishing.

Following from the theories outlined above, an examination of the affective infrastructures of populist environmentalism helps illuminate populism as a genre and transition. Scholars of populism examine its "political style" or "performance" (Canovan 1999; Ostiguy, Panizza, and Moffitt 2021); in Moffitt's estimation (2016, 29), the stylistic approach is a major step forward from theories that render populism a discourse or strategy of the political. Yet Moffitt's (2016, 38) definition of style emphasizes the traditional language of performance studies (e.g., leaders on stage performing speech acts for audiences) in a some-what restrictive manner. Marino (2018, 21) productively extends our understanding of performances of populism as "merg[ing] the senso-rium with social practice and the environment in the mechanics of *doing*: in backstage production, the rehearsals, the planning, and the networks that make up the performed act." Much like my assessment of performances of environmentalism above, such an analysis of populism does not indicate it is phony because it is theatrical or affective, as in some liberal assessments. Instead, analyzing populism's performance again shows us its genesis in, relationships with, and transitions toward other forms of politics.

I contend that it is not style but genre, however, that describes the formal elements—affective scenes or zones—that organize composi-tional elements of political styles.[11] By *political genre,* I understand "an aesthetic structure of affective expectation, an institution or formation that absorbs all kinds of small variations or modifications while prom-ising that the persons transacting with it will experience the pleasure of encountering what they expected, with details varying the theme. It mediates what is singular, in the details, and general about the subject." (Berlant 2008, 4). Berlant highlights that genre is "repeated, detailed, and stretched while retaining its intelligibility, its capacity to remain readable or audible across the field of all its variations" (4). To be in a "populist moment" means not just the stylistic element of rhetorical persuasion but why that persuasion historically makes sense. Drawing on genre and performance theory, Shannon Davies Mancus argues that "environmentalists can and do use genre as part of a contest among themselves about the correct politics of relating to the environment, because generic conventions quickly convey what the viewer should perceive as right and wrong" (2016, 11). Populist environmentalism makes sense to subjects because it works through the generic conven-tions through which (some) social subjects come to understand their everyday lives, their political landscapes, and the broader spaces that they—and others—inhabit.

Following the effects of genres of politics is especially illuminating, Elizabeth Anker writes, because they "double back, challenge them-selves, fail in their intended deployments, blend with other genres, and depict the same situation in multiple ways" (2014, 20). This approach highlights that despite hanging together, genres can be transitional. Studies of populism sometimes hypostasize it as an object or discrete social formation, in which individual people or groups are "populists." Instead, this book seeks to take populism as more distributed—in its genesis from everyday lives, transformation in political collectivity, and internal and external contradictions and supersessions. I offer scenes through which affective infrastructures of generic populism emerged and describe how its counterhegemonic battle faded from view in favor of other approaches (e.g., liberal, decolonial) or tactics (e.g., lawsuits, pipeline blockades). Without suggesting a teleological trajectory, each chapter highlights the swelling of populist sentiment, its growth into more vocal pipeline opposition, and the problems that the latter encountered in building coalitions, confronting white supremacy and settler colonialism, tarrying with the state, and locating its enemies. The open question, which I return to most clearly in this book's conclusion, is whether these affective infrastructures can be routed elsewhere.

NOTES ON METHOD

The initial research question of this project was "How does pipeline populism, as a collective social phenomenon, emerge from and transform contemporary ideologies of environmentalism?" The question delimits an interest in grasping the singularity of populist responses to the pipelines within the field of different approaches to environmental politics. This meant that I did not examine as direct objects of study the Big Greens themselves (excepting local chapters of the Sierra Club), the state (except as it interfaces with populist groups), or radical left groups. Similarly, although questions I ask in this work are in conversation with critical Indigenous and environmental justice scholarship, *Pipeline Populism* does not claim to foreground Indigenous anticolonial organizing or epistemologies/ontologies. I remain most interested in the self-understanding of white settlers in antipipeline opposition and environmentalism more broadly. As explained in this book's preface, the genesis of the project was in an immanent critique of my own political background as a climate activist and uninvited settler in South Dakota. One risk of this sort of analysis is that it recenters white settler ways of knowing and organizing politics and consequently could thus decenter "Indigenous peoples' own articulations of Indigenous-settler relations, their governance, legal, and diplomatic orders, and the transformative visions entailed within Indigenous political thought" (Snelgrove, Dhamoon, and Corntassel 2014, 26). I do not claim that this research contributes directly to a political project of decolonization. Instead, I describe adjacent individuals and movements in ways that help us understand where and how affective infrastructures contribute to the reproduction of racial capitalism and settler empire within environmental and antipipeline mobilizations.

For these reasons, it is important to state quite clearly that I do not see this book as a work of scholar-activism. Following Tuck and Yang, situations exist wherein "research may not be the intervention that is needed" (2014, 813) by on-the-ground political movements. I have devoted time and energy to opposing pipelines via extra-academic methods, including spending some six weeks in total in July, August, and October 2016 at the Sacred Stone Camp on the Standing Rock Sioux Reservation in North Dakota. I conducted no research activities while there, deciding that such activities were unnecessary for ethical, political, and security reasons. Nonetheless, the politics of the blockade deeply condition what, why, and how I think. Following Sylvain Lazarus and Alain Badiou (see Badiou 2005, 50), thought is conditioned by (rather than entails) such struggle. These authors argue that Spinoza's statement *"homo cogitat"*—"people think"—is an axiomatic statement that thinking is by no means reserved for philosophers. Ideology critique is still indispensable, I believe, to the project of demonstrating the conditions that block thought from happening, drawing our attention to different scenes than we would expect. But this process of the "selection" of different affects, Deleuze reminds us in reading Spinoza, is "extremely hard, extremely difficult" (1997, 145). Such knowledge is not privative or final but expansively formed by collectives within, against, and beyond the university, and at risk of attenuation and capture therein (Casarino 2019). I recognize this can be unsatisfying, though thankfully no shortage of generous Indigenous scholars have undertaken work framing DAPL and other pipeline struggles.

Methods of humanistic and qualitative social science inquiry ground this account of pipeline populism, including interviews, participant observation, and analysis of documents and media. I conducted a total of twelve months of empirical fieldwork in South Dakota, North

Dakota, Nebraska, and Iowa, a timeline that allowed me to respond to the changing political landscape of pipeline opposition from 2013 to 2016. In the summer of 2013, I lived in Winner, South Dakota, a small town of around two thousand people near the southern border with Nebraska. In the summer of 2014, I lived in Rapid City, South Dakota, the most populous city in the western part of the state. This allowed me to travel north to Harding County, east to the state capital of Pierre, and to sites along the KXL route. In the summer of 2016, I lived in Brookings, South Dakota, in the eastern part of the state, to track opposition to the newly proposed DAPL and to be able to drive to research sites in both North Dakota and central Iowa.

The broad parameters of pipeline populism afforded numerous sites of research and interlocutors. I interviewed members of, attended events organized by, or analyzed documents or discourse from around twenty nonprofit organizations, informal citizens' groups, and activist collectives. Although only a few of these organizations, such as Bold Nebraska, explicitly used populism as a moniker, the populist generic form saturated these groups. I also used ethnographic methods to examine campaigns against pipelines in public spaces. These included observation of the "spatialities of contentious politics" (Leitner, Sheppard, and Sziarto 2008), mobilizing strategies for studying emotion in protest (Gould 2009, 2010; Brown and Pickerill 2009; Clough 2012; Routledge 2017).

While interviews were very important to elucidating the political field and strategy behind the scenes of political melodrama, I found that observing these spaces of collective action and subjectification was most relevant. These include, first, participant observation in public participation meetings and evidentiary hearings associated with the federal environmental impact statement and South Dakota Public Utilities Commission reviews. I also drew from recordings, transcripts, and news accounts of meetings I was unable to attend or that preceded my field research. Second, I attended around thirty public gatherings not interfacing with state institutions. These included three protest concerts, seven marches, four potlucks, three blockades or direct actions, one direct action training, and one eminent domain condemnation hearing. These events took place across the research area in South Dakota, North Dakota, Minnesota, Nebraska, and Iowa.

Third, I conducted twenty-three semistructured interviews with key individuals in the pipeline opposition movement. These included community organizers, landowners, lawyers, activists, and environmentalists. One group interview was conducted with four interlocutors. I also interviewed some marginal participants in the pipeline opposition, including an attendee of but one public meeting, a pipeline skeptic who became a supporter, and a vehement pipeline opponent who was not connected to any political organization. Despite its aspirations, the movement against the pipelines on the Great Plains was not a massive mobilization. To protect individual identities and sensitive information, all names of interlocutors, as well as some identifying details, have been changed in the narrative book.

Finally, a vast array of documents and online relationships were important to this analysis. I surveyed the written comments of several thousand unique submissions made on the 2013 draft supplemental EIS, consisting of six documents totaling over six thousand pages. I did not read and then code all of these comments in order to inductively discover discursive patterns, but instead sampled based on keywords derived from a close reading of the first five hundred pages. I closely followed texts, flyers, pamphlets, email blasts, social media conversations, and other electronic documents through which social movement organizing over large distances of space is increasingly communicated. I have included some analysis of the way in which local, national, and environmental media and literature represent pipeline populism. Taken together, these sources allowed a rich if nonexhaustive analysis of the changes in public discourse and strategy of pipeline opposition from its inception to the present.

Outline of the Book

This introduction began by situating the movement against the pipelines in the history and contemporary field of environmental politics in North America. The following chapters more closely follow individuals and groups in the Dakotas, Iowa, and Nebraska, with occasional reference back to those broader climate politics. Each chapter further historically situates populist environmentalism in relation to private property, democratic institutions, scientific processes, and the politics of oil. In doing so, each also proposes a named affect: a loose feeling that I argue plays a role in the many determinations that led to the emergence—and problems—faced by populist generic forms. Overall, these chapters trace the waxing and waning of populist environmentalism, contributing to the argument that populism here must be seen as genre and in transition.

Some of the most strident settler opponents of the pipeline were landowners whose property was likely to be crossed by the KXL pipeline. Chapter 1 examines how the material and performative perforations of private property by land agents conditioned a feeling of territorialized resentment. Interpreted as a politics of land, this affective infrastructure set the conditions for landowners engaging in collective action, forming landowner groups, and engaging in coalitional, oppositional politics. Anxieties of property congealed into the social demands of pipeline populism. However, territorialized resentment also meant that private property reappeared in the movement against the pipelines in a manner that posed contradictions for which "people" and "land" were at stake. Some settlers compared the individual, white experiences of eminent domain to the historic and ongoing dispossession of Native Nations by suggesting pipeline firms and the state were "treating us like Indians." To account for the eventual limits that populist environmentalisms face in building common coalitions, I argue that we must understand how its oppositional politics link to both economic interests and political desires—in this instance, for the maintenance of landed private property.

Forums of public participation in environmental permitting and review were centrally important spaces for the raising of demands like the restitution of property rights. But they were also important staging grounds for populism's metaconcern with a supposed deficit in democratic decision-making and the corrupt influence of oil. Historically, Midwestern populism has a strong commitment to both public participation and radical democratic governance. But like desire more generally, populism is never satisfied with the actual performance of public participation. Chapter 2 analyzes the supposed insignificance of official public participation to the actual decision-making processes of environmental permitting. I demonstrate how spaces and norms of public participation are another source of frustration that cohere into populist environmentalism. Here, I am interested in why pipeline opponents kept returning to these spaces and demanding more participation despite the knowledge that participation is ineffective. Rather than understand these subjects as duped by democracy, I argue that they approach public testimony with resigned pragmatism. Populists do not think public participation constitutes "real democracy" (and there are good reasons to think they are right). But they do feel like institutional avenues must be exhausted before moving elsewhere. In showing the tension between idealized democracy and its actual performances, this chapter challenges scholars and activists alike to think through whether participation in democracy is exhausting or prefigurative of more radical politics.

Central to desires for security expressed by some pipeline opponents was a sense that the heartland, taken to be a particularly important and threatened part of the nation, was being exploited by foreigners. Chapter 3 scrutinizes how populist rhetoric structured an interior part of the United States in opposition to a foreign power through melodramatic affect. The pipeline corporation TransCanada and the Canadian government alike represented the corrupt power of foreign oil, while the export of oil to other parts of the world—especially East Asia—seemed to betray "energy independence." This chapter first shows that heartland melodrama has a long history, stemming from the populist reaction to the globalization of oil and agriculture in the 1970s. Yet pipeline opponents in the 2010s brought "the foreign" into heartland melodrama in new ways, focusing on new regions like Canada and new arenas of the supply chain, like consumption and transportation rather than simply production. Opponents compared the supposed invasion of foreign oil corporations to colonialism and the defense of the American Revolution. At the same time, they reconstructed an image of the rural Midwest as a geopolitical and economic breadbasket of the nation. Ultimately, I argue that heartland melodrama in progressive populism relies upon and reproduces anti-Asian sentiment as a symbol of abstract capitalism, thus securing the concrete grounds of opposition in national settler colonial control of land while forming the latter as a global, competitive project with other settler nations.

Antiexpert sentiment is crucial to populist rhetoric of all kinds, but environmentalism's reliance on ecological science might seem to preclude it from such a structure. In chapter 4, I address this contradiction by demonstrating how populist political identity was predicated on a particular experience of the affect and disaffection of performed expertise. In evidentiary hearings, pipeline opponents attempted to prove through collection of knowledge and evidence and the development of expertise that the pipeline should not be built. Although they were staunch in the belief of the truth of their position, the frequent dismissal of scientific evidence in evidentiary review proved to be the last straw for many. Cynically, opponents increasingly viewed expertise as simply a matter of money. But rather than simply oppose expertise to common sense, pipeline opponents instead began to use the knowledge and collective practices—"minor sciences"—accumulated in these spaces even as they took leave of the institutional process. This chapter demonstrates the utility and limits of contesting evidence via counter-expertise in a landscape where knowledge is seemingly available for purchase and facts seem to be contingently constructed.

How should we evaluate the ambivalences of pipeline populism in its attempts to create a mass movement to address climate change? The conclusion of *Pipeline Populism* reflects on how the concept of affective infrastructure can help reveal the limits of left populism. In particular, I attend to how "the desire to be popular" can constrain liberal, progressive, and even socialist imaginations in ways that might throttle possibilities for a revolutionary socialist transformation necessary to adequately confront the climate crisis. The substantive chapters of this book demonstrate both tremendous potential and crucial limits to the scenes through which pipeline populism emerged. Reflecting on the affective infrastructures from whence our desires are shaped can help us become more active composers of our movements and their spatial politics, thus emphasizing the transformative potential of political struggle.

1

"THIS LAND IS OUR LAND"
PRIVATE PROPERTY AND
TERRITORIALIZED RESENTMENT

ON A SCORCHING EARLY FALL AFTERNOON in September 2014, a crowd of several thousand antipipeline activists gathered in the remnants of a harvested cornfield excited to hear the protest music of Willie Nelson and Neil Young. The concert was held on farmland in the direct path of the Keystone XL pipeline just outside of Neligh, Nebraska. Though sparsely populated, the rolling hills through corn and soybean fields on Nebraska Highway 20 were interspersed with occasional homemade road signs denouncing the pipeline's construction. The thousands assembled in the baking sun were there for many reasons: to oppose local environmental destruction wrought by the pipeline and the global climate effects of tar sands mining and combustion, the exploitation of migrant workers from Alberta to the Gulf Coast, the theft of and damage to Native lands, the use of eminent domain to cross landowner property without consent. We affirmed the solidarity that appears through art, music, and celebration; the opportunities of local food, clean energy, and community organizing; and—as always when Nelson is involved—the legalization of marijuana. Though the sticky-sweet scent of pot mixed with that of a nearby hog farm to create a particularly acrid odor, none of this put a damper on the event. Cowboys, ranchers, hippies, activists, elders, T-shirt hawkers, nonprofit leaders, hemp growers, party members, corn and soybean farmers, and children were all seemingly united in opposition to the pipeline.

Donning a T-shirt bearing the First Nations movement slogan "Idle No More," partway through his set Young began a rousing rendition of the classic left protest song "This Land Is Your Land" with lyrics modified to be about the KXL struggle.[1] It struck me that the proposition of the pipeline opponents who had revised the song's lyrics was that our different identities were united by a collective desire to protect the land. This was particularly true for a gathering that sought to signify an alliance of Indigenous Ponca and Oceti Sakowin opponents with the menagerie of settlers to build common ground, as several of the speakers intermittent between bands told us. Yet given the important staging of Indigenous resurgence, which was (and continues to be) particularly potent in North America during this period and since (Coulthard 2014; Estes 2019; L. B. Simpson 2017), the large crowd singing of a desire for a restoration of land—understood by many as a defense of an inalienable right to private property—suggested that such unity might be tenuous. Many of these political organizations would help stall the KXL and Dakota Access pipelines, but moments like this rendition of "This Land Is Your Land" demonstrate how pipeline opposition is also capable of rearticulating settler desires for the defense of landed private property.

The concert was emblematic of the general problem of stitching together a broad coalitional politics without sacrificing diversity, a dilemma that has beleaguered political activists of all kinds, not least the populist genre's attempts to construct a "people." Many theories of populism focus on the interests that are woven together in such coalitional politics; interests, in a liberal-capitalist context, are frequently understood with reference to the supposedly rational self-interest of individuals seeking to accrue and defend economic profit. Both pipeline opposition and accommodation could emerge from self-interest in landed private property. However, in this chapter I argue that in addition to interests, we must also consider desires for land, which include psychosocial frameworks through which interests are filtered. Desires and interests can be coincident, as when landowners simply sought greater financial compensation from pipeline firms in exchange for the right to cross their land. But although economic interests are crucial, they alone cannot explain the entry of many landowners into the political sphere; violations of one's desires to possess and control property (rather than only realizing economic value) led many to pipeline resistance.

The environmental writer Jedediah Purdy suggests, in a book aptly titled *This Land Is Our Land,* that "every political contest over claims on the land is, in part, a contest over what will be remembered and what will be forgotten" (2019, xvii). Purdy attends to the ways in which land is at the heart of civic enmity in North America—it unites and divides us, he frequently writes. In settler colonial and supposedly postslavery contexts like those of the United States, however, the wealth ensconced in landed private property and the sense of belonging that land denotes can tip the scales of coalitional land struggles toward the maintenance of settler colonialism and white supremacy. A certain incommensurability lies in what is being fought over: Is land really a *thing* over and on which different groups make claims, however unequally? Or is land, as numerous Indigenous political revolutionaries and theorists suggest, a set of social, more-than-human political *relations* that entail normative obligations that can only flourish through the abolition of landed private property?[2] If the latter is the case, then struggles for the defense of private property should be examined with extreme suspicion.

Around the same time as I was doing research with landowners in South Dakota in 2014 and 2016, the libertarian property rights activist Cliven Bundy and associates had been stirring up trouble in the U.S. West again (Keeler 2021). In 2014, Bundy had led a standoff with law enforcement over federally administered grazing rights fees. In 2016, Cliven's son Ammon Bundy led a seizure of the Malheur National Wildlife Refuge in Oregon, occupying federal buildings for over a month in defiance of the federal government. Though such rebellions can pose minor annoyances to the security interests of the settler state and capital, the property rights activists appear to be consistent in their myriad actions: their attempts to privatize land coincide with an opposition to federal Indian law (A. Smith 2018). Similar white dissent could be found on the other side of the country as well. In Washington, D.C., in April 2019, a group of white nationalists protested a book reading of sociologist Jonathan Metzl's *Dying of Whiteness: How the Politics of Racial Resentment Is Killing America's Heartland.* The self-described "identitarian" activists were filmed chanting, "This land is our land" (Herreria 2019).

One might posit a certain resemblance between these actions and some of the more conservative and libertarian pipeline opponents. Yet through years of political organizing, their interests were remade to be put in solidarity with pipeline opposition. Jacqueline Keeler (Diné/ Ihanktonwan Dakota), in describing how the Cowboy and Indian Alliance differs from the Bundy movement, suggests that the ultimate question the former ask is "Can the land make us one people?" (2021, 200). Such a question would have to remain open because, as I describe in this chapter, aspects of the alliance were unstable and its populist organization flawed. So, if it has become common to understand the contemporary politics of rural white settlers through the concept of resentment toward urban elites and driven by the intersection of race and class, this feeling needs to be understood in its construction. Resentment is the feeling of bitter indignation at having been treated unfairly, which in this chapter I argue emerges from the territories of property interrupted by pipelines. Tracing the role of territorialized resentment requires an understanding of the economic interest that landowners seek to maintain. It also requires understanding contradictory political desires, which can maintain the possessive individualism central to white settlement or push past its limitations.

The first part of this chapter examines the difference between some landowners who felt that pipelines primarily threatened their economic interests in land and those who felt that it also threatened a more fundamental affective attachment to the land. The latter violations of private property were produced by, and further productive of, territorialized resentment, as landowners were affected by material violations of their (supposed) right to govern their plot of land. Territorialized resentments are material-affective; it matters, I show, that the property under question is not just titled but also bordered by fences, riven by creeks, aquifers, and irrigation lines, and trod upon by people and cattle. The second part of the chapter works through how, by exceeding the economic threshold of protecting one's economic interest, such territorialized resentment opened multiple political possibilities for resolution. Territorialized resentment led to social demands and identities that became organized as populism. Landowners began to collectively identify as "the people," in doing so "perceiving that their neighbors have other, equally unsatisfied demands," as Ernesto Laclau puts it (2005, 73). Most troubling, populist politics led landowners to channel their territorialized resentments into too-easy identifications with Indigenous resistance to pipelines. The federal government's use of eminent domain to expropriate parts of settler private property meant that landowners thought of themselves as, in effect, being treated like Indians. Land was understood as the equivalent signifier that bound together this collective people, that in which landowners, environmentalists, and Native Nations all had an interest in defending.

Populism also transformed desires in a manner that was more complex than simple economic interests can account for. It created spaces for reflection on desires not for reductive identification but for solidarity through difference. We can see these when some landowners did not reterritorialize their initial resentments back on to struggles to defend private property from eminent domain but instead leveraged them to critique the settler state's power to expropriate for the supposed public good of oil pipelines and economic growth in an appropriated representation of "the people." We can also see such desires in moments of comradeship, or when landowners have ex-appropriated their property back to Native Nations or put their bodies or wealth on the line for the ex-appropriation of federal land or wealth stolen from Indigenous peoples. Though still fraught, such moments should be particularly exciting for socialists and other radicals who desire an end to the private property system that governs land and livelihoods, making oil pipelines seem like necessary pathways to the good life. Consequently, this chapter presents populism as both a viable and limited entry point for the organization of desire; its strategy of lowest-common-denominator identification must transition for more radical politics to grow.

Land Agents at the Door

"It all happened so fast," Rick remembered. "There's land agents in the field already, you barely have time to assimilate it." A rancher in a sparse county in western South Dakota, Rick was in the middle of calving in spring of 2008 when he first experienced the impacts of KXL. "I didn't first *hear* about it . . . the first I *knew* about it was when the surveyor showed up on the county roads." Though Rick was suspicious, he was not initially alarmed. Until, that is, "they pulled down on my private road. They made a mistake," Rick suggested, "but I won't, well [actually], I *will* hold it against them. They should have been more professional'n that." Rick, like many landowners might, took affront to the sudden appearance of strangers on his property. If he had known in advance, perhaps things might have gone differently. It could have been a trivial encounter. "They should have just loaded up and left." Though the Keystone I pipeline had recently been completed on a north–south route through eastern South Dakota, it did not make many news headlines. Third-party surveyors and land contractors began scoping the KXL route in 2008 on the other side of the state. According to Rick, these surveyors from a third-party contractor based out of Oklahoma escalated things.

To understand this story, it helps to understand Rick. A rancher his entire life, Rick's hands were weathered, and he had shoulder problems. He struck me as a prototypically direct person, not one to be taken by bullshit. The first question Rick asked me when I called him to set up an interview was "Who are you funded by?" I explained that I was a graduate student from the University of Minnesota and that I had a small research grant to support the development of a project looking at land and pipelines in South Dakota. He persisted in questioning me. Finally, I realized that Rick assumed I was obliquely funded by TransCanada. Though my 605 area code denoting a South Dakota number alleviated enough suspicions to meet me, our interview the following week still began with a certain amount of skepticism. Rick coyly asked about family: "What do your parents do?" "Do you have folks out in the Chamberlain area?" It was only then that I realized he was concerned that I might be further linked to Annette Bosworth, a Republican seeking nomination for U.S. Senate whose campaign had been somewhat scandalous. I assured Rick that we had no relation, and our conversation became increasingly amicable.

All this is to say that Rick seemed like a person unlikely to avoid confrontation. At first, he just euphemistically told me that his encounter with the surveyors "wasn't very pleasant" and he was a bit "confrontational." Then details emerged: "Somewhere in the point they *did* load up and leave, 'cause they didn't like getting spit on." But this unpleasant encounter did not reveal anything about why the contractors were there, as they would not reveal who they were working for or what they were doing. A few days later, they returned to the same county road. Rick proceeded to hold them there until the county sheriff arrived.

"That was the first time I knew who they were and what was going on."

I initially did not consider how Rick had delayed them. That is, until we circled back around to the topic as he explained his philosophy concerning land agents. Many landowners first heard that the pipeline would be crossing their property from land agents rather than surveyors. Land agents, also usually third-party contractors, offered landowners financial benefits to secure easements to dig through their private property. An easement is an agreement to forfeit certain rights to part of your property to another party. Though we might think of private property as a complete, bounded thing—say, a plot of land—legal scholars frequently describe property instead as a "bundle of rights," an increasingly strained legal metaphor for property (Kay 2016; Steinberg 1995). In the U.S. West, this bundle often includes surface or underground water rights, mineral rights for oil or other resources, or conservation rights to leave land fallow. Rick was particularly concerned about mineral rights. "That was one of my arguments [against] the pipeline being on my property, because it would hinder my lands from being developed for oil and gas." But when push came to shove, Rick understood the incursions into land not so much through this legal framework but through one of performative exclusion:

> I've learned a lot through the process . . . One thing about land agents is, the first thing you do is throw them off your place. I mean, no sense even negotiating or dealing with them! . . . I finally told them, I said, "You know what? This is the last time you're coming out here. I'm not going to see you again. You're going to get shot if you come out here. Unless you have a document that has Barack Obama's signature on it, don't come back."

Rick told me that the land agents did not bother him much after that encounter.

In 2009, Stan first spoke with land agents who visited his property in south-central South Dakota. He was reluctant to sign an easement immediately and told the agents that he preferred to mull over the offer. After attending permitting hearings and information sessions, doing his own research, and talking to his neighbors, Stan felt uncertain. The price that TransCanada had offered was too little for the risk he would bear. Additionally, he did not like that they made the pipeline seem inevitable and that he had no say in the matter, noting: "This is supposed to be a democracy, after all." But it was not until he found surveyors "snooping around" his property without his permission that he decided to oppose the pipeline in earnest: "They were unlawfully trespassing before I had signed anything. It was the kind of thing that put a bad taste in your mouth." Many landowners felt "bullied" by the looming threat of condemnation—the process of land transfer via eminent domain, the legal seizure of specific property rights by the state for the common interest of vital infrastructure systems like roads or dams. It was difficult for me to assess precisely what land agents said, as easements usually included a nondisclosure agreement of some kind. But rumors swirled. Land agents suggested that delaying a contract agreement would result in a lower financial offer. They might also have hinted that condemnation would result in a much lower price in the easement, an experience that seemed to be confirmed by the condemnation hearing I attended in Iowa for a DAPL-crossed property. As another outspoken South Dakotan rancher put it: "Negotiating with TransCanada having right of eminent domain is like having somebody trying to rob you at gunpoint and arguing for your billfold when there's nothing in it" (quoted in Mufson 2012).

The sudden appearance of land agents was a jarring moment because it revealed the freedom and exclusive authority that property rights supposedly granted could be made more flexible than expected. I asked Betty, a landowner in eastern South Dakota whose land was crossed by DAPL, when she first heard about the pipeline: "November 13th of 2014 is the exact date when a land agent came to my home and informed me there would be an oil pipeline crossing my property. . . . I was handed just a few pieces of paper, told a few facts, and I refused to sign anything. I told her I wanted to do more research and find out more about it." These economic incentives and legal pressures resulted in widespread—if sometimes reluctant—acceptance of the KXL and DAPL projects from most white landowners.

Property, Dispossession, and the White Settler Subject

When reading such accounts, an initial interpretation might be that landowners are trying to protect their economic interest in their land.

How should we understand the character and origins of such interest? Landowners mix their own labor with the earth or seek rents from others who work the land in some way. In a capitalist economy, landed private property has a very special role—so important that classical political economists argued that along with capital and labor, land comprises one pillar of the "trinity formula" that would be so heavily critiqued by Marx (1981, 953). Land has also been a central (though not only) component in what the classical political economists called originary or "primitive accumulation," which Marxist scholars today sometimes refer to as "accumulation by dispossession" (D. Harvey 2005; Glassman 2006). These concepts refer to the processes by which peasants—or in the contemporary, subsistence farmers and smallholders—are dispossessed of relations with land through privatization, which is frequently accomplished through violence and with the backing of the state. Dispossession has long been central to critiques of—and Indigenous militancy against—the violence of settler colonial regimes of accumulation (N. Brown 2014; Coulthard 2014; Nichols 2020). Dispossession is realized through imperialism, racialization, and heteropatriarchy, as the common "wasteland" of "frontier" spaces and their supposedly "uncivilized" populations are understood by colonial powers, firms, and publics as requiring incorporation, subjugation, and development (Chakravartty and Silva 2012; Singh 2016). Dispossession also functions to submit ecologies of nonhuman life to the accumulation process, "separating the bulk of humanity from the productive power of nature" (Nichols 2020, 83). Such punitive extermination of nonhumans via their separation from people and land has been a genocidal tool to subjugate Native Nations, as when the slaughter of buffalo was used to quell the late 1800s resistance from the Oceti Sakowin in this region (Estes 2019). Dispossession thus has both an economic and a political function. Surplus capital is accumulated on top of that which is accumulated through the exploitation of labor, while peasant livelihoods are rendered more precarious and subject to domination. This dampens resistance and, in Marx's ironic term, renders the people from the land "free as a bird" (*vogelfrei*)—that is, free to participate in the labor pool and thus their further exploitation.

In addition to the destructive elements of dispossession and privatization, political subjects are constructed by private property. C. B.

Macpherson (1964) helpfully describes the everyday philosophy that accompanies private property as "possessive individualism," most clearly seen in John Locke's *Second Treatise*.[3] Locke describes the subject of property as working on himself through mixing labor (his and that of those he might hire or own as enslaved people) with the land, thus demonstrating ownership of the land through its improvement. Such labor also demonstrates individual ownership of his person and body—and consequently, its moral improvement—ideas that both presuppose and shape the theories of capitalism, liberalism, and empire (Mehta 1999; Rose 1994). Though not delimited to "white people" in anything like a strictly empirical fashion (since, after all, the "real" existence of race is social and historical, not biological),[4] the possessive individual's role in imperial capitalist accumulation historically and structurally reproduces what Denise Ferreira da Silva (2007) describes as "the transparent subject of whiteness." For Silva, this concept describes the Euro-American subject's understanding of itself as undetermined by spatiality—unaffected—and thus sovereign, or capable of self-command and mastery.[5] Aileen Moreton-Robinson (Goenpul) further argues that the sense of "possession" upheld in such patriarchal whiteness is understood as "having an *excessive desire to own*" (2015, 67, emphasis added). Opposed to such a transparent subject, Black, Indigenous, and poor people and migrants are socially deemed unfit property owners—as, for example, research on homeownership demonstrates (Chakravartty and Silva 2012; Roy 2017; K.-Y. Taylor 2019).

Scholars and activists further argue that moments of accumulation by dispossession and the resistance movements that they spawn demonstrate that no accumulation is accomplished without struggle (D. Moore 2005; T. M. Li 2014). The "origin" points of private property in the transition from feudalism into capitalism—and property's expansion into different territories such as the intellect, data, and genetics—are instructive. But sometimes scholars act as if all the action is completed during privatization. Property has been instituted, accumulation chugs along, and capital expands elsewhere. This would be an incomplete story. Private property did not only arise in a swift, single moment and expand incrementally through privatization from thence onward. Already-constituted property also continues to produce an ongoing libidinal and material investment through arranging bodies, spaces, signs, and subjects. Along with legal codes and state enforcement subject to interpretation, materials like hedges, fences, and signs signify and stabilize property boundaries. Furthermore, intercapitalist struggles remain over which uses or functions of property are most profitable. Should this plot of land support public housing or a new condo development? Do this land's capacities best afford corn and soybean production or a pipeline? It is through these investments that we can understand that settler desires to own must be constantly reactivated. This production is ongoing, both a site of struggle itself and the assumed grounds for other partisan struggles. Property takes ongoing work.

Struggles and contradictions continue for three reasons: economically, capital puts constant pressure on the rate of profit realized in relating to land via agriculture or rent. Take, for example, corn: following a historic spike after the 2007 financial crisis, corn prices plummeted in the mid-2010s. This can further result in competition to realize value through different land uses. The state may advocate for multiple or different land uses—through, for example, zoning laws, conservation easements, or eminent domain—which can spark resistance from smallholders or corporations.[6] Second, politically, the ongoing existence and persistence of Black and Indigenous peoples puts psychic pressure on the supposedly coherent subject of possessive individualism, as the disavowed history and present of the contradiction between expansion and security that formed the subject of possessive individualism must be addressed (Guenther 2019). Finally, the materials that private property attempts to subjugate and bound can be more unruly than expected (Steinberg 1995). Trees grow over property lines, fences break down, toxins seep from next-door waste dumps. Through defense and reinscription of these borders, property is not only sedimented but also extended. But it is only a tenuous achievement. As in Rick's response to the land agents above, the potential instability of property's territory registers in affective responses.

How, then, should we understand the relationship between emotion and landscape in property struggles? Cultural geographer Yi-Fu Tuan suggests that a sense of place attachment is formed through the "steady accretion of sentiment over the years" (1977, 33). Such an accretion occurs unevenly, shaped by power and politics, but Tuan is careful to suggest that it occurs nondeterministically. It is not that a rural farming landscape teleologically leads to resentment but that a complex combination of spatial characteristics are involved in the generation of such emotions. In suggesting that a territorialized resentment lay behind the emergence of pipeline populism, then, I want to point us toward the fact that affective reactions emerge from relationships between places and bodies as primed by racialized regimes of ownership. Furthermore, such affective infrastructures recursively create the conditions for multiple forms of political response. A feeling of lack of security in property can be the source of resentment and thus an object of defense and recuperation (as in, I must defend my land from incursion) or a source of resentment and thus object of negation (as in, I must rid myself of this defense from incursion). The meaning of *territorialized* is thus processual—it refers to the source of the feeling of resentment in the performative territories of property and the consciousness and transposition of that resentment onto one's relationship to other elements, such as body, coloniality, land, the state, or corporations. The moment of territorialized resentment is thus potent with political possibilities.

Such a theoretical framework helps us understand how the potential appearance and construction of a pipeline can thus disrupt the realization of value, the relations of materials, and the political psyches associated with the possessive individual. In the rest of this chapter, I show how this disruption resulted in the production of territorialized resentment, which primed settler subjects for political involvement in new ways. Would this affect then be reterritorialized onto capital, such that pipelines could become a method by which landowners could seek further rents and thus meet the pressures of a global marketplace? Would it be generalized into a populist struggle against pipelines, which violate the supposed sovereignty of the possessive individual? Or would it free up desires for alternative decolonial recompositions? The next sections examine each of these in turn and how they contributed to the formation of a populist political response to the pipelines.

Profit and Self-Interest

Dan, a farmer in eastern South Dakota, first heard about DAPL in 2014 when he talked to a surveyor driving around near his property. A few days later, he learned that the pipeline would be passing through his land. "You have to understand the demographics of land ownership in the Upper Midwest," he explained to me. "Most of the people that own land are probably in their sixties, seventies, and eighties, so an offer of X number of dollars sounds like a pretty good deal. So I think quite a few people took that first offer." But Dan, who was a bit younger, emphasized that he "was not satisfied with that first offer." Unlike other landowners, he was not overly suspicious of the pipeline company, ETP. They are a business just trying to make money, and Dan explained that he too was a businessman:

> One [land agent] came back to me and said, "Well, what do you have to have [in terms of a price]?" And I told him. And he used a baseball analogy, he said, "You're not just out in left field, you're clear out in the parking lot." Now, did I find that insulting? A little. But I'm like a businessman, and so basically this was a negotiation. And so I said, "Well, what's your number?" And they said, "Well, I can't give you that." [After that,] they would never, they would *never* say another number. So I think that the land agents were always quite [*pause*] "let's lowball these guys as best we can."

For Dan, the primary emotion resulting from initial negotiations was one of indignation resulting from the low offer. This was attached to the threat of eminent domain, which "loomed" in Dan's mind. He explained to me that, as "a former banker," numbers are something he frequently works with. As he did some back-of-the-napkin calculations, he quickly figured that "somebody's going to make some money on this thing."

> I went back and calculated what they had offered me. I said if they offered me that much, and then everybody north and west would get that much, and then everybody south and east got triple what I got (because it's more valuable land), then [ETP] would have their pipeline easements paid within about six months. So, for that reason I didn't settle. I sought out legal counsel.

From this point, Dan never had direct contact with ETP. His lawyer negotiated a deal that came close enough to satisfying his financial expectations. Dan's approach to the pipeline was almost entirely self-interested. If the rate of profit of the pipeline company was so high, he figured that he deserved more money for signing the easement. The negotiation process, for him, concerned profit—here described as value—and rent. His interests also led him away from politics. He did not get involved in organized pipeline opposition, explaining to me that his neighbors and other landowners all "seemed to do their own thing." Dan's political perspective also colored his eventual support of the pipeline, which he recognized as "more economical" than transportation by rail.

Still, Dan recognized something unfair about the whole process, even if he did finally support and benefit from DAPL's construction.

> You know how [ETP's] stock has done over the last ten years—including the Great Recession? 7 to 8 percent. Their standard increase in value has been that much. That's my rationale for saying, you know, "Somebody's going to make some coin, I need to make a fair amount as well." . . . My frustration is that as a farmer, I have to negotiate my cash rent. I'm providing food and fiber to the world. . . . I don't get to declare *I'm* going to go [use] eminent domain and say, "You have to accept my low cash rent, so that I can do this at a profit." No. I have to do that [work to make profit]. So, I find a little bit of frustration that this stock holding company that makes 7 percent dividend and 7 percent increase in value gets to say, "Well, we're coming through with this pipeline and if you don't accept it, we're going to [use] eminent domain."

Dan's story shows that economic self-interest was thus a crucial denominator in both sparking and resolving some landowner struggles with pipeline firms. When the price of easements and compensation for loss did not match the expectation as to the revenue that could be realized through land use, landowners balked. Other landowners felt like they would be unjustly compensated for a spill or damage to their property and that the risk of such an event was redistributed from TransCanada or ETP to them. This led skeptical landowners to seek negotiations for greater financial benefits. But though there were grumblings, many others were satisfied with the financial benefits of the pipeline. This suggests landowner resentment toward pipeline firms could serve as either an instigator for populist political movements or an instance of the internal struggle between landowners (including states) and extractive firms that bedevils the political economy of oil (Labban 2008). Some landowners were simply most concerned about whether a pipeline would affect their ability to continue to seek rents or realize the revenue of their farming or ranching labor. This interest demonstrates how landowners are compelled to protect and defend the profit that is realized through the sale of their agricultural commodities. Transferring limited property rights via an easement was a way for many farmers and ranchers to add further revenue through essentially renting out an underground portion of their land for a pipeline.

Even though the market ultimately disciplines assessments of value through the measure of price, individual choices still involve a certain amount of subjective evaluation, from which contradictions can emerge. But a contradiction is not a limit—it can be resolved without changing the terms of negotiation. Dan saw himself as a businessman. He translated his concerns via "numbers" into a comparison, using money as a general equivalent. The questions that a limit poses are: "What is a social formation capable of, what can it tolerate or bear, in function of its internal relationships, its codes, its institutions, its semiotics, and its collective practices? What on the contrary are the processes that exceed its conditions of reproduction, or call them into question?" (Sibertin-Blanc 2016, 55). Passing beyond the limit of economic assessment entails posing a problem that interest and its possessive individual cannot easily resolve. A limit wards off the transformation that passing such a threshold would induce: here, we can look back at how Dan talks about "the looming aspect of eminent domain" for a cogent example. "There's always that [sense that] 'well, you never know . . . we might have to go to court and if that happens we don't know.'" People are conscious of the potential of the situation to be transformed and can fear crossing that line. But if differences in the assessment of potential profit and risk could not provide a sufficient contradiction to induce such a transformation, then why did some farmers rebel against the pipelines?

Leakage, Depth, Attachment

Among pipeline opponents I spoke with, the calculative approach taken by Dan was an exception—those who signed easements more willingly perhaps were persuaded by the thousands of dollars offered by

TransCanada or ETP. Most opponents, by contrast, began narrating their experience with border crossings, such as Rick's disdain with surveyors appearing on his property. As he put it, "They claim it's still my land, but it's really not. They have the right to go out and do whatever they want, whenever." Rick's feeling of being dispossessed of his property rights contrasts with that of Dan, who said his concern with the pipeline was "not so much [that it would] economically *impact* me, because [regardless] I was going to get paid." Rather, for landowner opponents, a laundry list of what seemed like excessively inconsequential potential impacts led to their political involvement. These were understood as perforations of their individual piece of property and thus cause for what sometimes became massive investments of time and energy in opposing the pipeline.

For example: pipeline construction would run close to a well that is used for livestock drinking. Workers failed to close a gate on their way out. One landowner in the path of DAPL was peeved that construction would require cutting down part of their shelterbelt (a line of trees planted on the north and west of a building to reduce wind and thus heating costs). Eventually, ETP agreed to drill under the shelterbelt rather than disturb it—I was told secondhand that this landowner still grumbled. I do not mean to trivialize these grievances but rather to suggest that their variation and seeming inconsequentiality denotes they were not infringements of an easily quantifiable or generic exchange value of the land. Instead, they threatened personalized visions of territorialized desires to control or live with land, to maintain and build a certain kind of settler way of life.

Perhaps obviously, getting several thousand-mile-long pipelines underneath six feet of earth requires a massive amount of work. Unlike the arid cattle ranching lands of western South Dakota crossed by KXL, the porous soil of eastern South Dakota supports corn, soybeans, and wheat. In addition to the labor that farmers mix with the earth, a vertical territory supports this agricultural system, a cause of intense anxieties for farmers whose land was crossed by DAPL. First of all, of course, any crops being grown at the time would have to be abandoned—farmers would be compensated for their losses, but the rates were a source of uncertainty. Then there is the actual construction. Topsoil, with its moisture absorbent qualities and nutrients, is of central importance for growing crops, while beneath the topsoil lie layers of clay and other subsoil materials. Construction crews were required to separate these layers in two and return them in order, but in actuality some mixture might occur and mistakes could happen. Additionally, if topsoil is too compacted by construction, then it will not have the porosity to support plant growth. Finally, there is rehabilitation—the planting of crops or grasses on the returned soil. Rumors, horror stories, and images circulated from the 2007 construction of the Keystone I pipeline through the region. Construction during and after excessive rains caused major disruption, resulting in some difficulty growing crops after the pipeline was installed. One person told me he heard the heat from this pipeline affected winter wheat germination times—as well as the spring emergence of ground-dwelling insect larvae.

These anxieties exposed the three-dimensional lack of boundedness or closure in property as it extends beneath the surface of the earth. Farmers and ranchers voiced concern about a pipeline leak contaminating either the high surface water table in northern Nebraska and south-central South Dakota or the deeper Ogallala Aquifer, which provides irrigation and livestock water for millions of people from South Dakota to north Texas. The argument from many landowners was that an oil spill would have the potential to contaminate the aquifer, a gigantic public resource on which so many private landowners depend. Private property appeared to be bounded on the surface, but the farther below the earth one traveled, the more permeable and public it appeared.

Drainage tiles lie beneath the cropland in eastern South Dakota, Iowa, and Illinois. During excessive rains, soil can become sodden and thus cause the roots of some crops to rot. Drainage tiles are pipeline systems that collect subsurface water, channeling it out of fields and into marginal ditches or creeks. Steven was particularly worried about the impact an oil spill might have on the tile lines beneath the ground:

> Yeah even on this property here, twenty miles away there could be an oil spill and it'll keep tricklin' on down through the drain tiles of the farms. And there's even county tiles. They're old and they're big and they move a lot of water. Some of them should be replaced now, but some of them are still allowing a lot of water to come down. And it just keeps on comin' on down. So it doesn't even have to be an oil leak

on my property! It can be way up the road and it's going to affect me as well as everybody else.

In Steven's account, the leakage of oil through existing infrastructure systems and across property borders induced anxiety and resentment. Though the pipeline crossed Steven's land, he felt it posed a risk to him even if a leak were to occur elsewhere. Another possibility, he suggested, was that a drainage tile line might be severed during construction. In fact, this occurred to several farmers in eastern South Dakota during the construction of DAPL, one of whom sued ETP for breach of easement contract.

Meeting with me at a local diner, Betty brought a large folder bursting at the seams with printouts. She pulled out a map and a pad full of notes, out of which a whole host of grievances spilled. She described her property to me and the places where she "had some concerns about where they might be crossing." First, she asked ETP to move the route, but this was not possible. Still, she petitioned that part of the property "is where I grew up as a young gal till I left home as a teenager" and a nearby spot was "an ideal place to build a home"—either for her later life or for her grandchildren. "I can't build there now [because of the pipeline], so that's pretty well done." Betty explained in detail all the features of the property that were put at risk by the pipeline. Though undoubtedly exchange value has a part to play here, the pipeline also would affect her memories of the place and the future she had imagined.

Next, Betty explained in detail how bisecting her property would affect the water sources for her cattle:

> I was concerned that if the cattle were here they would not be able to get to the water. It did prove to be a problem. [The construction crews] left openings, but on Thursday, Friday they proceeded to weld all the pipes. It was a hot weekend. They left a tiny little opening on this end and assumed the cattle over here would know to go all the way around and come back to the water. I had cattle that broke a fence here 'cause they could smell water here so they broke a fence here and did damage in a cornfield. From day one when I started negotiating with them I said that's going to be a problem. I even offered to get a hook up to rural water over here. They would not even consider it.

[The land agents] said, "It's never been an issue, it won't be a problem, [the cattle] will always have access to water." I even had it in my
easement agreement because I didn't believe them! And it still was a
problem. So yeah, when landowners say, "This is going to be an issue,
we need to deal with it," and [the land agents] say, "No it will never
be a problem." [And] they said, "There will be a trench and the cattle
will not fall in it." Well, [the cattle are] curious! There was a calf and
it fell in and had to be rescued. So, you know, that's just one area.
There's so many other issues and I wish they would listen to landowners, you know.

These are cascading concerns with multiple boundary crossings:
tile lines, trenches, wayward cattle. Digging trenches for pipelines
threatens that security materially and, by consequence, psychologically.
A common yard sign encapsulated the philosophy of property at work
here: "Good Neighbors Mend Fences, They Don't Dig Trenches! *Stop
Keystone XL!*" The neighborly thing to do, the sign implies, is to help
each other—mend a fence to prevent cattle from escaping, thus repair-
ing the boundary relationship of property. As one landowner put it in
early PUC testimony, "How about crossing fences? They must cross me
four or five times. Are those fences going to be repaired to their original
condition? Because I'm very, very—you can ask my neighbors. I'm really tough on fences, and I want those fences right" (South Dakota
PUC 2009c, 12). The geographer Nicholas Blomley recounts his own
experience mending a fence, recalling the adage that "good neighbors
make good fences." "As subjects that perform property as we build our
fence, [we] do not stand before that performance. We neither precede
nor follow the act of fence building, but emerge as subjects of property
through these very performances" (2013, 36).

It is worth unpacking this argument. Property boundaries required
tending, reinscription, or reinvention, revealing that property is a "con-
ditional achievement, dependent on continuous practice" (Blomley
2011, 213). Despite the fact that property is ideologically presented as
a container or a bundle of rights, its boundaries presuppose failure,
decay, or leakage. The work of maintenance that a piece of infrastructure like a fence requires will reproduce the property boundary (S. Jackson 2014). But it is not just a matter of reproducing the property itself.
As Étienne Balibar argues, "property . . . constitutes the generic essence

of the proprietor, his internal capacity to act. . . . The individual (what we will then call the subject) can *identify himself* with this property that he is, or recognize his identity in his movement of appropriation and acquisition" (2014, 75, emphasis added). If property constitutes the subject through identification with appropriation and acquisition, it follows that breakdown, leakage, maintenance, repair, and dispossession perform work on such a subject as well. Territorial resentment can in part be explained by bodily identification with the threat of border crossings. A desire to avoid transgression is thus reproduced in and through landownership. Property "hijacks the inherent paranoia of the body and diverts it for its own purposes" (Schuster 2016, 172). The constant anxiety of property resonates in and through the insoluble problem of attempting to resolve the psychic and corporeal boundaries of the subject itself (Guenther 2019).

The vertical materiality of the land further grounds myths of belonging to land—what scholars sometimes call autochthony—that work through settler subjects' understandings of history and culture. The frequently voiced concerns about an oil spill threatening the Ogallala Aquifer certainly speaks to such subterranean attachments. To mend fences rather than dig trenches is to repair not only the real borders of property but also the imagined borders of one's self, family, rights, nation, way of life. It is to reproduce transparency and sovereignty in the self. But depth is also capable of becoming a metaphor that works against property. One journalist's assessment of the coalitional politics of pipeline opposition to which I turn below pushes back against my suggestion that property was at the heart of some pipeline resistance. "For some landowners it's merely a problem of property rights. For most, though, it goes far deeper, down below the grass and soil to the very roots of their identities as either cowboys or Indians, to a sense that they are irrevocably tied to this land, that if you poison it, that they will be poisoned too" (Moe 2014). While I am sure that this assessment is well-founded, to move beyond property rights to something deeper would entail extinguishing property. If it remains, then the move to depth is in fact superficial.

The threat to property rights was registered in transgressions that congealed into territorialized resentment, thus offering us a glimpse of subjects coming to be affected rather than sovereign or transparent. Because the subject of property assumes freedom from determination by outer forces, the pipeline was a jarring reminder of capital's ongoing dissolution of some social relations with land as new forms of value are realized through exploitation of workers and ecological relations. Understandings of freedom and capacity are relative. The comparisons to foreign regimes that I examine in chapter 3 further demonstrate some racial content of that understanding. The previously disavowed relationality and spatiality of the possessive individual is belied by the fundamental dependence of individual well-being on a regime of property predicated on ongoing dispossession. Such reminders were threatening not only at the level of white settlers' economic well-being but also through the affective loss of both security and freedom. The resentment at being treated unfairly, and the desire to reclaim such individual sovereignty, thus conditioned an emergent form of populist politics.

From Territorialized Resentment to Populist Struggle

I have demonstrated that many initial landowner grievances against pipelines were based in a defense and recuperation of landed private property. There were two origins of this defense: those based on interest and those based on desire. One version of populist opposition stemmed from a coalitional approach that joined landowner interest in defending property rights with other pipeline opponents. Such coalition operated by a logic of equivalence wherein *land* functioned as a term that could appeal to each group opposing the pipelines. But *land* meant different things to environmentalists, landowners, and Native Nations. How did this process of populist assembly occur, and what were its political consequences? What made the property rights struggle populist, and what were the thresholds beyond which it had to be transformed?

As landowner animosity against KXL grew, rural community organizers who had organized against Keystone I began reaching out to farmers along the earlier pipeline's route. They suggested that farmers and ranchers along the pipeline form a landowner association to negotiate better contracts with TransCanada. In 2009, around fifty landowners along the KXL route formed Protect South Dakota Resources to negotiate better easement benefits. Landowners also began to organize with Dakota Rural Action, who facilitated relationships among citizens, landowners, and Native Nations to oppose KXL. These groups facilitated involvement in public testimony and hearings conducted by the EPA and South Dakota PUC, which I examine in chapter 2. Through collectivizing efforts, as one landowner explained to me, "we did have some bargaining power." The South Dakota landowner groups eventually reached an agreement with TransCanada, though many were still resentful. As Rick explained to me in 2014, "We could have done way better if we had known [the pipeline] was going to get held up. We should not be signed now, today. We were under the assumption we were going to be in court in two weeks, and we *would* have been [if we hadn't agreed]."

In Nebraska, more landowners found themselves unable to stomach any negotiation or compromise. There, the nonprofit Bold Nebraska served as a node for landowner discontent. Bold Nebraska was an outspoken opponent of eminent domain, making "no eminent domain for private gain" a phrase that would appear on roadside signs around the region. The main problem the pipeline represented was the use of eminent domain in support of a large, private, and foreign corporation that would transport Canadian oil to the United States only to be exported to East Asian markets. This ideology was saturated with a classically populist agrarian producerism that I examine more thoroughly in chapter 3, noting that the U.S. American family farmer and rancher, and the heartland more generally, were constructed as that which was at risk.

At this point in pipeline opposition, both Nebraskan and South Dakotan political organizations also worked through the conventions of the populist genre of politics, though their political orientations were slightly different. Recall that populism is the use of the language of the people to build coherent political tendencies across difference. Bold Nebraska followed contemporary nonprofit political strategies for building what they described as populist "unlikely alliances" across party divides and political beliefs, including among landowners and Native peoples fighting the KXL pipeline. Community organizer and Bold Nebraska director Jane Kleeb (2016) self-describes as a "pipeline fighting, populist and proud Democrat." This nonprofit's savvy media team spread the stories and images of their impressive organizing efforts effectively through national media sources. By 2011, they had built relationships with national environmentalist groups and funders, elevating the KXL struggle through popular media platforms across the country.

One result was high-profile protests of KXL in Washington, D.C., in 2011, in which thousands were arrested in symbolic civil disobedience in front of the White House. Another consequence was that by securing the territory of representation, Bold Nebraska circulated a representation of the revival of the Cowboy and Indian Alliance, a loose group of Native and non-Native people who opposed resource extraction projects in the region, which I described in the introduction (see also Grossman 2017). In demonstrating the possibility that rural, non-Native people could join in coalition with Lakota and other Native peoples, the Cowboy and Indian Alliance quickly became a favorite example of the media and the ecological left. The 350.org leader Bill McKibben describes the headline "Cowboys, Indians Unite against Pipeline" as his favorite of fall 2011 (2013, 61), while Naomi Klein describes their opposition to KXL as a "flashpoint for a resurgent US climate movement" (2014, 140). Members of the alliance were prominent parts of a 2014 event in Washington, D.C., called the Reject and Protect rally, as well as the 2015 People's Climate March in New York City.

Though not often noted, property rights continued to be central to the generic scenes of populist pipeline struggle as the pipeline of concern shifted from the stalled KXL to the fast-tracked DAPL. When the permit for KXL was rejected by President Obama's State Department in 2015, Bold Nebraska had already used their success to expand into pipeline fights in Iowa and Louisiana. Fierce opposition to DAPL grew on the southeastern part of the pipeline's route due in part to Bold Iowa's defense of property rights. During DAPL public hearings in the fall of 2015, Iowan landowners repeatedly emphasized the violation of their state constitution's bill of rights, which enshrined as inalienable citizens' rights of "acquiring, possessing, and protecting property" (Iowa Const. art. I, § 1). In the words of a landowner at a 2015 permitting hearing, eminent domain to transfer land between private owners was "the most unconscionable thing of all" (Iowa Utilities Board 2015, 69). Another testified that "private property rights are as dear to us as our right to life" (n.p.). Property thus continued to be the main reason for some opposition.

For antipipeline organizers, such populist rhetoric and performance was beneficially flexible. Anyone opposed to pipelines could become part of the unlikely alliances that constitute "the people." Community organizers enthusiastically represented their work as bringing together farmers, ranchers, Native Nations, environmentalists, and concerned citizens; Republicans and Democrats; the Tea Party and Occupy Wall Street; and urban and rural communities. This also represents a tradition of "meeting people where they're at" common in many types of political organizing (an assumption to which I return in this book's conclusion). Furthermore, party elites and corporations were easy for each of these groups to demonize. Here is how Rick thought about the situation: "I'm not going to go too far but what if the Democrats were in power down there [in South Dakota's state capitol, Pierre]? It would be the same way." When land defense could be equated with property rights, many conservatives and libertarian landowners could become involved in these coalitions—and this extended to actions at the other leg of KXL's route in Texas and Oklahoma. As organizers with a group called Tar Sands Blockade put it in a 2012 editorial, "In an age of political polarization, it was refreshing to see older, self-identified Tea Party members who deeply value property rights literally holding hands and linking arms with bright-eyed young environmentalists and Occupiers. . . . The traditional categories often applied to climate justice activists break down when we look at the coalition of pipeline resisters now ready and willing to put their bodies on the line" (Wooten, Bernd, and Seifert 2012). The coalition did not just bring these people together, either. It also created opportunities for transformation, breaking down perceived social barriers that would have otherwise prevented such communication.

The performative unity of the concept of "the people" also easily recalled the common U.S. rhetoric of "we the people." While I will return to populist interpretations of constitutional overtures toward democracy and nationalism in chapters 2 and 3, respectively, here I want to take a moment to stay with the question of property and its centrality to public understandings of the constitution. Though Article V of the Bill of Rights also sediments the right of eminent domain for public use, it is citizen pursuit of "life, liberty, or property" that sometimes became equated with democracy. However, the U.S. Supreme Court had recently ruled in *Kelo v. New London* (545 U.S. 469 [2005]) that eminent domain could also be used to transfer property from one private owner to another, if there was some overall public benefit (including, broadly speaking, to the economy). This ruling has thus further created a political soup of opposition to eminent domain. Leftists could be furious that the property of smallholders was being taken in support of "the corrupt and fascist Koch brothers and their ilk," or more generally for corporate gain (U.S. Department of State 2013d, 1472). Conservatives could be brought on board because the state's role in coercively facilitating this transfer, and the potential negative impact on property values that a transfer might entail, fundamentally violated their understandings of freedom and property. Referencing "we the people" recalled for many participants the foundational violation of their imagined rights.

What allowed populism to maintain a minimum coherence in stitching together local pipeline opposition was the slippage of property into other ideologies of land. For environmentalists, land recalled the land ethic of Aldo Leopold, the preservation of ecological systems, and recreation in public lands. For the Lakota, Dakota, Ponca, and other Native Nations along the length of the pipeline, defense of land encompassed a wider normative domain of politics, including protection and reclamation of the relationships and obligations with each other and the earth violently besieged by settler colonialism for the last several hundred years. But as I suggest above, for many landowners I spoke with, defending the land meant a return to their prior experience of an untrammeled, exclusive relationship with their own property. Though their land defense involved partnership, it did not usually entail concessions to Native Nations. The populist coalition formed against the pipelines blended these meanings of land in a sometimes uncomfortable way, as in the rendition of "This Land Is Our Land" described above. "Protecting the land" could remain vague enough to allow enough people with vastly different politics to feel more or less satisfied with the coalition, an impressive goal given the difficulty of stopping oil infrastructure in the largely rural Upper Midwest. Because "the land" was rendered into a fungible signifier or "mediating device" (Nichols 2020, 83) out of and in place of the material economic modes of relationship that define Indigenous understandings, it functioned as a general equivalent without always rebuilding such relations of responsibility and caretaking.

A critical practice of dismantling racial capitalism and settler colonialism could have emerged from these conditions. Indeed, some lessons learned during the earlier, KXL phase of the struggle informed the blockade of DAPL, which more clearly diagnosed the pipeline as part of these social processes. But such an analysis would have to highlight how capitalism necessitates liquidation of meaningful relationships with land and disposability of Indigenous livelihoods in a necessarily uneven fashion to that of landowners. Not all accumulation by dispossession is the same. Yet for many of the organizers and landowners I spoke with, populist resistance had to remain open-ended for pragmatic reasons. Coalitions with former right-libertarian Tea Party activists, for example, offered the opportunity to fracture the emergent reactionary populism that was sometimes also built out of territorial resentment toward corporate power (see Grattan 2016, 157). But this pragmatic orientation sometimes formed the horizon and orientation of the populist pipeline opposition rather than simply a strategic component. One consequence was settler identification with Indigenous dispossession.

"They're Treating Us like Indians"

South Dakotan organizations took what they described as a "more grassroots" approach to organizing pipeline opposition than those in Nebraska, one that appears messier and thus seems to me more honest than some representations of antipipeline organizing. Rather than an easy coincidence between Native and non-Native people discovering their common cause, organizers told me of false starts and baby steps, conflict, and sometimes only begrudging collaboration. One revealing example of such a deviance exemplifies the lack of coincidence of desires in coalitional politics. When populist coalitions against pipelines fought for the protection of property rights, their diagnoses frequently rested on understanding eminent domain as analogous to the dispossession of land from Native Nations. The feeling of territorialized resentment was understood by landowners to be a common experience and a common cause for struggle. With the federal government authorizing a taking of their land in a manner they saw as against its own laws or the constitution itself, the refrain some landowners repeated was that "they're treating us like Indians."

This sentiment was first relayed to me in 2013 by Sheila, a rural community organizer working with both landowners and Native pipeline opponents in South Dakota. Sheila used the phrase to describe how difficult it was to get everyone "on the same page," a frustration at trying to find common ground. In making the analogy in organizing meetings, landowners seemed to, in her estimation, "put their foot in their mouth." But Sheila, among many others, was committed to trying to build not just a political coalition to stop KXL but a broader politics of reconciliation in the state. Landowners can be "terrified of the militancy" that Indigenous peoples have, she suggested. "So we try to get them to see they have some shared interests. It's then when you see some of them realize, 'Oh, they're doing to us ranchers what they did to the Indians.'"

After this interview, I began to do some digging and discovered that the analogy was neither new nor uncommon. In an ethnography of 1990s Bennett County in south-central South Dakota, an anthropologist recounts the loss of land due to eminent domain that was used to establish a contiguous wildlife refuge. She notes the resentment that broiled, leading one non-Native person to remark that "they treated us just like Indians. They just came and pushed us off our land" (Wagoner 2002, 53).[7] In the 1980s, fights against the use of eminent domain for power lines and resource extraction in Minnesota and South Dakota mobilized similar analogies. As one Native activist told non-Native power line opponents at the time, "'Now you know what it feels like' to be dispossessed of land" (Grossman 2002, 85). Similar phrases can be found scattered around media accounts of pipeline opposition.

The history and contemporary politics of environmentalism is littered with numerous forms of "playing Indian" (P. J. Deloria 1998), in which Indigenous knowledge, aesthetics, and ontologies are reductively and uncritically appropriated by settlers. To be "treated *like* Indians," however, was not such a romantic act of imitation. Instead, it was an attempt to understand oneself as being produced by a shared—if uneven—experience of being trod upon by state and capital alike. It was almost as if white settlers felt themselves being reduced from transparency to the "affected" subject position of the racial subject. For many

Lakota, Dakota, and other Indigenous peoples, such an understanding of shared identity was understood with a bit of wry humor. For example, prominent Yankton pipeline opponent and leader Faith Spotted Eagle analyzed the prevalence of the analogy with humor: "I think that it affected our white neighbors in a way that has really shaken their spirits to realize how it felt when our land was taken, and so we jokingly call them 'the new Indians'" (quoted in Rodriguez 2014).

Such felt marginalization could lead to several different kinds of political formations in pipeline opposition. In a study of Native and rural white alliances, geographer Zoltán Grossman notes that while "it is highly doubtful that rural whites have become 'new Indians' . . . many are being forced to rethink their relations with Native neighbors when they are both 'slapped in the face' by white outsiders" (2017, 26). This has the potential of "disengaging [white settlers] from the ongoing project of colonization and engaging them in solidarity with decolonization" (30). The immense amounts of organizing work poured into rebuilding and sustaining the Cowboy and Indian Alliance demonstrates the degree to which such solidarities have to be forged. Sheila called this "long-term structural change" in an interview a few years after our first meeting, reiterating that this was "stuff that takes a long time." Nonetheless, even in the short term such coalitions challenge the assumed complete disjuncture between Native Nations and rural white communities and, in some cases, can "redirect [the] anger" of rural whites "toward state and corporate structures" (Grossman 2017, 28).

However, scholars and activists must be attentive to the parameters that populist forms of political alliances place on the transformative potential of such coalitions. If land and property are taken to be interchangeable, then the violent dispossessive and racial role of property can reinforce the basic status quo of settler coloniality.[8] The complexity of forging and sustaining such alliances also did not travel with the eager media representations produced by settler environmental groups. Rather than a framework of decoloniality, then, the version of pipeline populism that circulated was narrated as multicultural or pluralistic liberalism. Though it might seem innocuous, the financial and credibility benefits that issue from the circulation of such representations had uneven consequences for political organizing against the pipelines. Sheila slightly resented that the name and image of the Cowboy and Indian

Alliance was being used to drum up funds for Big Green groups that had little presence in or relation to the region. At the same time, her actual grassroots organization was financially struggling while "doing the difficult and thankless work [of reconciliation] on the ground."

These limits were exposed when the narrative of populist pipeline resistance was broken by the prayer camps and blockades of DAPL at the Standing Rock Sioux Reservation, led by a reunited Oceti Sakowin Oyate and in solidarity with at least four hundred Native Nations from across the planet. When this high-profile political response foregrounded not white settlers but decolonization, the populist approach struggled to maintain its analogic understanding of Native and settler dispossession. Settler activists, landowners, and community organizations responded in two different ways: either accepting the politics of this shift or doubling down on the analogy. On the one hand, many organizations began to engage with the struggle for sovereignty and land by Native Nations all along the pipeline's route whose historic land bases were dispossessed by the state and private property. Understanding the struggle for justice at Standing Rock as part of a much longer resistance movement was "humbling," as one Iowan pipeline opponent told me. There, as in the Dakotas, some individuals and groups began to interrogate their own complicity in settler colonialism and work toward practices of commoning and solidarity beyond simple analogy (Carter and Kruzic 2017). Some KXL landowners participated in blockade activities at Standing Rock, especially in the early days. They contributed when and however they could and (unlike other settlers) did so without seeking recognition from the press. Thus, the populist coalition-building created conditions for some more transformative relationships to be built. A few landowners committed their private property to be returned to trust status on the part of the Native Nations who originally inhabited them or who were forcibly removed to the region. Though the individualized nature of such transactions—and their mediation by the federal government, which maintains ownership (via "plenary power") of Indigenous lands in the United States—can and should be critically examined, such land reclamation is a nonmetaphoric operation of decolonization, however piecemeal. To engage in solidarity adequately and humbly with Native movements for decolonization, the populist politics of lateral alliance through shared interest had to be superseded by a politics of shared desire for another world. That it could evidences the bread and butter of base-building political organizing, more important than any campaign slogan or action in producing the "long-term structural change" Sheila and others sought.

On the other hand, a second response from landowners and property-centric pipeline opposition was less hopeful. Some resistance groups doubled down on the analogy between settler and Native struggles over land, attempting to reclaim their resistance to eminent domain under the "water protectors" identity popularized at the Standing Rock blockade. At a 2016 anti-DAPL protest in Iowa, for example, a "No eminent domain for private gain" sign featured the visage of "Chief" Powhatan, leader of the Algonquin-speaking Powhatan people native to the region around my current home in Richmond, Virginia. Below his face was a presumptive quote from his 1609 speech, as recorded by settler John Smith, reading, "Why will you take by force what you may share quietly with LOVE?" Why did such analogies make sense as an interpretation of eminent domain in faraway Iowa? Why invoke the Powhatan people when organized Meskwaki resistance was occurring more closely in space and time? And it was not uncommon to hear a presumption of allyship where relations did not exist. At this same rally, an organizer described the "we" that had assembled hundreds of miles away. "We're standing with the farmers, landowners and our tribal allies to stop this assault on our water, climate and property rights. . . . There's been a lot of media attention up in North Dakota but [we should] recognize the landowners who have been most important down here in Iowa." Having just driven several hundred miles from the blockade at Standing Rock, I was struck by the difference in rhetoric and tone alike. The spatial account of pipeline opposition drawn by this organizer disaggregates the interests of the different constituent groups opposing DAPL. "Over there" were Indigenous activists, while "down here" it was landowners. Such moves absent Native Nations from the Iowan landscape, assuming (as many settlers in the Upper Midwest frequently do) a spatial division between the Dakotas as arenas of both Indian Country and conservative backlash and the more liberal or progressive Minnesota and Iowa, where reconciliation had supposedly already happened (Biolsi 2005).

A Sunday *New York Times* photo essay from 2017 performs a similar maneuver aesthetically, which I find to be helpful for understanding how the somewhat-myopic settler orientation to land continued to cite territorialized resentments of private property. Journalist Mitch Smith introduces KXL opponents in Nebraska by suggesting that "the pipeline opposition here looks nothing like the dispute that emerged last year over the Dakota Access Pipeline in North Dakota, where thousands of demonstrators erected a protest camp near a Native American reservation" (2017). Though the phrase "looks nothing like" could be understood as a reference to the form of opposition ("So far there have been no mass encampments on the Nebraska prairie, no tense standoffs with the police, no highway blockades"), the article was accompanied by a series of diptych photographs of landowners and their private property. In doing so, the reference to what opposition "looks like" also functions to denote a racial difference (no further mention of Indigenous resistance is made, including that of the Ponca and other Native Nations in Nebraska, though the author has written elsewhere in the *New York Times* about Native involvement in pipeline coalitions). Thus, similar

Figure 3. A diptych of two photographs from a *New York Times* article depicting property and landowners. On the left, a naturalistic-looking prairie landscape with a river bisecting it; on the right, a person stands in a green field looking offscreen. George Etheredge/*New York Times*/Redux.

to the organizer above, instead of the Indigenous tactics "up there," we see opposition led by (white) landowners "down here."

"It's the people who are tied to the land . . . who understand what's at risk," notes one of the landowners (quoted in M. Smith 2017). What could "tied to the land" mean here? The same interviewee noted that "the land is worth more than what they offered me." Smith's commentary notes that the landowner's "family ties run deep." The photo essays perform the "ties to the land"—and resentment at its disruption—that the text largely skirts around. On the left side of each diptych, a photograph depicts a landscape. Though not every photo is described as private property, all opponents and supporters of the pipeline interviewed are understood to be landowners. On the right side of the diptych is a photo of the landowner in question—all individuals or families, and one photo contains a dog, but none showing more than two people.

The photos of the land vary. Some appear to be classically naturalized landscapes, like prairie fields and streams. The foreground to background focus shifts to display either the windswept and dry grass or the

Figure 4. A diptych of two photographs from a *New York Times* article depicting property and landowners. On the left, a landscape with rolling hills and farm buildings in the distance; on the right, two individuals stand side by side in an empty field. George Etheredge/*New York Times*/Redux.

long, receding buildings in the distance. Some are clearly "working" landscapes—pictures of fields harvested and fallow, muddy and barren. Empty county roads appear and, of course, fences. The photos of pipeline supporters and opponents also vary. Pipeline opponents and supporters each appear defiant, though opponents perhaps a bit weary. "TransCanada not only wants to steal our property, they have stolen eight years of our lives," says one opponent (quoted in M. Smith 2017), and this shows.

Without belittling the material and political struggles these individuals are engaged in or suggesting an easy determinism, it is necessary to critically examine the function of the aesthetic of private property/landowner diptych here. What is naturalized is not the landscape itself but the relationship of ownership (and the security that is supposed to have provided) in and as the threatened form of being "the people who are tied to the land." In the face of Indigenous resistance, the desire to return landowners and property rights to a prominent aesthetic and narrative position could still continue relatively unabated. When President Trump signed an executive order approving KXL in January 2017, Bold Nebraska's director claimed that the best strategy for defeating the pipeline a second time would be "focusing on the landowners. . . . We are going to focus on property rights" (quoted in Bleifuss 2017).

The contradictory role of landownership in pipeline opposition demonstrates how the political desires at the heart of pipeline resistance continue to be a site of struggle. Territorial resentments produced by violations of private property rights affectively condition a grasping toward the settler experience of propriety. In this account of populism, I do not downplay the material, economic, and affective dimensions of property rights defense in favor of the symbolic—these were each infrastructural conditions for agrarian populism. But just because such territorial resentment underlies pipeline populism does not mean it was coherently determinant of the character of political struggle. On the one hand, property's constituent production of white subjects and their desires for transparency through possessive ownership, protection, and freedom animated many settlers' pipeline opposition. Centralizing the fragility of property rights consolidated a return to white subjectivities in populist politics. If private property is rendered merely one interest among others, the centuries-long and ongoing resistance to settler

Figure 5. A diptych of two photographs from a *New York Times* article depicting property and landowners. On the left, a working landscape features a rutted road next to a series of power lines and a browned farm field recedes into the distance; on the right, an individual kneels looking down at a dirt-clod-ridden field while holding a shovel for support, with farm buildings in the background. George Etheredge/*New York Times*/Redux.

colonialism led by Native Nations is trivialized or generalized. On the other hand, people are capable of change. Without the starting point of territorialized resentment, these individuals and groups likely would not have entered into the political struggle, remaining atomized and isolated subjects.

The varied reactions to the pipeline—acceptance, negotiation, or opposition—highlight the insufficiency of an analysis solely based on economic conflict. Layers of affective attachments to land condition subjects fractured in different ways by private property's role in mediating tenuous economic freedom and political rights and privileges. And many of the landowners were not seeking financial restitution as much as respect, that their property should be recognized by the state and corporations as properly belonging to them. This recognition was not only for legal rights but also of their long-standing labor and life on the land. Landowners described the continuity of their relationships with land in both spatial and temporal terms, by citing their individual and family history on that property. Homespun sympathies for stories of the hardship of settlement littered public hearings and comment sessions. They referenced "we the people" and the ideals of U.S. framers, arguing that the latter saw taking of private property as a "sacred act." Even stewardship, the combination of a Christian value ethic with environmentalism, was sometimes framed as an outcome best supported by enshrining private property rights.

These affective attachments to property are constituted by desires in land. Desires congeal in property and its subjects a whole range of memories, labor, family relationships, corporeal experiences, technologies of knowledge and control, and natural spaces. As Beenash Jafri argues, desire "is integral to the construction of settler subjectivities, to settler narratives, and to the project of erasure underlying the indigenizing efforts of settler projects" (2013, 79). Desires in land are not merely an ideological supplement to more-real economic interests perceived to be at stake in pipeline struggles. Nor can desire be circumscribed as a product of cultural politics. Instead, "desire belongs to the infrastructure" (Deleuze and Guattari 1983, 348), which is to say, desire is a meeting point of the economic and the political in racial capitalism. It is through apprehending, redirecting, and expanding these desires that populism emerged.

The multiple returns to private property in antipipeline environmentalisms demonstrate the difficulties settler subjects have in relinquishing the affordances of transparency that they have come to expect. Private property produces subjects invested in the economic interest that their property grants and the desire for recognition of inalienable ownership and sovereignty by their peers and the state. When this proprietary position became more tenuous than anticipated, resentment pooled as settlers felt thrown into the realm of affectability. Landowners begrudged being determined by some force larger than oneself and of the loss of rights at the hands of outsiders or foreigners. But while the threat of dispossession created for some the opportunity to reflect on the limits of property as grounds for opposition, for many others it entrenched the populist demand for the recognition of exclusive possession. Such a demand constitutively relies upon displacing the dispossession of Native Nations as only a particular historic act, not an ongoing structure of violence inherent to racial capitalism.

Conclusion

Desires for exclusive private property continued to be drawn upon to enhance the state's ability to maintain violent responses to anticolonial pipeline resistance at Standing Rock. While early blockades against DAPL were on land adjacent to the pipeline's path appropriated and managed by the Army Corps of Engineers, in October 2016 water protectors established a Frontline (or North) Camp directly in the path of the pipeline. In the process, water protectors occupied—or, better, "ex-appropriated" (Balibar 2014, 311)—private property that ETP had recently purchased from a landowner after the blockade's rise to prominence. Citing the land as unceded territory of the Oceti Sakowin Oyate under the 1851 Fort Laramie Treaty, the water protectors claimed they were using the power of eminent domain.

Although day-to-day police violence and criminal trespass arrests had been ongoing at the camp for months, the establishment of the Frontline Camp appeared particularly intolerable to law enforcement. The response by the police three days later was one of the more visceral shows of force to that date. Water protectors were evicted from the Frontline Camp in a raid by hundreds of riot police using Mine-Resistant Ambush-Protected (MRAP) vehicles, Long-Range Acoustic Device (LRAD) sound cannons, mace, and beanbag cannons. At least 140 water protectors were arrested that day after hours of nonviolent struggle, prayer, and ceremony. The Frontline Camp—containing numerous sacred objects—was bulldozed, and its contents were haphazardly returned to the adjacent Oceti Sakowin camp.

Morton County, North Dakota, police chief Kyle Kirchmeier said in a statement afterward that "individuals trespassing on private property can't claim eminent domain to justify their criminal actions" (quoted in Grueskin 2016). He described trespassing on private property as a "public safety issue." Defenders of the pipeline would repeatedly argue that DAPL does not cross any land "owned" by the Standing Rock Sioux. To suggest otherwise would, North Dakota congressman Kevin Cramer (2016) posited, "turn America's property rights upside down." Blockades were suggested to be a "dangerous occupation of property" that threatens lives (Wiederstein 2016), especially disrupting to nearby white landowners (Healy 2016). These statements further demonstrate the centrality to settler colonialism of maintaining both private property and its subjects, constituent elements of white subjectivity and modes of dispossession. The firm response by the police might not have been just due to the violation of the sanctity of private property but also because the water protectors attempted to enact a relationship with land as something other than property. Altogether, the courageous actions of water protectors, the ideological response of the state, and the violence of private police forces demonstrate the stakes of transforming private property.

In this chapter, I have demonstrated how a variety of landowner concerns emerged from the affective infrastructures of territorialized resentment. Such an affective relation undergirds the formed interests landowners have in maintaining value and, whether consciously or not, their own positions as transparent subjects of whiteness. Relinquishing desires for land could appear to be an impossible ask for many settler pipeline opponents—it was unlikely to be an effective starting point for building an alliance, given the deep naturalization of private property rights. Nonetheless, radical politics always entails demands that might seem, at the time, to be impossible. The populist strategies centered on property rights did not overshadow the resurgence in anticolonial resistance led by Native Nations that takes the protection of water to be incompatible with the dominant property regimes that maintain settler colonialism and produce the transparent subjects of whiteness. And for some, populism worked as an entry point for a more decolonial orientation. However, more robustly, the generic form of populism emerging from territorial resentment created expectations for the dramatic scenes of opposition that took place within the institutionalized environmental review process. It is to these public hearings that the next chapter turns.

2

"KEYSTONE XL HEARING NEARLY IRRELEVANT"
PARTICIPATION AND RESIGNED PRAGMATISM

PRIOR TO A 2015 SOUTH DAKOTA PUC HEARING on a renewal for a right-of-way permit for KXL, a *Rapid City Journal*/Associated Press news article provided the astute and entirely serious headline "Hearing on Keystone Pipeline Plan Nearly Irrelevant." That summer, a preevidentiary hearing was held in order that the PUC could better "formulate questions" at the (presumably more relevant) evidentiary hearing planned for the end of July. The public input, testimony, and participation at the preevidentiary hearing would not be used in any decision to be made about the permit for the pipeline. KXL was now entering its second round of South Dakota PUC hearings after the original four-year permit to construct had expired. Nonetheless, the meeting turned out sixty participants, who were shocked to learn that what they had taken to be democratic participation was procedurally empty. With a detached and dry tone that could almost be mistaken for humor, the AP wrote that "by rule, while any comments made Monday might affect a commissioner's private thoughts, nothing said at the public input session is supposed to matter" (Associated Press 2015).

In South Dakota, a cynic might suggest that the totality of public input could be seen as irrelevant as the evidentiary hearing in question. After all, the South Dakota PUC would take the time to approve the

KXL right-of-way permit in December 2015 even after the Obama administration had rejected the pipeline. The disconnect between pipeline opponents and administrative state and federal decision-making bodies became a major source of frustration for many participants. By 2014, Sheila started to have difficulty turning people out for public meetings and hearings. "Six, seven, eight times they've put in comments on these things and they never get listened to. So why the hell are they going to put in comments again?" she told me. Other words participants used to describe the hearing included "frustrating," "a farce," and "disrespectful." One colorfully described the experience as having put a "burr under [his] saddle." Mark, a landowner, went to his first public meeting concerning KXL in 2009. Though he still planned to go to the meetings in 2015, he instructs newcomers (like me) that they should not expect much. "You going in there testifying . . . it's just making you feel good."

One way that the populist genre shaped pipeline opposition was by fitting otherwise diverse grievances and demands into a more general frustration at the loss of democracy. Citizen rights, it was often said, were being eroded by corrupt political representation, requiring a renewed recognition of "the people" as the proper authors of politics. This is perhaps unsurprising, as "the people" as an imagined political subject is, of course, part and parcel of the democratic imagination.[1] These calls for a renewed democratic participation did not emerge ex nihilo. Since the 1890s, the regional political culture of the Northern Great Plains has emphasized the moral necessity of engaged participation in political decision-making, well beyond simply voting. South Dakota owes its status as the first state to pass initiative and referendum laws to the 1890s activism of the socialist-populist and disbarred Catholic priest Father Robert E. Haire.[2] KXL public hearings seemed to shirk such participatory principles that inform some aspects of political culture in the state. And there were nonlocal forces at work on the imagination of democracy at these hearings, as well. The historian Timothy Mitchell argues that oil-fueled technological and economic processes built mass democracy in the United States, while shaping the limits through which politics could be imagined. This included routing flows of oil through pipelines, both to crush the democratic power of coal miners' unions and to build the other sense of democracy, that of participation in "the market."[3] Though certainly oil is not alone in this regard, the legacy of its effects on democracy was felt to be in regulatory capture: the corporate influence on the permitting process, as well as the appointees or elected officials who serve on decision-making committees. So each of these, along with the rise of participatory planning mechanisms alongside environmental regulation, is an important precursor to the story I tell in this chapter. However, history was not so much on the minds of participants in public hearings. Instead, it was the experience of a democratic deficit that proved to be most frustrating. Attending and testifying at hearings was ideology slapped on so thick that it could only seem to be circus-like. Taking it as honest would be self-deceit, just "making you feel good," to recall Mark's words.

Such a frustration with what Nancy Fraser (1990) calls "actually-existing democracy" might still be surprising for those who would take populism to be an affront to the democratic tradition rather than a desire for a deeper or "real democracy" (A. Taylor 2019, 49). In particular, liberals are skeptical of populism's real interest in deliberative decision-making, seeing in "the people" an irrational distrust of institutionalized norms of governance. The political theorist Jan-Werner Müller (2016, 29) rhetorically asks, "Don't populists often demand more referenda?" Maybe yes, but for Müller this is an inauthentic demand. "[Populists] do not want people to participate continuously in politics. A referendum isn't meant to start an open-ended process of deliberation among actual citizens to generate a range of well-considered popular judgments." For Müller, populism is antidemocratic because it eschews the deliberative public sphere, which requires a certain dispassion and a willingness to compromise. This argument results, in part, because abstract political theory addresses itself to solving the problem of dissonance between institutions and publics, or between public discourse and law. If popular sovereignty is not denigrated outright, then it must be channeled into well-designed procedures and institutions (Habermas 1997). This position highlights one of the basic paradoxes of liberal democracy—that the people are "at once a constituent and a constituted power" (J. Frank 2009, 7; see also Mouffe 2000; Negri 1999; Riofrancos 2020; A. Taylor 2019).[4]

Much like populists themselves, critical geographers, environmental planners, and scholars in numerous other fields have been skeptical of institutionalized means of eliciting participation. Marxists frequently take populism's supposed desire to participate in real democracy as an idealist fantasy (e.g., Swyngedouw 2010). If procedural democracy exists to fulfill certain instrumental ends, Marxists argue that one of these is the capture or attenuation of constituent power. "The people must have their say, but their options must be limited," for example, to "the familiar landscape of 'participatory planning'—public comment periods, community boards, planning commissions, design charettes and a host of other interventions" (Stein 2019, 37). Other scholars have much more faith in deliberative or even "radical democracy" that occurs in extrainstitutional collective decision-making processes. But both positions can struggle to explain why groups of people continue to participate in the frustrating and debilitating institutional landscape of liberal democracy. They implicitly assume that participants in such processes are either being duped by the promise of democracy or simply wasting their time with a poor strategy doomed to failure.

With these debates in mind, this chapter takes a step back to ask: Why do people keep organizing through public comment and participation meetings? Are they deceived, or do they recognize that such events are, in the words of the newspaper headline, "nearly irrelevant"? To answer these questions, I track shifting experiences with public participation meetings at the federal (National Environmental Policy Act, NEPA) and state (PUC) levels from 2009 to 2015, following the dialogue recorded in archives as well as the reflections of participants. What I found was that exhausted organizers, opponents, and activists approach public meetings not with the spirit of resurgent radical democracy we are told exists in protest movements worldwide but instead with what I call resigned pragmatism. After briefly describing the history of public input in environmental permitting, I describe the collective affect of actually existing participation meetings. As participants increasingly formed a collective identity as "the people," they concurrently became resigned to public participation, which is to say they have accepted it as something unpleasant which "the people" cannot alter.

Contrary to the received wisdom of democratic environmentalism and without the full cynicism of radical critique, resigned pragmatism evidences the Beckettesque feeling of exhaustion that despite the feeling that one "cannot go on" one still "must go on." This is the "groping in the dark" (Deleuze and Guattari 1987, 461) of everyday politics in actually existing democracy, wherein one feels that one must vigilantly remain active, but without necessarily an overarching political vision or theory of change (Deleuze 1997, 153). Antipipeline organizers became further resigned to public participation because nonparticipation was effectively disallowed due to charges made by pipeline firms and supporters. Yet rather than value participation as a strategy in itself, it was increasingly treated pragmatically rather than romantically. Testimony offered an attempt to produce an understanding or consciousness among participants that political change would not likely happen within the legitimated institutional routes, a point I return to in chapter 4. Furthermore, testimony by Indigenous leaders sought to relocate popular sovereignty as an element within Indigenous sovereignty rather than stemming solely from the dyadic people–state relationship. Though resigned pragmatism is not endemic only to populism, such an affective infrastructure drew on the aspirational expectations that the genre conventions of populism lay out while ultimately superseding them. In doing so, it expanded the ideological and spatial field of pipeline opposition in unexpected ways.

Desires for Participation and the Populist Subject

Scholars frequently suggest that public participation in technoscientific review, public consultation, and popular protest should be valorized as a sign of a healthy democracy that would produce more just environmental futures (Fischer 2000; Klein 2014; Marres 2012; Whatmore 2009). The public deserves to be a part of the decisions that might affect their lives, even if these decisions involve complex scientific or technical problems. This stance is also repeated in the context of climate change. If global climate change is a contemporary problem for democracy, then local deliberation, participation, and activism should have the power to produce the proper response. The EPA itself, for example, suggests that public capacity is enhanced through such encounters, as the public emerges better educated about the complexity of scientific matters and better prepared to face future scientific controversies that might arise from climate change. (Downplayed in this institutional narrative is whether or not government institutions or corporations might benefit from such an encounter, but we will leave that aside for a moment.) Accounting for more actors in the democratic field should result in better decisions, thus reducing public harm and leading to a more equitable society. As mentioned above, public participation is also highly valued in South Dakota's political culture, stemming in part from a populist distrust of Washington politicians, as well as the legacy of the Farmers' Alliance and the Populist Party, embodied in both actual legislation and the regional political culture. This section selectively reviews the origins of public participation and its role in liberal political theory before moving toward a concept of resigned pragmatism.

The emergence of public participation in environmental review in the United States can be traced back to the legislative efforts of the 1930s, when participation was seen as a possible check on governmental and corporate power alike. Many begin with John Dewey and his seminal *The Public and Its Problems* (1927), which argued that the changing impacts of industrialism and trade create an increasing distance between citizens and the decisions over the processes that affect their lives. Those "indirectly and seriously affected" (15) by industrial economic activity deserve to be recognized by a name and as a subject: the public. Dewey argues that the public was not some abstract preexisting group, but instead that material problems create their own various interested and plural publics. He thought that if these publics could have some say in the way they are affected, then democracy could be salvaged from its contemporary crisis. Dewey was himself a staunch believer in liberal democracy and a sometimes-opponent of communism and other leftist movements (Kuznick 1987). But he also sought to reshape the role of public intellectuals not as the unseen engineers of his critics but as advocates for freedom and circulation of information (Ewen 1996).

Although Dewey's ideas were extremely influential at the time of writing, it was arguably not until the legislation of the 1960s and 1970s, especially NEPA, that the environmental aspect of the affected public was fully recognized. NEPA required that the environmental review process include public hearings prior to any decision, an aspiration somewhat unique for its time. But even then, participation was immediately fraught with political problems. Some argue that the participatory aspects of the legislation were in part a strategic attempt by the

Nixon administration to regain legitimacy and public license with environmentalists, who were "the least radical and threatening aspect of the counter-culture" (Dryzek et al. 2003, 59). Others see NEPA and public comment as significant victories for citizens, suggesting that participation need not be held to the standards of "radical democracy" to be a healthy and important practice (Fischer 2000, 36). And it is important to note that participation is a slippery concept even in practice, especially since the EPA has tweaked its participation procedures and recommendations with changing political administrations. Still, most of the executive administrations since Nixon have also claimed that participation is broken in some fundamental way. For example, during the Clinton administration and its institutionalization of environmental justice, "fair and meaningful participation" was upheld as one route to remaking the institutional structure of the executive branch (Foreman 1998; Holifield 2004). But the institutional approach relied on viewing participation as consultation, an act that gathered information from publics while retaining decision-making power for state institutions. In this model, publics participate to tweak the details of a proposed project.

Environmental justice scholars and activists have frequently pointed out the limits of this model, calling instead for participatory justice beyond the simple distributive justice named in official policy (e.g., Schlosberg 1999, 145–72). The focus on exclusionary processes of democracy with reference to marginalized groups clearly demonstrates a lack of local control over health and environmental impacts of industrial extraction and production. Yet scholars and activists alike also recognize that the demand for fair and meaningful participation can still be vague or even harmful (Young 2001; Pulido 2017). According to whose perceptions and definitions of "fair and meaningful" should any process be judged? The Clinton administration's 1994 environmental justice executive order (Exec. Order No. 12,898, 59 Fed. Reg. 7629 [Feb. 16, 1994]), for example, has largely resulted in limited recognition-based fixes to the problem. The EPA's institutionalized processes are limited in their ability to resolve a central democratic paradox between the affected public's supposed ability to represent itself to a distinct, institutionalized decision-making body.

So, despite faith in the ideal of meaningful public participation in environmental review, standard participatory techniques to involve publics in issues of science, technology, and the environment are widely recognized by scholars in the United States and around the world as partial and ineffective (Cooke and Kothari 2001). Skepticism in public participation techniques is certainly not at all new to our current moment (Arnstein 1969), nor is it confined to the left. Participation activities are critiqued for their strategic role in trying to derive consent from skeptical publics of the supposed safety, security, or social good that a project or technique will provide. In Brian Wynne's perspective, science studies scholars have adequately demonstrated how "entrenched powerful constructions of actors' capacities, agency, interests, concerns, rights, and identities, are silently reproduced, perversely through participatory processes which are supposed to be challenging those implicitly assumed categories in accountable ways" (2007, 100–101). Participation does not exist solely in the ideal world of political theory but is structured by conditions, contexts, and the capacities of participants to speak or to be heard. Such scholarship frequently attends to practices of resistance, refusal, and protest—again, both within the U.S. NEPA process (Hébert 2016; Hébert and Brock 2017; Phadke 2010, 2011) and in environmentally controversial projects around the world (Barry 2013; F. Li 2009; Riofrancos 2020; Welker 2012).

Such critiques of public participation broadly align, and are sometimes in conversation with, a more general criticism of contemporary democracy. Although democratic governance is sometimes taken to be a panacea for our contemporary ecological situation, it rarely seems to produce the outcomes that environmentalists desire. Erik Swyngedouw (2010) argues that the vast majority of what passes as "democratic politics" has had a chilling effect on political antagonism, foreclosing transformation of the political field toward justice. Similarly, Jodi Dean argues that "participation and deliberation, immanence and inclusion" (2009, 75–76) are democratic fantasies that orient political activism toward supporting the very institutional processes that hamper it. The somewhat technocratic nature of Habermasian participatory governance in practice tends to neutralize dissent, antagonism, and divisive politics to produce outcomes of consensus or at least legitimacy. Addressing our institutions and politicians through a counterdiscourse claiming that democratic participation is lacking seems to further entrench the power of leaders to make those decisions for and instead of people. This is also particularly notable within extractive industries, in which "environmental governance initiatives frame the politics of extraction as questions of inclusion and participation, rather than justice, rights and distribution" (Bridge and Perreault 2015, 482). The infrequency by which publics can affect broad-scale decisions about energy use, infrastructure siting, and a collective response to climate change could thus be seen as symptomatic of a broader disaffection with democracy. The result is a situation in which publics are constantly compelled to participate, though with no clear political benefit to doing so.

Public participation in environmental review is broken, and the discourse of redemptive democracy will not necessarily build political justice. However, these critical and normative positions—to which I also adhere—fail to explain the range of desires and ambivalences subjects feel with regard to the actual spaces of public participation. Critical social scientists critique the state's solicitation of consent, in contrast to the unambiguous resistance, refusal, and counterprojects that groups undertake against or outside of the state. But between these two positions a whole range of political organizing occurs in which people tarry with and repurpose state institutions (Riofrancos 2020, 122). Within these ambivalent experiences circulate the affective infrastructures of populist desire and dissent. So why do people participate, given they find the process so unproductive and exhausting? Do they express the ideology of democracy and popular sovereignty uncritically, or do they do so strategically? Do their experiences and actions confirm that public participation meetings are a political sidetrack, or do they reveal political excesses in the institutional structure of soliciting public input?

While complaints about "not being heard" ring in participation forums, I argue that most pipeline opponents—whether consciously or not—actually treat such spaces pragmatically or even strategically. This chapter argues that activists use public participation forums to demonstrate the state's impotence or incompetence, to help organize feelings of indignation into somewhat coherent collectives and alliances, and to broaden rather than shut down the political field of intervention against oil pipelines. To make this argument, I describe this affective ambivalence as resigned pragmatism. By *resigned pragmatism,* I wish to indicate that public participation is experienced as an unpleasant process to which one must still be partially committed. Despite recognizing the

farcical nature of public hearings, Sheila told me: "You have to participate in that process anyway. Because if you don't, then it's just like you're
lying down on the ground. Even if you don't think you can win, you
have to participate." The resigned pragmatism she and others felt indicates that public participation was not about performing for an institutionalized democracy per se but instead an experience and demonstration of the limits of actually existing democracy for the collective
political subject constituted in relation to this failure. Organizers
and pipeline opponents treat spaces of public testimony as a collective
ritual of fatigue and disaffection, thus opening up alternative political
strategies.

Resigned pragmatism is a sister concept to those of intimate publics
and cruel optimism, as described by Lauren Berlant. "Public spheres are
always affect worlds," Berlant argues (2011, 226). The ties that bind
you to a loose, mass public by, say, a newspaper (Warner 2005) or everyday public infrastructure (Wilson 2016) can be among those spaces
that produce a kind of "immediacy and solidarity" in which it feels like
"matters of survival are at stake" (Berlant 2011, 226). Intimate publics
are produced in "cramped spaces" (Deleuze 1989, 216; Thoburn 2003),
those sites of exhaustion and exploitation that elicit creative political
responses. Intimate publics work, in part, because they produce a feeling of belonging. But this is not just any collectivity; it is "the affect of
feeling political together" (Berlant 2011, 224, emphasis added). Berlant
is not sanguine about the potential of intimate publics—they can "confirm our attachment to the system and thereby confirm the system and
the legitimacy of the affects that make one feel bound to it" (227).
These attachments can include cruel optimism, their concept for the
persistent connection to an institution or scene that remains an obstacle
to broader flourishing.

Like cruel optimism, resigned pragmatism describes a relation in
which "despite an awareness that the normative political sphere appears
as a shrunken, broken, or distant place of activity among elites, members of the body politic return periodically to its recommitment cere-
monies and scenes" (Berlant 2011, 227). We might become attached to
the scene of the political event itself rather than strategically reflecting
on its possibilities to produce change. Berlant's interest in intimate publics and cruel optimism, however, describes not the people who revolt

but rather those who have "chosen primarily not to fight" (249).[5] By contrast, the affective infrastructures of populist politics do not pivot away from politics as antagonism. But neither do they simply embrace opposition or resistance. This is because populism orients its subjects to the feeling of being unfairly rendered marginal to the political sphere. Populism thus amplifies political melodrama, which I return to in chapter 3. And in this situation, I argue, it does not produce or rely upon either cruel optimism or cruel aspirations. A different sort of affective scene emerges from public participation in pipeline environmental review, with several nondeterminate pathways for political action.

The affect of resigned pragmatism is in no way limited to populism; we can find it emerging in all sorts of political movements. Think, for example, of the generic attitude taken by many professional community organizers, nonprofit employees, and government workers committed to reform. Though workers and activists in these spheres might wish for better conditions, they operate within the general parameters of "the possible" delineated by existing institutions. However, when hitched to populism, resigned pragmatism takes a somewhat different form because it emerges within and through a collective subject. It helped compose populist subjects by resurrecting a romantic position—"we the people"—that both demonstrates the limits of actually existing institutionalized democracy while functionally remaining vague enough to enroll others within its nostalgic democratic fantasy. I say "fantasy" because while "we the people" could name an actually existing democratic subject who might reject fossil fuel infrastructure, the empirical reality seems to have been that most people in the region accepted the pipeline.[6] Ultimately, the disaffection with public participation must lead to alternative practices that take democracy as neither ideal nor historical but speculatively and practically reinvigorated through an internal relationship to Indigenous sovereignty. Though it is not my goal to speculate on precisely what that might look like, it would require a fundamental transformation given what legal theorist John Borrows (Anishinaabe) calls the "filtered participation of representative democracy" that fails to recognize "Indigenous peoples, past and future generations, nor the environment itself [as] proper subjects of democracy" (2002, 44). Such possibilities lie tantalizingly beyond the construction of subjects in democratic spaces through resigned pragmatism, who emerged with the first public meetings held concerning the KXL pipeline.

The Circulatory Affect of Public Testimony

Public participation meetings are tied to regulatory requirements at the federal and state levels, but due to various hiccups in regulatory review this process unfolded unevenly over the first several years of pipeline resistance in the region. Following the official announcement of KXL, TransCanada filed for permits with the U.S. State Department, the South Dakota PUC, and the Nebraska Department of Environmental Quality in 2008. The State Department began the review process in 2009, holding twenty scoping meetings along the pipeline's route to determine the criterion that should be assessed in the review. Upon completion of a draft EIS, the State Department was required to solicit and respond to public comments from affected institutions and individuals. Nineteen public comment sessions were held in spring of 2010 along the pipeline's route, alongside solicitation of comment online. In response to the overwhelming number of comments received, the State Department decided to extend the public comment period and add two more public solicitation meetings in 2011 in Texas and Washington, D.C.

The first final EIS was released in August 2011, which corresponded to another open public comment period and public meetings in the state capitols of each of the states through which the pipeline passed. Aspects of the EIS were seen as shoddy, incomplete, and inadequate by many individuals, groups, and even other federal agencies (see chapter 4). Through responding to these criticisms and to public comments, the State Department also determined that the pipeline should not pass through the Nebraska Sandhills region. An alternative route was proposed, which resulted in a draft supplemental EIS produced by a new consultant. At this point, TransCanada also separated the southern part of the pipeline system in Texas and Oklahoma into a different project from the northern, international portion. Because the southern portion did not cross an international boundary and was not so clearly linked to the Canadian tar sands, it was approved, much to the chagrin of landowners and activists who had opposed and blockaded that portion of the pipeline system.

The final supplemental EIS for the northern part of KXL was completed in 2014 and yet another round of public comments were solicited, with a large public meeting held in Grand Island, Nebraska. The permit for the pipeline was finally rejected by the State Department in the fall of 2015, pausing the project after some 1.5 million public comments on this round of the EIS alone. By this point, there had been almost fifty public participation meetings. When KXL was reapproved by the Trump administration, the State Department's next public comment period solicited over three million comments. The reopening brought yet another round of public meetings in 2017 and 2019, which the Trump administration chose to structure as "open house" events rather than traditional public comments. Due to Covid-19, three virtual public meetings were held in 2020, associated respectively with Montana, South Dakota, and Nebraska. That is a lot of meetings.

Concurrent to the federal review process, states through which the pipeline passed also held permitting review periods. In South Dakota, for example, the PUC managed the state review process for a right-of-way permit for KXL. The PUC public engagement process was divided into two different parts: an informal solicitation of public comments and a more formal evidentiary hearing in front of the PUC commissioners. The South Dakota PUC held four public hearings in 2009, at which a total of 83 individuals offered their comments and 326 people attended. With the pipeline frequently delayed at the federal level, the permit expired and a reapproval process began in 2014. A second public hearing was held in 2015 concurrent with the request to reapprove a permit, followed by an evidentiary hearing later that month—referenced in this chapter's introduction.

Most public comments I read at both the federal and South Dakota PUC level were against the pipeline, even in the early years. Three of the initial twenty public input or scoping meetings in South Dakota in 2009 were hosted by TransCanada and the South Dakota PUC. These meetings were primarily informational and served to solicit possible concerns that would be addressed in the EIS. Even then, the meetings were described by one attendee as "a dog and pony show" and "very skillful in presenting a good propaganda package" (Wiken 2009). In the area around Winner, South Dakota, where I lived in 2013, a few people I spoke with remembered the meeting. "None of us really knew what we were in for," Jack, a landowner and rancher, told me. "It's not often that you get that many people in a room together around here, so it was a bit exciting."

In rural and small-town South Dakota, the public frequently brought up issues of local impact rather than the broad politics of climate change or environmental justice. The effect of the pipeline on property tax revenue and possible depreciation of property valuation elicited questions at many public meetings. Small-towners worried about "outsiders" bringing immoral activity to their rural communities. They were concerned about the effects of construction equipment on rural roads, which receive infrequent maintenance. Eminent domain concerns were immediately present, as were questions about potential impacts to rural water supplies. But so too were emergent reflections about public participation forums themselves. As Jack told me, "The first meeting I went to, we already could tell that they were taking us through a spin cycle." Why was this suspicion present from the very beginning? Though historical and regional factors play a role, the generic form of a public comment session creates the conditions for how it is viewed by rural and small-town residents.

The generic meeting is held in a public space big enough in rural South Dakota—a high school auditorium, a gymnasium, a community theater, or an austere hotel desperately in need of a remodel. As you filter in, a sign-up sheet is posted at the front of the room, asking for names, email addresses, and phone numbers. There might be handouts or pamphlets from TransCanada or the PUC. The unadorned room is set up with rows of chairs, and a board of officials from the governing body at hand sits at the front. Rarely do these rooms have windows, and you are lucky if they feature a water cooler or drinking fountain.

Scoping meetings are supposed to be informational. Sometimes, the meeting is preceded by a brief description of the regulatory framework, as well as past permitting and meeting activities. Then, a PowerPoint from TransCanada is presented. As this is frequently the first in-depth presentation of the pipeline, the presentation might be up to forty-five minutes. The firm meticulously documents the pipeline construction process, presenting images of past pipeline construction and describing remediation. The officials instruct the crowd gathered as to the rules of public question. Usually, they limit comments to two minutes, sometimes allowing as much as five. They instruct participants to stay on topic, narrowly defined. Then, comments or questions can be asked, which are followed by responses from either the governing body or TransCanada. Take these instructions from 2009: "Public comments today, any written comments that we receive, those will all go into the file and are instructive to the Commissioners as they make their deliberations" (South Dakota PUC 2009d, 4). Participants are told that what they are saying is going "on the record" and will thus be considered. Things start out cordial enough. Questions are innocuous, probing for possible weak links: Who will pay for electricity line upgrades? What about damage to roads? How are your stocks doing? What happens if there is a spill?

Answers from TransCanada seem meant to be disarming. The firm cites statistics that make themselves out to be a responsible, experienced company. They demonstrate the recognition of their safety and environmental record and the economic health of the company. And they are sure to emphasize the local benefits to rural communities starved for financial resources. Assurances are made: "In every county in South Dakota that the pipeline crosses, real property taxes will be reduced to all of the other landowners. If you want an example of that . . . real property taxes in Harding County will go down by half as a result of the construction of the pipeline. In other words, the pipeline company will pay over half of the cost of education and government in Harding County" (South Dakota PUC 2009d, 34). These promises were important for quelling some early misgivings. One farmer I spoke with had his mind changed by one of these early meetings: "At first, I was worried about whether this was a legitimate company or more of a scam artist, like the hog farm that went out of business right away a few years back. But they seemed professional, so I wasn't worried." As this comment indicates, the performance of expertise and professionalism could be a key affective component to producing consent.

In November 2009 at South Dakota PUC evidentiary hearings, a PUC staffperson would look back on the public input hearings positively. PUC Chairman Johnson and the staff member reflected on the benefit of public input to their process in a manner that gives a window to the institutional ideology that structured the process (South Dakota PUC 2009a, 229–32). The staff member described their role as to "go out and *try to get a feel* at these meetings what the concerns are, what the issues, what the general sentiment of the landowners" (emphasis added). Expressing surprise at "how little opposition we heard at these hearings," the witness then described how they incorporate concerns from landowners. The PUC chairperson asked the PUC staff if "those concerns that were raised during that process, were those internalized in any way to staff? . . . Did those [public concerns] guide how you proceeded with regard to how you dealt with your witnesses, the Interrogatories you submitted to the Applicant?" They responded by describing the process in detail:

> Definitely. I think you'll see throughout the witnesses that we have coming today after the experts that are actually going to testify to all of this, these input hearings give us an opportunity to form a lot of our questions you see in those data requests. So while in our data request it might not say specifically this landowner or this individual asked this question . . . what you'll see is all of those issues brought up are addressed through either our witness testimony or through staff data requests as well too.

Following up, the chairperson posed a leading question, asking, "Would you say . . . that the vast majority of the beneficial impact that landowners and other interested citizens have as a part of this process comes through their involvement with these public input hearings?" The PUC staff affirmed: "Definitely. It's very helpful that we get as much input that as we can, and we got a lot of input, yes." Here, we can see the argument that public input must be channeled by experts, while such relations benefit the public as well.

The process of public input was laid bare as a listening exercise in gauging "general sentiment" before finding more specific witnesses and data requests, all in the name of "beneficial impact." Nonetheless, the general tone and tenor of the earlier input sessions was described as friendly, not oppositional. It is reiterated that the concerns of the public were heard and shaped how the PUC approached regulating the pipeline. But what is really interesting here is not the role of public input for the state but rather that the performance and acknowledgment of the benefits of public input to both participants and the state is actually grounds for further resentment in that very process. To put it in more colloquial terms: in suggesting that this was a functional process for recognizing concern, it felt like the state was gaslighting the participants who registered serious complaints. The idea that such participation has a beneficial impact for interested citizens, we will see, was not shared by many pipeline opponents.

Unlike the scoping meetings, which are meant to answer questions, assuage fears, and build legitimacy and consent, public comment sessions—held several months later—feature no such activities meant to convince the public. In my limited experience (which also included attending hearings on proposed uranium mines in southwestern South Dakota during this period), these meetings can sometimes feature little dialogue at all. A session might begin with a five- to fifteen-minute presentation about the project from the company. Officials from the PUC, State Department, EPA, or whatever agency is tasked with decision-making sit at the front of the room. Then, for the next two to four hours, they are almost completely silent, barring the occasional notification that "time is up." They listen stoically and take notes occasionally as the comments pile up. They rarely nod and only occasionally pipe up to ask for repetition or clarification of a comment.

The audience is likely much tenser and more disgruntled during these meetings than the earlier scoping meetings. This could be in part because community organizations had brought many of us together and given us talking points. Or it could be because a feeling of assurance had faded in the wake of more information and experience with TransCanada. Emotions run high among opponents lodging their concerns, comments, and outrage. The seeming crossover genre of courtroom/science drama elicits self-identification as experts and attempts to produce credible scientific evidence. Landowners do not simply identify themselves as ranchers, they cite their years of experience in the area. "I live ten miles straight north of Okaton, South Dakota up on Dry Creek. My parents and grandparents have been there one hundred years. My wife's family, the Iversen family, has been in Jones County over one hundred years. We're good stewards of the land. We always have been and try to be. And I have some real concerns about TransCanada" (South Dakota PUC 2009c, 10). Residents will cite their personal experiences left uncaptured in dry statistics, or they will dig up their own evidence from news articles or scientific studies to try to disprove the experts. I address expertise more extensively in chapter 4; for now, I just want to note that most attempts to provide scientific evidence in testimony seemed unsuccessful. It is at the emotional level that public testimony had the upper hand.

One by one, courageous individuals step up to the microphones and identify themselves. This could be the first real public speaking experience for a lot of people. Even if you have a decent amount of experience, the event can be harrowing. During my first public comment, I stumbled over my credentials, spoke too fast, and made several wholly incomplete sentences. I felt woozy before, sweaty during, and disappointed afterward. By comparison, those around me—whether seasoned community organizers or first-time participants—far outclassed my own attempt. Speakers spill their souls over the perceived harms of the project at hand. "Why are you doing this?" "What gives you the right to make the decisions?" "Won't you think of future generations?" "I know you are a good person, look into your heart and know this pipeline should not be built." Or: "You shouldn't even have the power to make these decisions." "Won't somebody listen to the people?" I was surprised by what Betty told me about the testimony experience at a later DAPL hearing: "Kai, I know God was taking care of my needs. I'm not going to rely on the pipeline company to make a payment. I'm not going to rely on the PUC to protect me, cause they're going to fail. They're humans, they're humans in all of this. These humans are failing. But God is taking care of my needs, so that's what helped me get through the hearing, that's what helps me get up and speak with people, in front of people. It's a lot of courage."

It is a lot of courage, but as Spinoza teaches us, "courage and generosity can emotionally bind persons together in pursuit of a collective project" (Stolze 2020, 166). After testimony, you sit back down to applause, smiles, thumbs-up, and comforting looks from your allies, many of whom you might never have talked to before. I experienced a wave of relief. "Good job!" "You're completely right." And so on. Something happens to you in this act. Despite the fact that testimony is individual, through it you become part of a collective. Your identity is reshaped. During bathroom breaks, you might share a few words with your new comrades. "I liked your speech." "Do you think we're winning?" "What a waste of time." During a lunch break, people share snacks or perhaps organizers have coordinated to provide free meals. A whole edifice of social reproductive care work sustains maybe a hundred two- to five-minute speeches. If you are lucky, there is a protest or march before the event. People stand around smoking cigarettes, drinking low-quality coffee, or eating cheap sandwiches that organizers, mostly women, have put together. Sometimes, there is a ritual led by Oceti Sakowin elders. If you are really lucky (which means organized), there might be fry bread.

Though you are becoming part of a collective, the testimony of your allies might not always make sense. Someone starts talking about healing crystals, chemtrails, or population control. But this is politics as hyperbole. You kind of just go with it. Occasionally a comment begins like all the others, yet features a massive "BUT . . ." in the middle, followed by "This is why I'm in favor of the pipeline." Hisses and even boos emerge. Someone yells, "Shame on you," as the speaker sits down. It helps to locate an opponent, a heel. Sometimes a protest chant or even a song erupts. But the comments, as the day wears on, are especially negative. Tension and excitement erode, through repetition, into anger and outrage. "This meeting is a sham!" "What corruption. The government has been bought and paid for by foreign corporations." Agitated heckles from those in the back grow increasingly frequent, directed mostly at the officials. Hand-drawn signs wave after every speech. At the end of the day, participants who say they "hadn't even intended to comment here" start to get up. One turns from an observer into a participant, a participant into a collective. The repetition within a day's testimony reminds us also that meetings are not exceptional events but iterative series. "When you guys came to my hometown of Buffalo, the Secretary of State's office held their scoping meeting there. In fact, it was in the same place, the rec center. And I asked . . . at that meeting about the financial condition and if we as landowners end up with [bounced] checks or a white elephant and she said that's not my department, that's your State Commission. They are approving this permit" (South Dakota PUC 2009c, 57). People reference their past testimony and the seeming lack of incorporation of their questions and concerns into the institutional response.

"How can you take private property?" "Water is a common resource!" "In a democracy, we, the people, are supposed to have the say!" Public participation meetings are intimate public space. They produce, above all, exhaustion. Lots of people shake their heads and never return. But they are also about heightening emotion. I will not pretend as if I do not tear up frequently at public hearings. Winona LaDuke similarly writes of the hearings taking place for the Line 3 pipeline in northern Minnesota. "At these hearings hundreds of people would stand there to talk. Or sign up. Many times, getting to talk was, well, sort of like winning the lottery. We were each given three minutes to ask questions and present our views. We, the people would cry, explain ecosystems, our culture, our wild rice, treaties, climate change and scientific data" (2020, 143). "Untrained" laypeople narrate their lives and their intelligent grasp of the politics of a complex situation, all to be churned up by a regulatory apparatus that appears to already have all the answers. It is both heartening and crushing to witness and take part in.

You go home, drained. Sometimes, you wake up the next day and do it again.

Forming a Collective Identity as "We the People"

As mentioned above, at early public comment and input sessions, landowners and other pipeline opponents were not particularly organized. Opposition was collective but spontaneous and could be characterized in the Deweyian sense as the formation of an ephemeral public. But as meetings were iterated, a collective subject began to cohere through the shared experience and conscious organization of individuals and groups opposing the pipeline. I used the pronouns "you," "we," and "our" in the above section to indicate the generic aspect of the process but also because I was and am a part of this provisional collective. Pipeline opponents started to think of ourselves not as an assortment of individuals but as a people. As *the* people. And it was through both collective identity and iteration that the binding experience of testimony eventually turned into resigned pragmatism.

The most common expression of this subject position was through reference to the U.S. American democratic tradition—phrases such as "We the People" from the Preamble to the Constitution or Abraham Lincoln's pronouncement of a government "of the people, by the people, for the people." Others preferred to cite invocations of the people closer to home—South Dakota's motto "Under God, the People Rule" seems to me to be a direct legacy of the Farmers' Alliance in the state (though of course settler colonialism is unmentioned). In 2015, when Iowans began organizing against DAPL, speakers at a public hearing frequently cited the opening stanzas of the Iowa Constitution, which begins with the line "We, the people of Iowa . . ." More forcefully, it makes the constituent claim that "all political power is inherent in the people." In drawing on the culture and rhetoric of popular sovereignty in the United States, these acts unravel and reperform the mythical and mystical foundations of authority. In demonstrating the insufficiency of these authorizing documents to adequately measure the will of the people, they "undo the purity of this origin" (J. Frank 2009, 9), in some way asking these founding documents to live up to a standard that they never have. As Margaret Canovan writes, if "we, the people are to take charge of our lives and to decide our own future," then we are "in deep and inescapable conflict with democracy viewed in the cold light of pragmatism, and the gap between the two is a fruitful breeding-ground for populist protest" (1999, 11).

In bearing the mantle of "the people," some comments certainly fall into the category of pleas for intersubjective recognition and a nostalgic return to purity of administration. In doing so, commenters reproduce the very impotence of the people, the submission of the people to an external authority that would recognize it. In continually calling on President Obama, Secretary of State John Kerry (and later Hillary Clinton), or the State Department at large to "make the right decision," commenters performed our own marginalization or lack of power. This sentiment was emphatically expressed by many written comments—this one among several hundred emails in the South Dakota PUC archives: "PLEASE LISTEN TO THE PEOPLE, ALL OF THE PEOPLE, NOT JUST A SELECT FEW THAT HAVE THE MONEY AND MEANS TO GET THEIR MESSAGE ACROSS LOUDER THAN THOSE OF US WHO DO NOT WANT THE PIPELINE." Implicitly, the people here are taken to have less power due to their lack of resources.

Others, however, understood the people not as subjects of proper representation but instead as the real constituent power from which this representation was derived. This mode of articulation was not an appeal or demand for representation or for the voice of the people to be heard. Instead, it was something more akin to a right to resistance or even a threat. "We, The People will not just lose trust, we will RESIST and mistrust all your words, your programs, your very core and the values we believe you stand/stood for. . . . It will then become our initial instinct and even perhaps our mission to fight your efforts every step of the way" (U.S. Department of State 2013a, 163). At the state level, speakers sought to portray the constituted decision-making process of the South Dakota PUC or the Iowa Utilities Board as illegitimate. The "public" interest was supposed to be embodied in the elected South Dakota PUC, while the appointed and thus unelected Iowa Utilities Board seemed to be a violation of the spirit of the Iowa constitution itself. Yet both were perceived as incapable of representing the people.[7]

Language concerning "the people's right of self-government" was also derived from another broad social organization in North America: the community rights movement. This rhetoric and strategy, developed by the Community Environmental Legal Defense Fund, grew out of rural anti-coal-mining organizing in Pennsylvania in the late 1990s (Campbell and Linzey 2016). The strategy of the community rights movement hinged on an interpretation of state constitutions taken at their word: localities have a right to govern themselves. Consequently, municipalities and counties should be able to pass laws that specifically ban harmful activities (frequently environmental) from their locations. Some localities in Pennsylvania had since been successful in passing zoning laws to prevent fracking, for example, leading to some hope that a similar movement could garner energy in the Midwest. In a 2015 hearing in Iowa, many testifiers seized on this people-powered movement philosophy to ground their arguments against DAPL. The archive of this meeting included statements submitted by participants, as well as a transcript. One emblematic statement was typed out by the speaker and brought to the hearing:

> We the people of Iowa deserve better than an unelected and unaccountable Iowa Utility Board having the authority to decide whether we get this dangerous pipeline, and whether private land owners will have their property rights taken away from them and handed to a corporation. This ~~whole regulatory~~ hearing ~~process~~ is illegitimate, as it violates our right to govern ourselves in our communities, and to decide for ourselves whether the pipeline is a good fit for our state. I encourage you to find out more about the Community Rights move-

ment which could help you pass a locally-enforceable law in your county that would ban the pipeline.

The "we the people" language, as well as the community rights movement call, appeared in many comments during this hearing and were offered by organizers with a group called 100 Grannies for a Livable Future prior to the hearing to many potential speakers. But the crossed out words in the testimony also show how the speaker's thinking changed as the public meeting was continuing—they modified the organization-supplied language to highlight that it is not just the regulatory process but this hearing specifically that appeared farcical. Another commenter had a similar typed-out statement but wrote in large handwritten script on the bottom: "This procedure appears to be rigged. And, is an abuse of the public trust." Citing the Iowa constitution in parentheticals, another typed comment read with selective boldface: "**We the people** must **act** to protect OUR RIGHTS, granted by the Iowa constitution. . . . We must never forget that '**all political power is inherent in the people . . .**'"

As political theorist Jason Frank argues, such a distinctly U.S. American sense of the people as a sovereign power extends back to eighteenth-century American political rhetoric and theory. Frank calls such fleeting sites where the paradox of representation is exposed by the people "constituent moments" that "enact their claims wholly on the democratic authority of the people themselves: out of these enactments a new democratic subject emerges" (J. Frank 2009, 8). Such moments are "felicitous," Frank claims, in part because they explicitly break with the procedure for recognizing or authorizing public democracy. Drawing on this work, Thea Riofrancos (2020, 136) contends that claims to collective peoplehood, "if felicitous . . . can shore up the collective identities and forms of participation they invoke." The people cannot preexist such enunciations or signatures. In composing itself as a subject through such acts, they expose the democratic deficit at the heart of representational democracy while reauthorizing itself (as the people) as a potential subject of claims-making practice (see also Derrida 2002). This practice of vox populi can emerge as the redemptive form of populism (Canovan 1999, 10). Such a sentiment can be seen in comments such as these: "The time is now for WE THE PEOPLE to be put back into this Democracy" (U.S. Department of State 2013b, 126). The demand is for a restoration of people's democracy. The redemptive form of "We the People" is directed at state representatives who are seen as having been corrupted by money, specifically from the oil industry. Recalling the public commentary Huber (2013) examines from the 1970s, oil companies were seen to be "squeezing the lifeblood out of democracy" (U.S. Department of State 2013d, 1381). Such accounts of a corrupt or fallen democracy are central to the redemptive moral power that "the people" holds in U.S. American populism.

Although behind-the-scenes meetings, Facebook posts, and email blasts could explain the emergence of the people, these internet worlds are individualizing. They are less public "spheres" (intimate or otherwise) than they are "archipelagos" (Dean 2010, 38). Spaces of nondigital public participation form more coherent collective identities. This is in part because the circulatory affect of the crowd is not as easily individualized during an in-person event. It is only through the affects of being together in a place that sensibilities can reverberate and cohere. Elias Canetti provides two reasons for this in his theorization of crowd behavior. On the one hand, a negative affect emerges: the "feeling of being persecuted, a peculiar angry sensitiveness and irritability directed against those [the crowd] has once and forever nominated as enemies" (1962, 22). While in chapter 3 I examine how this feeling could be directed toward a foreign outsider, in public participation meetings it was far easier to locate the enemy as a TransCanada representative, for instance. On the other hand, more positively, Canetti suggests that "all demands for justice and all theories of equality ultimately derive their energy from the actual experience of equality familiar to anyone who has been part of a crowd" (29). The flattening or equalizing feeling of public testimony provided the basis for the possible emergence of a collective subject.

Participation Fatigue and Resigned Pragmatism

The problem is that these felicitous moments of constituent power are by definition fleeting. As Marxist theorist Antonio Negri poetically describes, "A web of a thousand threads defines the originary radicalness of constituent power. The coherence of the weave, however, is always in danger" (1999, 24). This is in part because such power is attenuated by the institutional democratic process. The composition of the redemptive subject of the people required the confidence of testimonial as "we the people" but also the (perceived) failure to be heard or recognized. One Keystone commenter asked the State Department to reveal what we all knew to be the situation: "Tell us the truth: Democracy in the US is a fantasy" (U.S. Department of State 2013d, 1344). Such sentiment emerges from the iterative performance of public input and comment, which, as noted above, wears people down. After years of testimony, it was clear to many of the people I spoke with in 2014 and 2015 that their voice was not actively reshaping PUC power. Participation events had become simply performative, without any discernible attachment to reality.

A particularly significant symbol of this feeling occurred at the 2015 KXL PUC evidentiary hearing. At that event, PUC commissioner Gary Hanson appeared to fall asleep during the hearing. He would later claim that he was simply on pain medication and was resting, but this defense did little to quell criticism. It seemed like a potent symbol of the disrespect that the democratic process held for participants. Sheila, the community organizer, related to me in 2016 the emotions felt by participants after that period of time:

> It functions as a dog and pony show where people sleep through it when they're supposed to be listening to you. And yeah, it's hard from our end too because we had a monumentally difficult time getting people to participate in the final environmental impact statement process because people were like, "We've done it enough times. They don't pay attention to what we think!" And you think, the final environmental impact statement, they had like two million comments, [but] I guarantee you they had five from South Dakota, at least from the landowners. Because they're like, "We've done this before. We've done a final environmental impact statement before." I mean, they had to do a different one because of the reroute, but now six, seven, eight times they've put in comments on these things and they never get listened to? So why the hell are they going to put in comments again? It's the same thing with the PUC process, and it's something where I think we're going to have a little bit more difficulty with—in terms of sort of engaging with sort of, being like, "We have to do this

again? Are you kidding me?" Because they don't feel like they've been listened to.

I will return to the question of "getting people to participate" in the next section. For now, I want to underline Sheila's argument that iteration—the very relation I suggested above formed the condition for subjective coherence—also eventually exhausted many pipeline opponents. While the iteration of participation can create a more cohesive collective identity through the affective circulation of public testimony, it also creates resentment and disaffection at the process itself. An iterative series can only go, after all, until it hits a threshold (Deleuze and Guattari 1987, 438). Participants will keep coming back to give testimony as long as they think it is the pragmatic thing to do; once the weight of the evidence of their experience accumulates, they must do something else or risk some form of psychic damage.

And it is true that, as Sheila put it, "they never get listened to," at least not meaningfully. Officials do not usually respond to the ardent criticisms emerging from the audience during events themselves. Instead, several months later, a document is posted on the regulatory body's website that claims to incorporate the comments of the public. At the federal level, each individual comment is transcribed and divided into its constituent parts. Then the criticisms are grouped under different themes (e.g., socioeconomics, risk, alternatives), not unlike a social scientific analysis. If you are intrepid, you can sometimes even find your name and comments (during my research, I was tickled to find the names of several academic geographers). Next to a quote from your comment, there appears a code word, like RISK 25, CLIM 13, or PN 09. Page to the end of the document, and you will find your response summarized. "Inaccurate characterization of lifecycle GHG emissions." "Lack of consideration of Keystone's safety record and safety culture." "Economic 'ripple effects' of the proposed Project." You then scroll down even further to find a response. "As discussed in section 13.9 . . ." "Regulatory oversight is detailed in Section 4.13.6.1 . . ." "Section 4.14, Greenhouse Gases and Climate Change, discusses the impacts of bitumen extraction in Canada on global climate change." The sense that these are responses is misleading. For example, the State Department summarizes all grievances related to "Process" in fewer than seven "themes." The EIS responds to these themes in a mere four pages. In those pages, it only once even argues that the participation process was sufficient. The "responses" merely describe activities undertaken, without ingesting critique.

In a legal review of the public participation process of KXL up to 2012, Elizabeth Brown concludes that "all indications are that the outcome of this project has been politically predetermined" (2012, 505). Many commenters agreed with this sentiment; as one put it in another email to the South Dakota PUC, "I know it's a done deal and this 'public input' session is merely for show." To the extent that the public was involved, its participation was meaningful not from within the NEPA or PUC process but from outside it. But were things as predetermined as many commenters claim—given KXL's ultimate rejection? Some evidence suggests it was not conspiracy but incompetence in managing an interagency review on the part of the State Department that led to regulatory snafus (Hersh 2011, 2012). Nonetheless, the public experience of meetings, open comment periods, and the immense amount of technical expertise involved in EIS review paints a remarkably cynical picture of the democratic process. Participants felt like "we weren't being heard," "our comments didn't matter," and that the entire participation system itself was in the pockets of the oil companies.

What is important to note about this quasi-exhaustion of desires is that in their disorganization, desires spill far beyond the class interest in maintaining democracy in its bourgeois form. So too do they exceed the interests that liberal, bureaucratic state organizers might have in maintaining public participation as a form of legitimacy. Many former participants expressed to me some variation on the refrain that they "just wanted the meetings to end." For others, giving public testimony reified their position against the pipeline and brought them into contact with political organizing that they had never experienced before. As one participant put it to me, "I have never considered myself a political person. But now, I feel like I have to take a position on everything." This is merely inchoate sentiment, but it is also one that exceeds the codifications of the public participation process even as it is produced in relation to it.

The contradictory desires of participants highlight the situation organizers like Sheila had to unravel. Given that everyone seemed to take participation as something of a theatrical performance without much impact, why continue to participate? And what good could come of participation? Sheila reiterated a point made above: "It's hard when you have those public processes and people participate in them and then they don't get any response from them. So then the question becomes: What can we do outside of that official governmental process to move the thinking so that when we get to that process we can get a win? And it's difficult." So, pipeline opponents took public participation events as a pragmatic site of organizing other kinds of political activities beyond their events. The events were sites of convergence of pipeline opponents, they strengthened opponents' resolve, and they served to highlight a democratic deficit. Through the resignation produced therein, organizing could increasingly move "outside that official governmental process" and thus toward a different mode of politics. Despite the seeming optimism of that assessment, Sheila told me: "I don't think we have a rat's chance in hell that [the PUC will] say 'no,' but we're gonna fight as hard as we can." It was crucial for people to participate:

> You [can] get a lot of media, and a lot of focus on like, "Wow, there are a lot of people in South Dakota who are opposed to this." So, it's one of those things where you kind of know that it's kind of maaaay-beeeee potentially a little bit of a farce. But there's a tiny chance of winning and you have to participate in that process anyway. Because if you don't, then it's just like you're lying down on the ground. Even if you don't think you can win, you have to participate.

Individuals, organizers, and groups approached the internal organization of such events with resignation. They have accepted it as something unpleasant in which they must participate and that they cannot do anything about. *You have to participate.*

Perhaps this can in part explain why in South Dakota political participation within the PUC review of DAPL permitting seemed much less contentious when compared to KXL. In the midsummer of 2016, I had thought that this lack of organizing was a sign that the movement had exhausted itself in opposing KXL. But it turned out that such exhaustion in the official process led in part to an exodus toward contentious politics: the forms of Native-led direct action and blockade that characterized the gathering at Standing Rock. And it is true that a handful of prominent non-Native KXL opponents, organizers, and landowners were active early in the DAPL resistance and blockade movement at Standing Rock, well before the international prominence of the movement. Neither is it frequently acknowledged in the existing literature on the DAPL blockade, for example, that four long-term prayer camps had been established along the KXL route as early as 2014. When some of these organizers and activists have suggested that the experience of fighting KXL was crucial to the NoDAPL blockade movement that later emerged, one of those lessons might have been the limits of public participation.

"You Have to Participate!"

Such an exodus strategy also had consequences for pipeline opponents, since the background discourse to official public participation became the delegitimization of other forms of political activity. From the perspective of TransCanada, ETP, and state and federal government officials and politicians, the process of public participation grants legitimation to construct a pipeline. This meant that, from their perspective, nonparticipation could be seen as proof of opponents' political degeneracy—their lack of democracy. It is important to highlight grievances from pipeline opponents and responses from officials in order to demonstrate the manner in which certain contestation of political participation could in turn consolidate the process.

Throughout the KXL and DAPL permitting process, Native Nations and Indigenous people contested the very authority of the PUC and the federal government to derive a ruling through public participation processes. At most public meetings, such individuals—either part of tribal governments or not—repeated the claim that the pipelines violated the sovereignty of the Oceti Sakowin Oyate and other Native Nations along its route. Although the pipelines did not cross administrative reservation boundaries, most Lakota, Nakota, and Dakota people contend that these are not legitimate boundaries due to the violation of the 1851 and 1868 Treaties of Fort Laramie. These treaties—as "supreme laws of the land," in the words of the U.S. Constitution—were developed in sovereign nation-to-nation meetings and condition the understanding that western South Dakota was, and remains, stolen land (Deloria and Lytle 1984; Deloria and Wilkins 1999; Ostler 2011; Ostler and Estes 2017; Estes 2019).

Tribal governments and Indigenous participants both expressed the necessity of government-to-government consultation on development projects, including pipelines. They requested to meet face-to-face with United States political leaders, not sundry administrative officials. They thus understood consultation processes in both KXL and DAPL to be incomplete. That the Oyate were only offered "meaningful participation" via public processes rather than nation-to-nation consultation was frequently seen as offensive. Jason Cooke (2015), elected leader of the Yankton Sioux Tribe, expressed this difficulty at the July public input session for KXL:

> I am disappointed to say that this public input session is the only way in which many of [our] concerns can be heard. I am here despite the fact that the commission has provided inadequate opportunities for tribal members to participate and an inadequate process by excluding relevant evidence because this forum is the only forum provided to us to address these issues. This is par for the course, unfortunately, when it comes to outside governments' treatment of indigenous people. And this is something that must change for the PUC's proceedings to provide due process to all South Dakotans.

Even the Obama administration acknowledged late in 2016 that it was necessary to create "a broader review and consultation as to how, prospectively, Federal decisionmaking on infrastructure projects can better allow for timely and meaningful tribal input" (Bureau of Indian Affairs 2016). Yet much like other forms of participation, such an assessment still takes tribal consultation as "input" to already-proposed projects. By contrast, the Treaty Alliance, an international coalition among 150 signatory Indigenous Nations against tar sands extraction and pipelines across North America, proposed a completely different articulation of sovereignty.

This form of political action is not the subject of this book. Nonetheless, I want to highlight an awareness of the difficult contradiction between Native sovereignty and popular sovereignty present in these spaces. Grounding political opposition in an understanding of abstract population or class dynamics can render Indigenous peoples a mere asterisk in coalition politics. As Tuck and Yang (2012, 23) write, "The '99%' is invoked as a deserving supermajority, in contrast to the unearned wealth of the '1%.' It renders Indigenous peoples (a 0.9% 'super-minority') completely invisible and absorbed, just an asterisk group to be subsumed into the legion of occupiers." Such a critique of "the people" as a numerical identity thus opens the question of the necessity of another form of sovereignty that a politics of decolonization would produce.[8]

Yet such an argument can give the impression that such sovereignty is futural rather than actively practiced. Instead, much like Borrows's account of the "filtered participation" of representative democracy, Jason Cooke (2015) inverts the account of who ought to participate in whose actually existing democracy. Rather than taking Native sovereignty as a minority position that must be protected within the broader context of popular sovereignty, Cooke argues that popular sovereignty is predicated on and derived from Indigenous sovereignty. During testimony, Cooke cited the importance of usufructuary rights reserved by the 1851 and 1868 treaties and asserted that the Yankton Sioux Tribe's obligation to this land did not end with the creation of reservation boundaries. He continued, however, by describing how meaningful participation for all is failed when Indigenous consultation is not undertaken:

> While we appreciate the opportunity to participate in this proceeding, and that others have been granted the opportunity as well, it now appears that the intervenor status was not granted to enable the public to meaningfully participate, but, rather, to give this proceeding the appearance of fairness to the public. Many of the commission's decisions in the course of this proceeding do not comport with what is required by South Dakota statutes, and this process has become almost unrecognizable as a quasi-judicial proceeding. The public involvement element of this process has been a matter of form rather than substance, which was not what was intended by the statutes. To protect all South Dakota, the voices of all South Dakotans must be considered in a meaningful way.

The open possibility here, it seems to me, is not one of recognition or belittlement but a redistribution of our understanding of where and how constituent power or popular sovereignty might be derived.

Although the Obama administration was sympathetic to fixing the broken consultation process, to the broader dynamics of the settler state and subjects such claims or possibilities were not just unintelligible but deemed to be dangerous. Nowhere can this be seen better than in the admonishment served by the oil industry and its political allies to the Standing Rock Sioux and their coalition for not properly participating in environmental or cultural review. Ed Wiederstein (2016), from the industry-funded public relations firm Midwest Alliance for Infrastructure Now, wrote in a *Bismarck Tribune* op-ed that "these groups did not participate in the public hearings held by the North Dakota Public Service Commission, [and] now they seek to push a radical environmental agenda through illegal action." North Dakota governor Jack Dalrymple (2016) went further and suggested that the blockade "tramples on a legal and orderly process in favor of mob rule." The supposed nonparticipation of the Standing Rock Sioux Tribe in consultation remained one of the major talking points of the pipeline lobby.

These sentiments saturated the earlier KXL public participation process as well. At a public meeting in South Dakota in 2011, a group of Indigenous pipeline opponents entered a meeting dressed in fatigues and stood silently around the room. The hearing continued and the masked people did not participate. The silent, nonparticipatory action outraged many local non-Native people. Journalist Bob Mercer (2013) suggested they were "dressed as real eco-terrorists." Mercer interpreted their dress and silence as "symbols of intimidation and threats of potential violence" that contributed to an "already tense atmosphere." The coding was thin and obvious; within the broader realm of racial signification as understood by settlers, masks and fatigues on an Indigenous person can only signify racial threat and terror, proving an ignorance of long-standing outsized enrollment of Native peoples in the U.S. military (LaDuke and Cruz 2013). Reference to "eco-terrorists" might have contributed to the State of South Dakota's financial relationship with the Department of Homeland Security. One of the claims made to secure such funds was "the chance that environmentalists might attack the proposed Dewey-Burdock in situ uranium mine or the Keystone XL pipeline" (O'Sullivan 2014; see also Bosworth and Chua 2021). The broader point is that from the perspective of the settler, silence and nonparticipation in democracy are seen as racial threat, whereas, as Kanngieser and Beuret argue, "the refusal to be counted, to speak . . . is a means of making silence into a de/colonizing device, one that works through the refusal of representation and incorporation" (2017, 376).

Conclusion

This chapter traced the broad experience of public participation in environmental review from the point of view of political organizers and regular people who were enrolled in its process. Though initially both skeptical and enthusiastic, political review at the state and federal levels was increasingly taken to be a feckless performance. Iterations of participatory events produced a feeling of collective identity as "the people" who might call for a renewed democracy but also produced a resigned pragmatism that tied pipeline opponents to the affective scenes of participation while also gesturing toward the necessity of political life beyond it. This populist opposition to KXL works against two common-sense claims in critical scholarship. First, the idea that more or better-designed participatory mechanisms will produce a better result is, populists demonstrate, something of a losing battle so long as histories of colonialism and the influence of capitalism structure such events. Populists are resigned to public participation. I agree with them (and learned from them) that the process and outcome feel very much "rigged" by industry and the state alike (even if the specific connections are not always convincing). Environmentalism's populist spirit allowed it to connect to the region's verve for grassroots democracy, so when supposedly participatory processes failed to reach expectations, the institutions appeared all the more illegitimate.

Second, the counterclaim from critical scholars that the people are ignorant of the ineffectuality of participation or captured by its process does not hold in this case. Participation was fueled by the desire to testify and render visible and affectable a social group's attachments, including to the fantasy of participatory democracy. Pipeline populists were pragmatic insofar as they somewhat consciously sought to demonstrate through such processes that democracy is a fantasy. The resigned pragmatism of populism, intentionally or not, exhausted the possibility of meaningful public participation. But at the same time, it also exhausted many of its participants. What resigned pragmatism does to environmental politics, in the context of revolutionary and anticolonial politics emerging in the wake of these participation meetings, is an open question of political strategy. But it is, in fact, a question of strategy, not one of quiescence or unconscious capture.

However, to me, when geographers and environmental justice scholars advocate for more participation, or for developing better structures of democracy, we are sometimes advocating for the very structures to which activists and the public are pragmatically resigned. It seems to me that such idealistic scholarship, if it fails to engage with the real political experience of participation, becomes caught in its own cruel optimism and settler colonial desires for a world in which deliberative consensus is achievable. It is no surprise, then, that those who advocate for a left-populist path toward agonistic democracy do so with a certain disdain for actual antagonism. I find it too easy to imagine such an agonistic process renewing a state that retains the juridical power to sanction acts of debility, exhaustion, and extermination directed at Native Nations, Indigenous peoples, and the global working classes. The experimental reformist creation of new institutional structures of participation, from this perspective, is an attempt to calcify academic authority to augment the conditions for the emergence of proper democracy. As Pulido argues, "the state has developed numerous initiatives in which it goes through the motions, or, 'performs' regulatory activity, especially participation" (2017, 530). The fact that these procedures almost never produce meaningful results demonstrates not a problem with "a lack of knowledge or skill" on the part of participants (as chapter 4 further demonstrates) "but a lack of political will that must be attributed to racial capitalism" (530).

Few participants in public participation processes believe these sessions to be politically fruitful, enjoyable, or meaningful. Participants devote countless hours to organizing through participation even though many experienced these meetings as exhausting. Most everyone involved sees the actual mechanism of deliberation as a charade mediated by a corrupt state under the influence of oil. Yet they are compelled to participate, since participation is used as a wedge by conservatives and the fossil fuel PR machine to delegitimize resistance as antidemocratic. So, pipeline populists were caught in a paradox wherein popular sovereignty is desired but its scenes, stages, spaces, and representations, alienated by technocratic modes of participation, seem to intentionally exhaust it. One way out would be a recomposition of a less-filtered democracy through the expansive and transformative mechanisms that Borrows describes. However, this might require a different valence of the subject of democracy—especially when even left-populist articulations of "we the people" resurrect a nationalist subject fearful of outside influence. It is to the melodramatic threat of China and Canada that the next chapter turns.

3

CANADIAN INVASION FOR CHINESE CONSUMPTION

FOREIGN OIL AND HEARTLAND MELODRAMA

IN 2014, THE POLITICAL ACTION COMMITTEE NextGen Climate Action spent millions of dollars to air an anti–Keystone XL television advertisement in the hours before and after President Obama's State of the Union address. Founded by billionaire philanthropist Tom Steyer, NextGen was making one of the most high-profile attempts yet to sway the president and the State Department to reject KXL. According to the *New Yorker*, Steyer had met repeatedly with climate activist and 350.org leader Bill McKibben to "discuss the strategy against Keystone," including while hiking together in the Adirondacks (Lizza 2013). Steyer had also pitched a KXL rejection to President Obama during an exclusive fundraiser. Nothing was successful. So, at the behest of his advisers John Podesta and Chris Lehane, Steyer hit the airwaves. He began a unique-for-the-time digital campaign called We Love Our Land in June 2013 and began purchasing ad buys in September. NextGen's strategy was built upon a message that had previously polled well: connecting the pipeline to "foreign oil," while singling out China as the ultimate destination for the fuel. There, foreign companies would use this oil to "make more products to sell back to us," a move the ad suggested was designed to undercut "*our* economy and *our* workers." According to Lehane (Lizza 2013), this "formula," in which an "enemy" oil company was portrayed as pursuing its own self-interest abroad while hurting America, was responsible for successes in recent Democratic Party ad buys.

The January 2014 NextGen advertisement entitled "Suckers" expresses exactly this philosophy (see Figure 6). The ad opens with the declaration "It's a sucker punch to America's heartland. The deeper we dig into the Keystone XL pipeline, the closer we get to the truth: China's become one of the biggest players in Canadian oil." An animation of a Canadian flag posted on a desolate-looking tar sands landscape morphs into a Chinese flag before select financial statistics scroll across the screen, lending authority to the claim.[1] The ad continues with a geopolitical map showing the destination of the oil flows across North America and eventually overseas, claiming that the Chinese government is "counting on the U.S. to approve TransCanada's pipeline to ship oil through America's heartland, and out to foreign countries like theirs." An image of a distraught-looking woman pumping gas plays while the voiceover reiterates that "the oil lobbyists and politicians—they take Americans for suckers." But upon ending, NextGen reiterates that the lobbyists and politicians are working for "investors like China," creating "more power for their economy, and more carbon pollution for the world." Images of Chinese workers in factories and extravagant Chinese cities at night flicker.

"Suckers" was not the only instance of such ideology produced by NextGen, as it followed an earlier ad in which a fictional deranged Canadian oil CEO sneers a similar message: "They said it couldn't be done—building an oil pipeline that cut right through America's heartland. I guess we proved them wrong!" As he jumps into a pipeline like a waterslide, the CEO lets us in on a secret: "All it took is a little old-fashioned lying. Like when we told the American people it would be good for the economy. . . . And this is my favorite part: We said that the Keystone pipeline was going to increase American oil independence! You want to see who it's really going to increase oil independence for?" He gestures toward Chinese oil tankers in the background, ending with a sardonic "God Bless America."

Situated within the geopolitical context of U.S. American economic and environmental decline, these advertisements channel heartland precarity into a resentment of foreign outsiders. Their melodra-

Figure 6. A still from the NextGen Climate advertisement "Suckers" shows Canadian Prime Minister Stephen Harper and Chinese Premier Wen Jiabao shaking hands behind flags from their respective countries. The photograph was taken in China at a signing of trade deals between the two countries. In the ad, the photo is in black-and-white except for the two flags, emphasizing the national component.

matic divides between "good American heartland" and "bad foreign oil" are designed to rescript regional experience of economic and political instability through negative interpretations of China's consumption of Canada's foreign oil. These ads also help us understand how the ideology of "energy independence," frequently touted by environmental groups, could easily slip into bipartisan and capitalist support for domestic hydrofracking. In the process, they reference and repeat a scene popular in populist genres: the melodramatic dramatization of the hardworking Americans prevented from reaping the fruits of their honest work by a corrupt or antidemocratic foreign outsider.

Analyses of populism have long attended to the xenophobic tendencies possible in "the people" as a subject, even when such orientations are ostensibly progressive. Richard Hofstadter (1960) infamously indicted the Populist Party with these very charges, though his analysis has been heavily contested by historians and theorists since. For these and other reasons, advocates and analysts of left populisms tend to dismiss charges of exclusive nationalism and, of course, ethnonationalism. Nonetheless, some left-populist advocates like Chantal Mouffe still argue that "it is *at the national level* that the question of radicalizing democracy must first be posed" (2018, 71, emphasis added). Even in radical movements, such as Occupy Wall Street and the global "movements of the squares," Paolo Gerbaudo finds a kind of populist civic nationalism. Gerbaudo suggests it is not an exclusive identity but a citizenism or a "democratic and progressive patriotism" (2017, 114). But while such left-populist stylings might rely on seemingly kinder civic nationalisms based on expansive concepts of democracy that are formally different from ethnonationalist identity movements (Moffitt 2020), this chapter shows that their diagnoses of global capital flows induces the generic rhetoric of "the people" toward still-debilitating xenophobias. As Spinoza argues (2016, 314 [TPT XVII 80]), "no hatred can be greater" than that born of devotion and piety, exemplified by the "hatred of other nations." To study such sentiment, I take an approach influenced by feminist and popular geopolitics (Dowler and Sharp 2001; Hyndman 2001; Dittmer and Gray 2010; Pain 2009) and, more generally, the affective scenes of national (in)security that attempt to bind together as intimate publics the settler subjects of contemporary North America (Berlant 2008; Masco 2014; Anker 2014; Crang and Tolia-Kelly 2010; Merriman and Jones 2017). I examine pipeline populism's nationalist expressions through ideologies of "the heartland" constructed relationally between the foreign oil seen to be produced by Canada for the financial benefit of China.

The examination of such heartland melodramas in the affective geopolitics of KXL challenges contemporary assumptions that nationalism and xenophobia are reserved for right populists and thus are of little concern for left populism and transnational environmental politics. Preceding the prevalence of the more explicitly right-wing and antisemitic critique of "globalism" by several years, the pervasiveness of anti-Chinese and anti-Canadian sentiment in 2013 places pipeline populism in a geopolitical and economic context shaped not only by contemporary globalization but also by ideologies of dependence on foreign oil and the felt necessity for energy independence. I first examine such histories of anti-oil populisms before unpacking the concept of "heartland melodrama." Public comments on the 2013 KXL EIS exemplify this affective infrastructure. Then, by comparing the discourses on Canada and China in this data set, I build on theories that examine the intersection of transnational antimigrant and especially anti-Asian nativism with the expansive project of settler colonial empire (Day 2016; Lye 2005; Karuka 2019). The odd context of a romantic defense of the wounded U.S. "heartland" through both anti-Chinese and anti-Canadian sentiment pushes us to think carefully about the ways in which settler empire as a project—and thus the production of settler citizens—is built through transnational rivalry. Not only is such a project based on the externalization of racialized populations of foreign others (e.g., China), it is also, importantly, conceived of through competition with other settler colonies (e.g., Canada). Only by developing stronger internationalist alliances—especially class-based—can we form adequate diagnoses of the relation between settler colonialism and global capitalism, staving off such reductive affective infrastructures like heartland melodramas.

Populism, Foreign Oil, and Energy Independence in United States Identity

Because oil extraction in the United States emerged during an era of capital concentration, large oil firms have long attracted populist ire. Beginning with Standard Oil and the Rockefellers and traveling through the energy and environmental crises of the 1970s, oil has served as a metonym for corruption, price fixing, monopoly, foreign influence, or unfair government interference with markets. Rural residents and the U.S. heartland have often served as a proxy for that which was threatened by nefarious oil activities. Before turning to the example of pipeline populism, this section examines the dynamic political history of populist rage directed toward oil companies in an international context.

Though the Populist Party of the 1880s and 1890s occasionally located its gaze on Rockefeller or Standard Oil, it was the Progressive movement of the early 1900s that set its sights squarely on the oil monopoly (Kazin 1998, 49–53; Williams 2020). Ida Tarbell ends her infamous critique of Standard Oil with a populist call to action that will soon become familiar: "And what are we going to do about it? For it is *our* business. We, the people of the United States, and nobody else, must cure whatever is wrong in the industrial situation, typified by this narrative of the growth of the Standard Oil Company" (Tarbell [1904] 1963, 292). Tarbell exemplifies the genre of muckraking critique that emerged from 1890s populists like Minnesota's celebrated orator Ignatius Donnelly. Both populists and muckrakers sometimes suggested that monopolies arose from the supposed broader project of international Jewish finance capital. Such anti-Semitism was directed at Rockefeller himself and also emerged through more symbolic references, such as depictions of Standard Oil as an octopus. With its expanding tendrils reaching around the world, the octopus was a frequently used stand-in among political cartoonists for imperial power, representing capitalism, monopoly power, Jewish finance, communism, and yellow peril. Even during this period, the figure of the Jewish financier was sometimes placed alongside that of the foreign/alien threat of the Chinese to agrarian lands. Though the popular creation of Alien Land Laws of the late nineteenth century were sometimes rooted in a distrust of ownership by centers of capital within the United States (say, financiers in Chicago), they also effectively racialized the ownership of land (especially mines) by preventing Chinese or Asian people more generally from owning such property in state laws and even constitutions.[2] Anti-Chinese sentiment also structured literary naturalism and its critiques of monopoly and finance capitalism. By frequently reifying the danger of monopoly and finance into the figure of yellow peril or Jewish finance, populist and progressive-era diagnosis could only remain, in literary critic Colleen Lye's estimation, "a failed critique of capitalism" (2005, 8).

Oil was so abundant during the Great Depression and the postwar political order (due in part to policies like Eisenhower's import quota limit) that it was not until the late 1960s that widespread populist rage toward petroleum began to spike again.[3] This changing perception of geopolitics and political economy was rooted in the experience of frustration at long lines and suddenly high energy prices. By the 1973 oil crisis, the public increasingly pointed the blame at the Organization of Arab Petroleum Exporting Countries (OAPEC) or oil corporations.[4] U.S. consumers understood the supposed price fixing engaged by OAPEC (and acknowledged by the broader Organization of Petroleum Exporting Countries, OPEC) to be linked to the disreputable market policies of "big oil" and "big government"—and thus there was a popular sense that the crisis was "fake" or "contrived" (Huber 2013, 99).

This form of anti-oil skepticism lives on today in the libertarian peak oil movement (Schneider-Mayerson 2015).

The cultural politics of oil in the 1970s "were shot through with a racialized politics of anti-Arab xenophobia" (Huber 2013, 107), thus consolidating the supposed independence of U.S. consumers. Orientalist tropes of shady sheiks presented an alternative explanation that displaced the responsibility of U.S. foreign policy or oil firms in precipitating the crisis. By contrast, the U.S. American heartland was full of honest producers, exemplified by radio personality Bobby Butler's 1979 song "Cheaper Crude or No More Food" and the concurrent trucker strikes. Historian Shane Hamilton writes of the period that "a truck driving man was supposed to be the king of the open road, the backbone of America, not a mere cog in the wheels of global energy politics" (2008, 218). The truckers, many of them former farmers, thus had an aesthetics and grievances shaped by prior agrarian populisms, but inverted: they were against state regulation and union interference.[5] Less frequently noted is that the 1970s' fears around foreign oil seeped into U.S. understandings of Canadian production. In routing natural gas pipelines from Alaska, the El Paso Natural Gas Company emphasized that a U.S. route would be "completely under United States jurisdiction and immune from foreign decision-making, thereby giving the United States consumer a 'secure' gas supply" (Lieberman 1974). At the same time as public ire railed against oil markets, populist environmentalism surfaced in reaction to the Santa Barbara oil spill in 1969, the proposal and controversy surrounding the Trans-Alaskan Pipeline, and Canadian drilling for gas in Lake Erie (Sabin 2012, 179; Bird 1970). These events thus served to reinforce anxieties about "foreign oil" and populist desires for "energy independence" and "energy security" as aspects of U.S. identity (Herbstreuth 2016).

The 1980s and 1990s saw an increasing focus on the globalization of the oil industry, especially its high-profile crimes in Latin America and Africa. "Foreign oil" also came to further signify corruption, war, and terrorism as purportedly supported or funded by Arab governments (Vitalis 2020). In the wake of the September 11 terrorist attacks and the subsequent war on terror, a simplistic relationship between oil, geopolitics, and violence has been frequently taken for granted by both the political right and the left. For the right, international oil dependency breeds terror organizations and weakens American values of freedom and self-sufficiency. For the left, the U.S. government's imperialism appeared to be driven by its thirst for oil (e.g., Caffentzis 2017; D. Harvey 2005). Much like the international development ideology of the "resource curse," oil firms sometimes receded into the background. Counterintuitively, perhaps, both the left and right also reconverged around the discourse of "energy independence" in the early 2000s. President Bush famously expressed a desire to end the United States' "addiction to oil" in his 2006 State of the Union address. Green groups and labor unions supported energy independence through development of the nation's wind, solar, and natural gas resources—the last of these eventually resulting in the hydrofracking boom. In the context of globalization's economic and geopolitical blowback on the United States, ending its supposed national pathology seemed paramount.

Yet when the political context was changed by the Obama administration, terrain for different populist ideologies against oil began to resonate. The Obama administration extended many of Bush's policies in support of energy independence through what President Obama would term an "all of the above" energy strategy, including support for renewables as well as domestic oil and natural gas production from offshore wells and through hydrofracking. Domestic oil production rose so high that in 2015 the Obama administration lifted the domestic oil export ban, which had been in place since the 1970s. The combination of deepening inequality after the financial crisis and increased domestic production also resulted in a new uneven landscape of energy production, transforming communities in the Dakotas, Pennsylvania, West Texas, New Mexico, and Colorado who did not always have historic experiences with oil extraction. The high-profile BP offshore oil spill and Kalamazoo River pipeline spill in 2010 highlighted the dangers of North American oil production; the latter had been transporting diluted bitumen from the Canadian oil sands. And while much deserved indignation was directed to the "Drill, baby, drill!" rhetoric of the insurgent conservative Tea Party movement (and their funding by oil magnates like Charles and David Koch), quietly some of the same Tea Party activists—especially in Texas—found their populist rage directed instead at the pipelines proposed to cross their property.

Imported Canadian oil had long been used as a contrast to that oil arriving from the Middle East or Latin America. Many scholars and activists have examined how Canadian firms and politicians have attempted to avoid being branded as foreign oil by promoting Canadian crude as an "ethical oil" alternative (Grant 2014). Canadian firms and politicians have also tried to reframe scales by suggesting the pursuit of "North American energy independence" (Carter 2014, 30). The efficacy of these ideologies relies on the history of U.S. perceptions of Canada as supposedly closer or even interior to its own national or racial identity (Herbstreuth 2016). TransCanada took up these frames by branding KXL as a secure source of oil in contrast to "unrest" in the Middle East (Bosworth and Chua 2021). But many in the United States do not readily accept the narrative of U.S.–Canadian continental solidarity. The evidence in this chapter instead shows how juxtapositions with improper Canadian production and Chinese consumption of oil consolidated a settler defense of the U.S. heartland. This aspect of U.S. national identity is independent from—yet in geopolitical and economic competition with—the rest of the world's countries. It is sustained by both racialized and competitive geopolitical and economic contrasts.

Below, I analyze the popular geopolitics of oil transportation through an examination of public comments made on the 2013 KXL supplemental draft environmental impact statement. The pipeline's crossing of the U.S.–Canada border was consequential for eliciting populist and nationalist responses that assessed international relations in three ways. First, the border crossing required a presidential permit, which meant that the pipeline required full review in accordance with the National Environmental Policy Act. Pipelines that do not cross such recognized political boundaries (such as DAPL) do not automatically garner this evaluation. Second, the determination of the presidential permit would hinge on whether the project would serve "the national interest." And third, rather than more experienced agencies like the EPA or the Department of Energy, the lead agency contracting the EIS was the U.S. Department of State. Together, these three aspects of the environmental review led many commentators to assess the pipeline on the terms of national interest in a global competitive landscape.

Public comments were made during March and April of 2013 and posted on the official KXL website later that year in six batches. Though

KXL has endured several public comment periods, the 2013 comments are the most complete set made available by the State Department.[6] Though millions of comments were submitted, most of these were simple form letters from organizations opposing or supporting the pipeline. Official statements from groups like the Sierra Club are also not included in this sample; instead, these are largely comments from individuals. Altogether, the sample amounts to over six thousand pages of comments, which I narrowed down by coding five hundred pages for keywords associated with populism and geopolitics, then querying the remaining document for further instances. Though identities of commentators (e.g., race, gender, or geographical region) cannot be determined, I do not treat these comments as neutral or representative of an abstract position. Instead, like other positions I have examined in this book, I treat these as public performances. That is, as with the embodied performances analyzed in the previous chapters, online commentators are expressing the arguments and emotions that they expect the State Department to most value. If a determination is expected to be made on national interest, commentators provided arguments for or against the pipeline based on that audience, which invited nationalism and invocations of "the people" alike.

The Populist Genre in Melodramatic Public Commentary

It is important to reiterate from the outset that an overwhelming majority of the opposition to KXL concerned the potential environmental impacts of the pipeline. Commenters highlighted the effects of tar sands mining and combustion on global climate change, water, and deforestation in Canada as well as the potential impacts of an oil spill on U.S. waterways. Though not universal by any stretch, frequently these environmentalist frames were elaborated through the melodramatic populist form with nationalist resonances. Take for example this typical comment, which positions the subject of the people in opposition to oil corporations: "Please do not cave in to pressure from the big money, big lobby energy companies. The people deserve a voice in this debate. And the people are speaking loudly. The Keystone XL pipeline is bad for the environment, bad for America and does nothing for jobs or our economy" (U.S. Department of State 2013c, 259). Such a contrast between "the people" and "corporations," "big oil," or the monied interests of the Koch brothers was one of the most dominant themes in public commentary and exemplifies the melodramatic tone of public commentary. In short: "This is the people vs. Big Oil. Please stand with the people" (2013d, 1462).

As a political style, melodrama indicates a heightened contrast between a "good" or virtuous interior subject (frequently an individual) and a "bad," villainous other. Both self and other in this framework are relatively pure, and their opposition is irreconcilable. Elizabeth Anker describes the U.S. American form of political melodrama as a "faith in ordinary people, a critique of unjust power, and a heroization of the underdog" (2014, 78). Though Anker emphasizes the importance of the individualism of the hero, I believe it is clear that such genre conventions can be equally found in the collective subject of populism (e.g., Hofstadter 1960, 73). I will further explore the tendency for melodrama to reinforce nationalist and exclusionist themes, but these were not necessary components of the heightened emotional resonance of melodrama. Numerous comments directed their ire toward villainous oil corporations and a corrupt government, all in defense of the little guy. For example: "What does an ordinary citizen have to do to be heard above the money din of those who now control our corrupt government[?]" one commenter ponders. "How can we begin to remove the pervasive and cynical collusion of our government with the corporate against the people, which is typified by this action[?]" (U.S. Department of State 2013c, 351). Such comments pit the "ordinary citizen" or "regular" people against the special interests of oil corporations. As another put it, "The Koch brothers and their like are rich enough, enough, enough, enough! In God's name the 1% is rich enough and We The People are crying for common sense" (2013a, 140). The latter is located not in elites but in the people.

Many comments staged direct conversations between the common people and President Obama or Secretary of State John Kerry, posing the problem of political representation in melodramatic terms. "Are you in league with the corporations, or are you a champion of the people, to whom this country really belongs[?]" asked one (U.S. Department of State 2013a, 232). This irresolvable problem of democratic representation is reduced to a matter of virtuous citizenry versus a cabal of evil corporations who have bought out the politicians. Frequent capitalization of "The People" or "We, the People" allowed heightened dramatization of the decision the Obama administration was to make as an action of representation. "You were elected to represent the PEOPLE of the united states [*sic*] but you appear to be representing the bottom line of the corporations of the world that do not have the best interest of the nation in mind" (2013f, 324). The question of ideological and political representation was thus consciously posed.

Melodrama is frequently connected to another common style of American political ideology: the jeremiad (Anker 2014; Meyerhoff 2019). This genre convention laments the loss of a past way of life while indicting the interior corruption and moral culpability of society, the nation, or a community. Jeremiad was used a few times by commenters who pinpointed responsibility for climate change not on big oil or political representatives but on privileged U.S. Americans: "The next generation is going to pay in unpredictable climate changes that will lead to dangerous storms, and devastating droughts. We the people of first world countries are responsible. Our descendents [*sic*] are going to look back upon us as the people who decided lavish lifestyles was [*sic*] more important than their basic lives" (U.S. Department of State 2013c, 648). As in the melodramatic comments excerpted above, this person dramatizes the pipeline decision. However, here, "We, the people" is not only a callback to the U.S. Constitution but also indicates the speaking subject who is a generic cause of climate change. Recalling the "addicted to oil" narrative promulgated by George W. Bush, such oil jeremiad was uncommon; instead, the populist wing of commenters attributed the problem to outside actors, whether oil corporations, politicians, or countries.

The Popular Geopolitics of Heartland Melodrama

Melodramatic styles consolidate U.S. national mythology and identity. The emotional resonances of woundedness and retribution allow an externalization of the causes of any failings onto others outside the nation. Anker is correct in pointing toward the sense of national belonging at stake in sentimental and melodramatic texts and performances. But how does melodrama mediate the scalar gulf between the vast diversity of the national community and the individual who feels its twinge? "The heartland" figures as a popular and especially virtuous hero for the dramas of the nation. The heartland elevates the world-historical importance of the wounded U.S. Great Plains region while centralizing the role of territorial defense in a global political economy. It thus contrasts with foreign interests, but in doing so it shores up not only the nation but also a specific and special region of it.

With ties to national belonging and national security alike, *heartland melodrama* is my conceptual name for this affective infrastructure. The U.S. heartland is a fuzzy region usually consisting of the interior states of the Great Plains and Upper Midwest. As historian Kristin L. Hoganson defines it, the heartland mythos appears "as static and inward-looking, the quintessential home referenced by 'homeland security,' the steadfast stronghold of the nation in an age of mobility and connectedness, the crucible of resistance to the global, the America of America First" (2019, xiv). The heartland is assumed to be predominantly white, though with specific regional heritage in the European immigrant communities that migrated in the late 1800s and early 1900s, especially Germany and Ireland. Living in the heartland is supposed to foster rural and small-town values of self-reliance, community, religion, and steadfastness, ideals taken to be exemplars of the best that the U.S. culture has to offer. Although resonant with widespread political melodrama in the wake of the September 11 terrorist attacks, heartland melodrama does not figure an individual as its heroic subject, nor the undifferentiated nation as a whole. Instead, a region stands in as the exemplar and social metaindividual on a global stage. As Stuart Hall argues, the character of such a response to globalization is a double movement: "It goes above the nation-state and it goes below it. It goes global and local in the same moment" (1997, 27). The heartland melodrama does not correspond to a self-same or normative experience of a diverse and fractured region.[7] Instead, the affective infrastructure created by heartland melodrama reinforces attachments to scenes of security in race, nation, and settler coloniality that allow it to go global and local, above and below the nation-state, at the same time.

The history of the geopolitical concept of the heartland is particularly elucidating for understanding its melodrama. The British imperial geographer Halford Mackinder popularized the concept in the early twentieth century. The heartland designated, for Mackinder, the crucial role that geopolitical control of eastern Europe has for global domination. In particular, he emphasizes it was this somewhat abstract region's natural resources (especially fertile soil that produced grains but also included oil) that made its control paramount for global power struggles (Kearns 2009; O'Hara and Heffernan 2006). Mackinder's legacy in global national security ideology is long and complicated; however, two parts of the heartland thesis and its hold over the myths of U.S. popular geopolitics are particularly important. First, Mackinder emphasizes the importance of the control of resources to geopolitical rivalries. The heartland thesis, as it travels through the United States, suggests that despite its comparatively low population, the plains region is a possible security risk and thus deserves special protection. Second, Mackinder's thesis contributed directly to the globally polarized melodramatic understandings of the U.S. geopolitical situation. This included Cold War melodramas, but also the post-9/11 melodramas of the war on terror, some of whose architects subscribed directly to some version of Mackinder's heartland thesis (Kearns 2009).

Heartland melodrama as I examine it here, however, was more of a popular geopolitics than an effect of actual geopolitical maneuvering. Its roots are in the agrarian mythos of U.S. democracy, which populisms old and new have elaborated upon. The Jeffersonian agrarian or yeoman hero has long been a fixture of populist texts, which focus on the role of such subjects as "producers." Yet with the consolidation of agricultural land and labor starting in the 1950s, images of the rural U.S. began to change as well. Although "the heartland" had functioned occasionally within U.S. geopolitics in the Mackinder style since the early part of the century, historian Toby Higbie argues that the popular use of "the heartland" in the United States peaked in the 1980s during and after the impacts of the economic restructuring or "neoliberal globalization" began to hit the U.S. agricultural sector even harder. In the 1980s, as evidenced by a number of popular films, "the evocation of the heartland in popular culture took a turn for the sentimental" (2014, 87).[8]

Heartland melodrama, as a named affect, can help explain this counterintuitive uptick in the 1980s when one might otherwise expect that the agrarian fantasy of the United States was fading. After all, "the industrialization of agriculture made even family farming so highly capitalized and commodity-oriented that the agrarian myth's ever-tenuous connection to rural reality became farcical" (Hamilton 2008, 188). Yet as a sentimental political convention, heartland melodrama requires a feeling of injury. The hero of melodrama must first be hurt, fractured, or incomplete in some fashion such that righteous vengeance drives him to locate and defeat the villain. In its populist form, heartland melodrama stages a scene in which white, rural Midwesterners have felt specifically targeted by the effects of globalization. The affective infrastructure of heartland melodrama is thus consonant in many ways with the effects of industrial agriculture on the U.S. Midwest. These include a dramatically lower workforce employed by agriculture in the wake of the Green Revolution of the 1960s; a depopulation of rural areas as people moved to cities, suburbs, and small towns; a shift in the proportion of economic activity from agriculture; and the consolidation of farms into larger size.

Public commenters frequently emphasized the risks of a pipeline spill to the heartland, which indicated the Midwest region and its prairie, farmland, ranches, and aquifers. Many included international references that I examine below, but others simply indicated that the risk to the heartland was being created by big oil. "We should in no way permit a pipeline to carry this oil across our fertile midwest, endangering the water and soil of our heartlands," wrote one commenter (U.S. Department of State 2013c, 572). Somewhat despondently, another contended, "Once air, land and water are compromised, what's left. This is our agricultural heartland we're talking about. We can't eat oil" (207). A third wrote, "It would cut across our great homeland/heartland at much greater risk than is admitted. It would feed into more Big Oil and Gas rather than developing sustainable energy sources" (308). As these comments indicate, the main feature of the heartland is its natural resources that support agricultural production, to which oil poses a risk.

Sometimes, the impacts of the pipeline were taken by commenters to be not just more than risky, but outright devastating. KXL would "destroy people's homes and ranches and farmlands," it would "be an ugly scar across thousands of farms and rangelands" (U.S. Department of State 2013c, 423, 216). Another highlighted a certain catastrophic irreversibility, suggesting that "this monster would cut through our Nation's grazing and grain heartland, which cannot be replaced nor restored"

(2013a, 255). Finally, the subject of the heartland was sometimes linked to the people or the United States writ large. "We the American people are aware that the majority of this fracked fuel will not even benefit the US, but it will leave our farmlands, homes and parks decimated and poisoned" (2013b, 174). Consequently, the terms of the deal were understood to be a "sacrifice of America's heartland to the industrialization needed to build this huge pipeline" (15). "What does *our* country get out of the deal?" another commenter asks. A biblical series ensues: "Contaminated drinking water, contaminated farmland, a plague of insects, crop failures, famine—and *none* of the gasoline or profits, no tax benefits, and hardly any wages for very short-term jobs" (2013a, 326).

It is thus the heartland that the pipeline puts at stake: prairie, farmland, water and soil, the breadbasket of America, "agriculture, small town living, and the strength of our farming and ranching communities" (U.S. Department of State 2013a, 203). This idyllic version of the Great Plains region is threatened by an oil industry that seeks profit above all. Consequently, the coloniality of "the heartland" could not be acknowledged in these comments, nor the environmental impacts of industrial agriculture in the region. Yet those working to stop the pipelines from ever being built were not unaware of the dangers of this frame. Iowans, for example, had to square the rhetoric of pastoral farm life under environmental threat from the pipeline with the on-the-ground reality of agricultural pollution in the region (Carter and Kruzic 2020). Waters are polluted by industrial agricultural runoff, much of which stems from petrochemical fertilizers. Concentrated feedlots create noxious odors that slowly waft across property borders. And the heartland mythos seemed to retain a certain propriety for the largely white farm owners, as I discussed in chapter 1. Yet the melodramatic form struggles to speak to complexity; instead, it works through clarifying actors into victims and villains in its purifying narrative plot. While big oil was a crucial component of this plot, the heartland melodrama also needed contrasting outsiders: China and Canada.

Foreign Oil and Energy Export as Yellow Peril

Several months before the NextGen advertisement "Suckers" was released, the pages of public comments I read were saturated with particular concern about the destination for the oil in question—most frequently figured to be China. Thus, pipeline opponents inherited the problem of energy independence from prior generations but, during an oil boom, figured it in terms of a dependence on foreign consumers rather than producers.

As with several of the comments examined in the previous section, opponents expressed concern that the benefits of the pipeline would largely flow outside of the borders of the United States. Some of the comments left the destination unnamed, perhaps correctly understanding that oil sold on the world market is not likely to have an easily determined destination, as TransCanada and the oil industry had argued. "The oil produced from it would be sold on the open market, not dedicated to US consumers. Where exactly is the benefit to United States & the American people if this pipeline is built[?]" asked one (U.S. Department of State 2013a, 374). "I reject the idea of a non American company pumping this caustic, nasty tar sand over our beautiful American lands, (including Aquifers), to send it offshore to the global markets" (431). One longer comment stood out to me for its working through of these details with more precision:

> I have heard from several sources that this pipeline routes to New Orleans—one of our largest shipping ports—for a reason: the oil is not actually meant to bolster domestic supplies, but instead will be sold on the open global market to the highest bidder (a global market which is big enough that this new additional oil will have virtually no effect on oil prices). In other words, the benefit to the citizens of this country is null, while these same citizens absorb all the risk involved in having a potential environmental catastrophe run through their back yards. The motive seems to be corporate profit at the expense of individual citizens' well-being. This is the common theme of our time, and if you want to be viewed fondly by history and posterity, you would do well to oppose this trend, on this front and on others. (405)

Such arguments preempted the narrative that the Canadian tar sands would be "ethical oil" destined for the United States, resulting in lower prices at the gas tank for consumers and reduced dependency on oil from the Middle East. Despite the fact that even in this case "not all imported oil is equally foreign" (Herbstreuth 2016, 116), the fears of being beholden to imported foreign oil were surprisingly applied to Canada. Commenters interpreted this oil as a specifically spatialized commodity, with concentrated and uneven risks and benefits. To the extent that benefits existed, they were too thinly distributed among the population to matter—and many of them seemed to flow outside of the country. By contrast, the risks seemed to be concentrated within the United States' national territory, and its especially important heartland.

Yet the possibility of energy export frequently led to analyses that focused on the oil's ultimate destination, often taken to be China. A typical comment demands to know the following: "Why are we going to rip our land apart, poison our underground waters to let this dirty oil spill over our farmlands and cities and into tankers for CHINA!" (U.S. Department of State 2013f, 210). "Our" territory was being put at risk, a risk that some noted was also distributed among humans and nonhumans: "I cannot see how our safety and the safety of our wildlife and wildlands can be traded for a short term job producing pipeline transporting oil that goes to China" (132). Overall, China was second only to Canada among countries singled out by name. Why was this the case, and what does it tell us about the effects of heartland melodrama on the populist political genre?

Analyses of xenophobia in U.S. environmentalism have mostly focused on ideologies that suggested migrants are pollutants of white and national ecological purity. The latter is sometimes figured as a racial and ecological operation (Hultgren 2015; Kosek 2004). Migrants from Central and South America, in particular, have been targets of ideologies of overpopulation and pollution that function to mask or excuse the ecological impacts of white wealth (Park and Pellow 2013). Scholars thus examine how the (nonwhite) immigrant has been figured as a symbol of poverty, ignorance, or perhaps a supposedly backward antiecological culture. Fewer analyses in environmental justice studies are directed toward figures of immigrant wealth and industry (Chan 2018), such as the dual "model minority" and "yellow peril" figures ascribed to Asians and Asian Americans. Lye argues that such myths work due to "the historical identification of an Asian presence in the United States with the social costs of unbridled capitalism," which "has its counterpart in the global signification of Asia" (2005, 2). It is particularly important to examine such romantic, failed anticapitalisms because they are also premised on settler colonial erasure of Indigenous history and sovereignty.

The "model minority" myth suggests that Asian Americans and the populations of Asian countries alike are proper minority subjects, which an array of other racialized individuals, populations, and states ought to strive to emulate or be negatively compared to. However, Asian "success" is measured in the terms of liberal multiculturalism and capitalism—namely, through supposed assimilation. Such assimilation becomes threatening when Asians and Asian Americans appear more successful than Euro-Americans in their own terms. Thus, everything from the growth rates of Southeast Asian economies to the supposed hyperefficiency of Asian migrant laborers are figured as that which is praised and to be mimicked, on the one hand, and that which is particularly threatening to Euro-American economic interests, on the other. Threat is frequently framed through the racialized themes of "yellow peril"—the mythic and racist threat of economic infiltration or takeover by East Asians. In fact, it is worth recalling one narrative through which yellow perilism emerged was Mackinder's heartland thesis. In suggesting that control of the heartland was paramount for geopolitics, Mackinder highlights in particular the threat that imperial Japan posed to British dominance. Yellow perilism has thus worked to produce "a looming dread where the potential threat is as good as any actual violation" (Tchen and Yeats 2014, 14), thus justifying proactive imperialism in defense of the heartland.

Lye puts these racial ideologies in the historical and narrative context of the U.S. political economic imperial project: the extension of the U.S. American frontier around the world and into the material history of global geopolitical relations (2005, 9–10). These include not only those "between" North America and Asia but also a shared anti-Asian nation-building project among the United States, Canada, and Australia—the white settler colonies of the Pacific Rim (Lye 2005, 20). What is most important for my analysis is Lye's attention to how populist and progressive critics of U.S. imperial power in the early twentieth century relied upon anti-Asian constructions in order to ground their opposition to monopoly power and capital. For populists (such as Donnelly), progressives, naturalists, and even some socialists, critical representations of monopoly and finance capitalism relied upon anti-Asian abstraction in order to frame the "popular rhetoric of decline with respect to Anglo-Saxon-led settler colonialism in the face of emergent and more abstract forms of imperialism" (Lye 2005, 54). For romantic anticapitalists, such as many U.S. American settler environmentalists today, China has become the most potent symbol of this hypercapitalist exploitation.

Oil export to China appeared particularly insidious to KXL opponents given that the Chinese economy seemed to be a direct competitor with that of the United States. One commenter suggested that they "believe that supporting the Keystone XL pipeline would be an act of Treason because it would facilitate the export of North American oil resources to countries like China. How can the State Department support this treasonous proposal that would supply energy to our global rival[?]" (U.S. Department of State 2013c, 341). Similarly, another noted that it is "greedy enrichment of corporations who will sell this oil and gas to China and other foreign consumers. This effort is being promoted ONLY by enemies of the people" (2013f, 349). Some commenters posited, as NextGen surmised, that China was heavily invested in the pipeline or in the Canadian tar sands more broadly. Though corporations are indicted alongside China, both seem to be driven by a similar thirst or greed. Global economic competition meant that the effects of the pipeline on the U.S. heartland were an indication of the nation's faltering position in the global order. Many commenters put their analysis in explicit cost-benefit terms: "The oil reaching Lousiana [*sic*] will be refined and then sold to highest bidder, maybe China. Why do people think that USA will get cheap gas below world market prices. Who gets any profit. Not the people of USA" (2013b, 195). Risks, like benefits, were at stake in this distribution. "So why should WE/USA take all the RISK for them to EXPORT their CRAP to China over OUR IRREPLACEABLE FARMLAND and Private Properties?" one commenter asked. "AMERICA must be self sufficient for oil, or why would we be exporting oil to OTHER countries, if we still don't have enough for our use??" (2013e, 1039). The heartland serves as the hinge in a scalar jump linking individual private property to national self-sufficiency.

The capitalist greed that oil seemed to satiate was complicated by a supposed history of East Asian land appropriations, sometimes associated with communism. Some critiqued the use of eminent domain as if it were an appropriation that primarily benefits foreign powers: "Eminent domain should not be used to benefit private companies and China" (U.S. Department of State 2013c, 368), one simplified. Another similarly wrote that "private land is being taken away from Americans who do not wish to sell, entirely for the benefit of two foreign nations, Canada and China" (678). In these comments, the main problem is the flow of benefits was primarily out of the heartland, seemingly replaying the post-1950s era of Green Revolution and neoliberal globalization. One commenter would have preferred a land appropriation that had redistribution as its aim: "Eminent domain has been used to seize private lands from unwilling sellers along the pipeline route. I am sad to see this confiscation of property from private citizens to benefit foreign companies happen here. Communist China also seizes land from private citizens, but at least in China, the intention is to help the Chinese public at large" (2013d, 1058). Similarly, another argues that "if Canada and China need this sandy oil then find an alternative way, through my yard is not the way for me. This isn't capitalism this is communism" (2013e, 1218). A striking extension of the logic of the tragic fall of the U.S. state occurred in 2016, when an Iowan was arrested for flying an American flag upside down underneath a Chinese flag to protest DAPL. A sign underneath the flags read: "In China there is no freedom, no protesting, no due process. In Iowa? In America?" The case was later dismissed (Pitt 2016).

More often, however, China was associated with pollution: "Let the Red Chinese sicken their people by fracking, Let the Koch Bros. drink the polluted subterranean effluent poisoned water, and STOP THE TAR SANDS FRACKING here in the USA. It is mainly motivated by greed, not by necessity. NO PIPELINES IN THE USA AND NO FRACKING ANYMORE The only financial beneficiaries of this destructive process, are the Koch Bros, The Red Chinese, and Big OIL" (U.S. Department of State 2013c, 614). Many commenters noted not only the foreign destination of the oil but also the transportation networks: "Oil going to Asia—All of it. Ships carring [sic] the oil—Foreign registered. Pollution from pipe line [sic] leaks and processing—potentially a lot, all on American soil. WHAT IS WRONG WITH THIS PICTURE?" (2013f, 352). Again, it is "greed" that is the motivating factor of both oil firms and Asian competitors, driven to disregard American lives and landscapes. Pollution is the symptom.

Contemporary yellow perilism has frequently turned to Chinese pollution as both a source and a symbol of that looming fear (Chen 2012; Sze 2015), which here was treated either as a threat for what the United States could become if it gives in to pipelines or a direct material threat to the United States were the pipeline to be built. An abrupt turn to all caps in one comment implores the reader to "ASK THE CHINESE HOW THE AIR IS IN BEIJING" (U.S. Department of State 2013c, 186). Similarly, another notes that the United States could "end up like countries such as China, where you sure can not drink the water" (2013c, 498), while another noted that in China "people are already wearing masks to breathe" (2013e, 695). Some suggested that Chinese pollution from burning tar sands oil would affect the United States directly. "Bejing [*sic*] is frequently in the 300 range in pollution and has been as high as 700. . . . California, Oregon and Washington State are all having difficulty meeting air quality standards because the pollution is drifting across the Pacific" (2013c, 292). Pollution does not respect borders: "I am distressed at the projects to send more fossil fuel to China to burn. China is already a massive polluter and their pollution does not stay at home" (2013a, 256). These comments thus do not analogize the Asian threat to pollution of the U.S. body politic in the rhetorical move that we might expect given the homology of "alien" pollutants. Instead, it is the actual pollution that will "blowback" to the United States (2013e, 747). As in Mel Chen's examination of the threat to U.S. children of leaded toys made in China, it is the "*transnational* (that is, extra-domestic) exchange that simultaneously seems to threaten representative individual bodies and criminalize Chinese trade participation" (2012, 183). The threat to the U.S. heartland is magnified, while any environmental effects in China exist to serve as a foreboding lesson to the United States.

In connecting Asian greed, big oil, and transnational pollution, commenters enacted a failed and romantic critique of capitalism. In this structure of heartland melodrama, one bad part of capitalism is vilified (the abstraction associated with finance capital and China that results in environmental degradation). However, a supposedly good concrete arena (of nature, "real" labor, or agrarianism) is absolved or reified, without recognizing that the latter is also produced by capitalism (N. Smith 2008). Environmental politics today, like turn-of-the-century naturalist writings, is susceptible to this political structure because it frequently relies on the sense of alienation between concrete nature and abstract capital to dramatize its calls for social transformation. As Iyko Day writes, "Expressing the antinomy of concrete and abstract, nature therefore personifies concrete, perfected human relations against the social degeneration caused by the abstract circuits of capitalism" (2016, 15). When nationalism figures the heartland as a kind of "pastoral retreat," it thus "must be read as inseparable from a history of yellow peril and anti-immigrant sentiment" (107).

The heartland melodramas of antipipeline public comments reproduce a similar structure. "Canadian Tar Sands are dirty and I don't want them running through our Heartland. How would [we] benefit from the sale of the oil after refinery? China? No thanks!!" (U.S. Department of State 2013f, 1). Though protagonists and antagonists are linked through the corporate avarice of oil, the Koch brothers, or even capitalism as such, a heartland melodrama absolves the subject from wrongdoing in the drama that is unfolding. Here I want to reemphasize that one of the effects of this kind of ideology is a reinscription of "*our* Heartland" at stake in the pipeline decision. As Day argues, one of the functions of the romantic critique of Asian abstract capitalism is to make available and normalize settler access to the position of the concrete. Heartland melodrama, as romantic anticapitalism, offers "an ideological framework for settler colonialism to respond to economic and technological [as well as ecological] crises." This is accomplished by framing whiteness through an "organic connection to land that function[s] to distort and deflect responsibility for capitalist modernity" (Day 2016, 36–37). Heartland melodrama functions to defend this supposed organic connection between a people and a landscape from further injury.

Though it is not an essential component of the populist genre of pipeline opposition, the scene of heartland melodrama frequently appeared therein. Heartland melodrama reinforces populism's claims to defend authentic (agrarian) democracy, while counterposing other identity positions that are represented as corrupt or nefarious. Dramatizing concrete relationships to place in contrast to abstract others reinforces an exclusive nationalism. In the case of the KXL pipeline, this resulted in fears over oil export to China. Like the oil companies who facilitated this transfer, China was seen to benefit from the risks that the pipeline posed to U.S. American farmers and ranchers, food supply, water, and wildlife. China loomed as an example of the threat of capitalism on the environment, of communist land expropriation that echoed eminent domain, and of transnational pollution threatening the national nature of the United States. The danger of each of these was to our land, a heartland that was experienced as a sacrificial region. The threat of Chinese oil consumption thus reinforced settler commonsense relationships to territory, precluding understandings of the interconnected nexus of nationalism, capitalism, and environmental exploitation. The result was a framing of looming catastrophe; the solution, listening to the people. Yet KXL did not exist only in a bilateral international axis; the loathing for China's purported oil consumption was matched with fear and hatred for the Canadian corporation, its government, and the treatment of First Nations and the Canadian environment. In an unexpected twist, Canada had become synonymous with foreign oil.

"Let the Canadians Do Their Own Dirty Laundry in Their Own Destroyed Land"

As described above, foreign oil has long played into the fears of populist political movements. Sebastian Herbstreuth convincingly summarizes the reason that China, like the Middle East, might be figured as a threat: "Foreign oil is dangerous because it comes from places that have themselves been constructed as foreign and dangerous as part of an ongoing process of establishing American national identity" (2016, 117). By contrast, oil from Canada has rarely been construed by policymakers as foreign in this same fashion because Canada is understood to share U.S. political and cultural identity. However, in the case of KXL opponents, the foreignness of Canadian oil was reconstructed. This occurred through identifying several problems with the northern neighbor: a potentially cozy relationship between Canada and China; the mistreatment of First Nations by the Canadian government or TransCanada; the use of eminent domain to support Canadian corporations; and the spatialization of environmental risk and economic benefit beyond Canada's borders. As with China, the Canadian contrast in the heartland melodrama served to externalize the threat, de-emphasize U.S. culpability for environmental degradation and impact on Indigenous Nations, reinforce norms of international sovereignty, and secure U.S. American identity in its heartland. As a common sentiment put it: "If Canada wants to damage their environment, that is their right. And they can figure out how to ship the material to China through their own territory." By contrast, the president's "allegiance" should be to "'the people of the United States of America' not Canadian greed" (U.S. Department of State 2013d, 1665).

Though anti-Canadian attitudes in the United States have a history, many U.S. Americans frequently think of Canada as something of an extension of the United States—if it is thought about at all. Anti-Canadian sentiment has usually been promulgated by the U.S. political right, for whom Canada serves as a cautionary tale of the ills of liberalism or socialism (Gravelle 2014; Harrison 2007). Though such differences can be inflated, the Canadian health care system and the Canadian government's choice not to support the U.S.-led invasion of Iraq in 2003 might indicate a shakier assessment of the North American friendship. Nonetheless, Canada and the United States remain deeply economically tied as one of the largest bilateral trading partnerships in the world, especially with regard to energy exchange. For these reasons, sustained anti-Canadian sentiment among U.S. pipeline opponents is novel and worthy of commentary.

Kinder commenters described Canada as a "wonderful country" (U.S. Department of State 2013b, 57) or a "close friend" (2013a, 59). However, most instead used pejorative descriptions of foreign oil, naming Canada in particular or omitting it entirely. What, if anything, would the Canadian oil do for U.S. energy demand? "The XL pipeline will not do anything for American energy needs, but instead will put more carbon into the air we Americans breathe" (2013a, 355). Selling the oil was understood as Canada's problem. Echoing a comment above, another suggested that "if the oil companies and the Canadians want to send this dirty fuel to market, let them ruin their own country. Let them transport it to the Pacific Ocean and straight to China. It's their problem. It's just not worth it for the United States of America" (244).

Negative sentiments directed toward Canada were far more frequent than those posed to China (though often they were mentioned at the same time). The most frequent kind of portrayal was one in which TransCanada was demonized as a foreign oil corporation seizing U.S. land to turn a profit. The issue of eminent domain was rendered a greater injustice by TransCanada's role as a foreign corporation. This was emphasized by many of the landowners I spoke with, as well as organizations opposing the pipeline. For example, Betty described the feeling as one of invasion:

> Kai, this is how this reminds me of when our country was just becoming the United States, when the British would come over here and they decided they wanted to take this plantation or that land or that house or whatever. It just looks like it's starting all over again. That's how I look at it: like okay, these big oil companies are coming in and they're just saying we're going to take your land whether you want us to or not. Basically then, they are in control of what can be done on my property. And I just feel it's [like] the British! The British are back!

Betty was particularly animated in explaining to me this feeling—she had underlined "The British" in the notebook she had brought to our interview. Many commenters highlighted a similar feeling of incursion, in which the U.S. federal government was called to halt a "foreign corporation's invasion of our land with a filthy, dangerous, disruptive tar oil pipeline" (U.S. Department of State 2013c, 71). A second suggested that "it is not right for a foreign company to use imminent [sic] domain to take away the land of red blooded Americans to fund this project. Support America not Canada" (2013a, 69). In these comments, the foreign transfer of land is likened to a geopolitical event in which the lifeblood of authentic U.S. citizens is sapped away to benefit another nation's greedy corporation. Such comments sought to head off the arguments that the pipeline would be a direct or indirect benefit to those whose lands it crossed. However, in doing so, their seeming sense of invasion by a colonial or imperial power positions their victimization outside of a historic timeline of settler colonialism or U.S. imperialism. A handful of commenters somewhat shockingly contrasted the great power of the United States with those of the Global South: "We are not some third world country to be used and abused, and left to fend from the damage caused by Imperialist's [*sic*] that only want to skim the wealth. Without protections of our air and water, we have nothing left" (451). The abdication of U.S. geopolitical power reignites fears of international competition and imperial decline.

Such a move also consolidated the heartland identity of "we the people" that was being affected by the pipeline and the land that was "ours." The importance of not simply knowledge but the repertoire of melodramatic affects in these scenes of injury were particularly crucial:

> I feel as tho my own country is being exploited to the max by outsiders. Hauling Canadian (shame on them for what they are destroying) oil on trains thru MY country to sell to foreigners is even worse than building a pipeline to carry the junk. Let the Canadians do their own dirty laundry in their own destroyed land. Send all our greedy capitalists to China and Russia for further exploitation. (U.S. Department of State 2013a, 142)

There is a lot going on here. The commenter highlights how alienating being harmed by non-Americans feels, especially when they previously felt ownership over their country. The author takes up the common suggestion that the Canadians should simply pipe the oil across "their own destroyed land." They end by suggesting that specific U.S. capitalists might be disciplined, presumably sent to China and Russia due to these countries' authoritarian or communist rule. The latter contrasts allow the author to speak to the threats the pipeline poses to their "own country."

Hyperbolic measures were pushed even further by those who urged the U.S. federal government not only to reject the pipeline to encourage its neighbor to end its destructive tar sands extraction project altogether. "We have pushed Canada many times in the past but seldom on the side on the environment," one commenter explains (U.S. Department of State 2013a, 466). Noting that they "realize that a rejection of Keystone XL has the potential to slightly sour relations with the Canadian government," another commenter nonetheless argued that "we have to stick to our principles and do the right thing" (271). Drawing a biopolitical analogy between the relationships at stake, another remarked that "the health of America's environment is of far greater import than the health of our relationship with Canada" (2013b, 254). One astonishing

comment suggests that the United States might go to war with Canada
to stop the tar sands:

> Not only should this pipeline never be built, but Canada should
> never be allowed to export its supply of tar sands anywhere. The US
> has been at war in one place or another, often in many places simul-
> taneously, since I was born, in 1951. These wars are almost always
> fought to maintain and expand upon America's interests in oil and
> other resources. Now there is a good reason to be at war, to keep
> Canada from polluting the Earth past the point from which it can
> survive. (2013a, 175)

This comment is striking, unique, and cynical. It acknowledges the role
of U.S. international war and policing, linking these wars to the country's supposed interest in securing foreign oil. Though the author implicitly critiques the driving role "America's interests" play in this history, the pessimistic twist is that war is now necessary to stop the export
of foreign oil. Wars to maintain and expand upon U.S. interests in oil
and other resources must instead be inverted! Whether tongue-in-cheek
or serious, the comment provides a window into the stakes that some
pipeline opponents imagined.

The purported influence of a foreign corporation on U.S. politicians highlighted that the governing power of the people was at stake in
these decisions. Addressing their comment directly to President Obama,
one commenter noted that "instead of keeping your promises you seem
willing to sell out to the oil companies of Canada. . . . Are you in league
with the corporations, or are you a champion of the people, to whom
this country really belongs?" (U.S. Department of State 2013a, 232).
Noting that "Canadian Corporations should not be permitted to
strong-arm their way through American public issues," another commenter threatened revolution: "Are we a Democracy? If the United
States is a Corporatocracy increasingly driven by powerful boards in
foreign lands and the Koch Brothers, then make no mistake: Grassroots Americans find this model increasingly intolerable; and we will
inevitably overturn that model" (2013a, 9). It is clear in these cases that
"the people" is principally a reference to specifically U.S. citizens, especially those who are "grass-roots." And numerous commenters drew this
connection explicitly: "There really isn't any other choice, or a better

choice for our future then [*sic*] clean renewable energy, OWNED AND OPERATED by US citizens, NOT Canada, Saudi Arabia, foreign investors, or crony capitalists bent on destroying our planet and leading us into WW3" (2013b, 403). The United States is by and for U.S. Americans.

The problem of energy dependence or independence is thus one that extended beyond the countries or regions usually associated with foreign oil. The potential influence of U.S. dependence on Canadian oil or Chinese customers threatened the heartland and its people, to whom the country "really belongs." But one might wonder whether commentators recognized that "the people" is not a unitary subject. Did they not acknowledge the differentiated impacts of the pipeline on Indigenous peoples of North America? Some readers might be astonished at how few references this commentariat makes to Native Nations, given that Indigenous leadership in pipeline opposition is more widely recognized today. But Native Nations and Indigenous peoples received far fewer mentions than references to Canada or China. In the over six thousand pages of comments representing, in my estimation, at least fifteen thousand submissions, only ten mention the impacts on Lakota or Sioux people specifically (none referencing Oceti Sakowin). Zero mention colonialism. By contrast, over three hundred mentions of *China* or *Chinese* appeared (though some of these comments were in support of the pipeline).

Just as striking, among the more generic references to Native Americans, American Indians, First Nations, or Indigenous peoples, most referenced poor treatment of First Nations adjacent to the tar sands in Canada, not to Native Nations living "within" the purported borders of the United States. Some noted that "the extraction process [of tar sands] is destroying the health, habitat, animals, and culture of indigenous Canadians" (U.S. Department of State 2013b, 454). Similarly, "the story of the Canadian Native peoples is tragic. They are losing their lands and getting sick" (473). U.S. Americans could recognize the human rights violations leveraged against people by other governments, but their own government's violations were not differentiated. The federal government was violating the rights of all its citizens by allowing the pipeline. Echoing the sentiment that "they're treating us like Indians," the pipeline invasion was akin to colonialism but extended to all people:

This is getting to be worse than what the Native Americans had done to them, when the Europeans entered this continent. The established powerful took most of what they had and then started killing them— even as they tried to protect their reservations that were given to them. We citizens—white, black,yellow,red, [*sic*] or whatever skin color—are having the same thing done to us, whether we are old, veterans, or Democrats or Republicans [*sic*]. Something is wrong with this picture! (2013e, 1258)

Such a comment generalizes colonial or imperial "invasion" as something experienced evenly by the people of a nation as a whole. In doing so, differentiated histories are meant to be forgotten, since doing so is supposedly a requisite for united opposition to pipelines.

The general absence of commentary on settler colonialism can lead to several provisional conclusions: First, it might tell us something about the demographic of public commentators. Many of the submissions were modified form letters distributed by email blasts via organizations like the Sierra Club, 350.org, or Avaaz. This section of pipeline opponents, I would hazard, is wealthier, whiter, and less concerned with environmental justice or Indigenous sovereignty than climate and ecological impacts. Second, this absence demonstrates how left-populist affective infrastructures—even when espousing civic rather than ethnic nationalism—are still subject to normative exclusions. The melodramatic populist scene need not necessarily result in a demonized foreign power (as Žižek 2006 suggests). Instead, it is its historical unfolding within settler colonialism and racial capitalism that entails diagnoses that the ill effects of these systems are the product of outsiders. Finally, as in this last comment above, the populist melodrama required a subject that was wholly affected rather than differentiated into particular segments. How should we view the multifaceted way in which heartland melodrama contributed to constructing this populist subject, and what can be done to direct such emotional reactions otherwise?

Heartland Melodrama as a Populist Affect of Settler Empire

The heartland melodrama of pipeline opposition was not the only or even the primary affective scene through which EIS commentators found a populist genre to be effective. Populist rhetoric was also used to emphasize that political power or environmental knowledge had been consolidated among an elite that had little interest in environmental justice or democracy. And as I have argued throughout this book, both the imbalance of power and the desire for a unified opposition made a reclamation of "we the people" strategically and emotionally appealing. But in the process of working out possible scenes through which this subject could be enunciated, I have described how some EIS commentators constructed its power differential through an imagined international geography in which Canada and China were exploiting the U.S. heartland. Understanding the parameters of this melodrama helps us diagnose the limits of left populism's reliance on romantic anticapitalism, normative producerism, and civic nationalism. These affective scenes easily nudge into reinforcing historical modes of describing international relations through felt power imbalances that ultimately hide or legitimate U.S. settler empire.

The concept of heartland melodrama helps us understand and diagnose the limits of contemporary left populism's reliance on a normative producerism. Scholars of populism have critiqued how the petit producer as the engine of the economy and the heart of the nation has reinforced "a vicious strain of white working-class ressentiment" (Grattan 2016, 60) directed toward not only elites but also those seen as nonworkers or freeloaders—the latter sometimes aimed at Indigenous people, Latinx and Black people, and Eastern European and East Asian immigrants. But the rhetoric of producerism was also a popular thesis of working-class power and thus could—in the nineteenth century, at least—reinforce tendencies toward class unity rather than division. The continued reliance on producerism in the twenty-first century after the consolidation of U.S. farming labor as part of a broader international division of labor is far more mythic. It tries to resurrect the rural producer as a more crucial component of U.S. industrial and international power than it is. Consequently, U.S. populism in the heartland—especially in the wake of the 1970s—is of a different character than that of prior generations. Its subject is not only materially exploited but affectively wounded—and thus is constantly in search of explanations for each of these felt characteristics. The problem with producerism thus was not only that it presented an exclusive and normative white subject but also that that subject was increasingly mythic.

The formal structure of injury requires working out both its causes

and the identity of that which had been wounded. For pipeline opponents, the cause was most notably big oil. However, big oil could also be
a metonym for other functions: capitalism, greed, monopoly, foreign
oil, or globalization. Though anti-Asian and anti-oil agrarian populisms
alike precede the 1970s, my argument here is that the character of the
felt causes and identities related to the heartland shifted in the wake of
the crises of the 1970s and 1980s. As Ruth Wilson Gilmore writes, "crisis . . . signals systemic change whose outcome is determined through
struggle [that] occurs at all levels of a society as people try to figure out,
through trial and error, what to make of idled capacities" (2007, 54).
After the farm crises, the "figuring out" of the causes of imposed idle-
ness increasingly turned from blaming free trade or even capitalism as
such (located in regional "outsiders" like Wall Street) toward condemn-
ing undue foreign interference for corrupting national markets. Subject
identities shifted from romantic producers to a landscape or region of
injury and nostalgia. Heartland populisms shifted register from a redemptive arc in which power was held by those who produced value to
the melodramatic arc that assumed the position of victimhood whose
causes were outside of the region. This is how even the minimal class
characteristic that some argue allows left populisms to work across difference was displaced.

The shift in causes dramatized big oil, but sometimes this was because (some) oil had entered from the outside of the nation. For those
using scenes of heartland melodrama, U.S. consumers were not culpable for the climate crisis. It is worth considering for a moment how
drastically different this populist frame is from the standard ideology of
U.S. environmentalism, in which the consumer is the source of environmental harm and thus action is taken via lifestyle changes. Such
moralizing discourse tends to be both disempowering and depoliticizing when it works primarily through stigmatization. By contrast, the
melodramatic scene's moral economy locates the problem of pipeline
construction not in individuals but in the undue power of corporate oil
firms. Yet here, the threat of big oil is magnified through the foreign
bodies it empowers. Chinese competition and pollution are both taken
to be a direct danger to the heartland and a potential sign for what the
heartland could become without drastic action. Canadian invasion sig-
naled the necessity of a reclamation of U.S. global leadership and hege-

mony, exercised through softer or harder forms of power also directed at the northern neighbor. The heartland melodrama rearranges how the "enemies of the people" would be located.

As mentioned above, the shift in causes works to consolidate a shift in identities from emphasizing producerism to a regional landscape identity. The self-reliant independent citizen of the heartland has been injured by dependence on producers or consumers elsewhere, whether of oil, corn, beef, or manufactured goods (recall the images in "Suckers"). It is not just the individual who is materially hurt by, say, the transfer of limited property rights or the rising price of gasoline. Instead, that individual harm stands in metonymically for the very foundation of the nation and of democracy. "We the people" emerge as the proper civic subject of environmental politics, a populist subject who must reclaim independence from the undue influence of outsiders. Though the subjects of the heartland are not all white and the identities of the public commenters are unknown to me, the structure of the operation is still racialized. It preserves the "transparent subject of whiteness" in a global spatial context, which operates as if it is capable of escaping determination, and thus ought to escape it (Silva 2007).

Sovereignty is thus doubly important here, indicating the manner that heartland melodrama relies upon both settler colonial operations and a reinforcement of that transparent subject. Sovereignty here can be understood first in the sense of the nation-state's exercise of power over territory in a competitive field of nation-states. It is taken for granted that it is in the "national interest" of the United States to provide an advantage to its citizens vis-à-vis the rest of the world. If the heartland is affected by a foreign state or a market influenced primarily by foreign producers or consumers, then U.S. sovereignty and interest is put at risk. Second, sovereignty can be found in the national subject's feeling of having constituted democratic state power. As elsewhere in the world, citizen activists try to remind the U.S. government that it exists only by deriving power from popular authority; thus, they try to "assert their constituent power over and against state institutions" (Riofrancos 2020, 113). If the felt autonomy of heartland people is at stake in these decisions, so too is the state's legitimacy and authority itself seen to be at risk. However, in this case, such constituent power was more powerful as an imagined force than as a real force. Finally, sovereignty is a story about the ecological character of a relationship of belonging to the land that settlers feel is under threat. Repeatedly, it is *our* heartland—our farmland, our waters, our economy, our wildlife—that is enunciated to be at stake in such a project. Thus, the possessive individualism I described in chapter 1 can jump scales into what Brenna Bhandar (2018) calls "possessive nationalism," in which "the psycho-affective dimensions of the possessive individual, including the desire to possess exclusively and to control one's possessions absolutely, to deal with the need for security and to calm the fear of losing one's property, are here transmuted to the stage of the nation-state." The heartland is the regional scale that mediates the dual movement of global and local, above and below the nation-state. Each of these feelings of threatened sovereignty beckons its return, and thus an evacuation of actually existing Indigenous sovereignty.

Heartland melodrama thus unfolds through the affective scene of a staged natural interiority pitched against abstract exteriority, reinforcing an articulation between racial capitalism and setter colonialism. By inhabiting the supposedly concrete relationship of a people to a land against the unnatural pollution of outsiders, the populist opposition buttresses settler propriety of the nation-state and its governance, thus displacing Indigenous relations of the land to a supposedly prior position (Povinelli 2011). Though popular sovereignty would undoubtedly be preferable to the corporate capture of state institutions, a romanticized version of the redemption of democracy through the civic nationalism of people power tends to suggest that the corrupting force of oil is due to its use by or in service of foreigners. While the feeling of having one's life invaded is certainly understandable, the analogies drawn between foreign invasion and international imperialism reinforce settler forgetting of the structural perpetuation of settler invasion through containing Indigenous modes of relating with the land (Mei-Singh 2016; Spice 2018; Wolfe 2006). It is not the totality of capital that is indicted but rather abstract Chinese capital, with its supposedly perverse characteristics of being authoritarian and undemocratic. Though it received little discussion in the antipipeline commentary examined in this chapter, such a vision of reclaimed popular sovereignty further relies on an operation of power that is fundamentally anti-Black insofar as these agrarian myths also rely to a certain degree on a plantation landscape and a disavowal of the afterlives of slavery (McKittrick 2013; Sexton 2010, 2016). To the extent that environmental populism relies upon staging heartland melodramas to critique pipeline intrusion, it will unnecessarily limit its politics to a reinforcement of U.S. sovereignty, settler nativism, and resource nationalism—resulting in odd suggestions that one should stop the pipeline in favor of better exploiting U.S. oil: "If we're going to use fossil fuels to supplement our renewable energy sources, let [us] focus on natural gas and the oil in [South Dakota]" (U.S. Department of State 2013a, 456).

Diagnosing such failed critiques is crucial to building and sustaining not just a more inclusive or comprehensive climate politics but also a more radical one that can point to the structural features of racial capitalism culpable for the crisis. I do not wish to suggest that environmentalism ought to revert back to its prior affective scenes of almost masochistic levels of individual responsibility for environmental damage. Instead, my goal is twofold: to work against the assumption of innocence that the heartland melodrama imparts upon its subjects in the service of leveraging instead shared, differentiated responsibility and international solidarity in the face of what is a very deep, very real crisis.

Conclusion

Heartland melodrama describes the affective scene in which an agricultural region taken to be central to geopolitical international power is felt to be wounded and threatened by a foreign power. When speaking through the genre of environmental populism, heartland melodrama diagnosed corporate power, foreign oil, and Chinese and Canadian governments and firms as threats to an imagined grassroots, democratic, and national subject. This dramatization reinforced the historic, representational division between foreign oil as an abstract, racialized threat and the concrete propriety of white settler subjects to an agrarian landscape.

Though heartland melodrama can be seen in many public comments against the KXL pipeline, not all pipeline opponents expressed an instrumental and myopic view of so-called foreign oil. Some, when drawing connections to China and the global economy, correctly noted that people in other parts of the world unevenly bear the consequences of the aggregate economic decisions made by the United States. Rather than seeing Canada as the primary perpetrator, only a few saw the pipeline as a symbol of the shared transnational project of settler colonialism. "It is 2013 we the US and Canada need to stop breaking our promises to native peoples" (U.S. Department of State 2013a, 70). But in this chapter's data set, even such mild indictments were uncommon. More often, commenters drew the conclusion that "America [should] reclaim and renew its participation as a global leader" (2013c, 506). The mood of this sort of comment also fails to recognize the past and present imperialism that such leadership has upheld. "The global" is taken as an abstract, disemplaced scale rather than one constructed through historic, asymmetric connections. Thus, to the extent that international concerns were considered at all, they were only with reference to the abstract level of global climate change, international climate agreements, and economic decision-making. "The people of the world" or "of planet earth" appears frequently, but this is the undifferentiated *anthropos* in "the Anthropocene" that has been so heavily critiqued by social scientists for flattening historical inequalities. Despite searching desperately, I could not find a strong internationalist counternarrative in the thousands of comments I read. Radical anti-imperialism was simply not a major part of this portion of pipeline opposition and environmentalist ideology.

Outside of the public commentary examined here, however, some pipeline opponents refused the heartland melodrama that NextGen Climate's "Suckers" ad laid out. My favorite of these comes from journalist Josephine Ferorelli, who drew on the history of leftist anti-Chinese sentiment analyzed critically by Alexander Saxton (1971) to critique the NextGen ad. Ferorelli, referencing an incidental family relationship to Saxton, writes: "It may seem expedient now to whip up an anti-Chinese froth, but as uncle Alex [Saxton] put it, 'tactics . . . have a way of becoming habits.' Whatever groundwork of allies and animosities we lay now will be the foundation of what must be a long-term movement" (2014). This is undoubtedly the analysis that is needed. Its rarity demonstrates that a lack of international solidarity remains a major problem for contemporary U.S. environmentalism and climate justice movements.

Though the international or global is frequently spoken about within the climate justice movement, it exists either through the negative frames of inequality, injustice, war, or disease or through the abstract, unifying figure of the species. Climate migrants are understood to be a looming threat in part because their movements disrupt sacrosanct borders. Frames of victimhood do not produce solidarity for humble learning. A more generous version of this discourse exists among political theorists of democracy (e.g., Honig 2009; Connolly 2013), who valorize the stranger or the foreigner in democracy and suggest working across difference strengthens democratic pluralism. Yet sometimes solutions that posit democracy through cosmopolitanism put the cart before the horse. The argument seems to be that if we recognize in the alien other a shared being, common project, or foundation on planet earth, we will be able to harmonize and balance these relationships. But what if the problem, posed in Spinozist terms, is that in the devotional act of positing "we the people," we already imagine we do not share enough in common with that stranger? To be maximally "in common" with these others, we need not recognition of some shared humanity or condition but rather that portions of that "we" must be materially augmented through redressing the damages of colonialism and capitalism, writ large and historic. Such a position would not foreclose alliance but instead would recognize that stronger coalitions are formed by material repair and reparations, which make common bonds more efficacious and powerful. Forging that potential is crucial given the rise of antiglobalism, which sees the problem of climate chaos to be solved by a stronger nationalism in which defending nature turns into defending *our* nature. Some environmental writers argue that this entails closing borders and defending nature from migrants in a "benevolent green nationalism" (Kingsnorth 2017) that inherits the xenophobic elitism of Hardin while dressing it up in a populist rhetoric.

These approaches contrast with movements historically and materially grounded in transnational struggle, such as Indigenous internationalism, anticolonialism, anti-imperialism, border abolition, and migrant solidarity movements (Walia 2021). While it is commonly pointed out that the movement against the DAPL gained international attention and participation (e.g., Tysiachniouk et al. 2020), Estes argues that its more critical features were its inheritance and enactment of "a tradition of radical Indigenous internationalism [that] imagined a world altogether free of colonial hierarchies of race, class, and nation" (2019,

204). At the DAPL blockade, a standard "United States" map was set up with a pinboard where representatives from Native Nations across the Americas (and later, the world) began to unmake and remake this symbol of the supposed coherence of the United States. As more and more Native Nations traveled to stand in solidarity with the Oceti Sakowin Oyate, the borders of that map were increasingly undone by the rewritten places inscribed on the map. Flags from these nations soon went up; these included other Native Nations from North America, alongside those of Palestinian and other international allies. Likewise, at an August 2015 march in Bismarck, North Dakota, the slogans emblazoned on four gigantic posters read: "All nations. All relations. All waters. #NoDAPL." What such slogans demonstrate and, likewise, what Indigenous internationalists argue—sometimes also as socialists, anarchists, and radicals—is that neither civic nationalism nor democratic cosmopolitanism can suffice so long as settler empire, racial capitalism, and border imperialism structure the material ways people relate to each other and the earth.

4

THE PEOPLE KNOW BEST
COUNTER-EXPERTISE AND
JADED CONFIDENCE

OPPONENTS OF KXL have long been worried about water contamination from an oil spill, such that the Lakota phrase *mni wiconi*—water is life—might be taken as the guiding philosophy of the movement. Many in the arid upper Great Plains are reliant on groundwater and aquifers for drinking water for humans and cattle and for irrigation for crops. Of particular concern is the extensive Ogallala Aquifer, which is significantly recharged in the Sandhills, a porous soil and high water table region in northern Nebraska and south-central South Dakota that early routes of the pipeline would have crossed. KXL also would have intersected several Missouri River tributaries, which supply drinking water to millions downstream. Yet in 2011, scientists and activists were divided among each other. What risk would a spill have to these bodies of water, and what kinds of evidence ought to be mobilized to support these claims? Hydrogeologist John Gates and civil engineer Wayne Woldt, both researchers at University of Nebraska–Lincoln, write in a 2011 comment on the EIS that "there is very little precedent on which to scientifically predict crude oil plume behavior in a place like the Sandhills." Scientific knowledge of contaminant behavior underground relies upon studying actual spills. But Gates and Woldt (2011) write, "Most of what scientists know about crude oil behavior in aquifers comes from a single study in Minnesota conducted by the US Geological Survey," stemming from a 1979 pipeline rupture that spilled 10,700 barrels of light, low-sulfur crude near Bemidji, Minnesota. But KXL, of course, was bringing diluted bitumen, a very heavy crude. What is the risk?

By contrast, James Goeke, University of Nebraska–Lincoln (emeritus) hydrologist and oft-described foremost expert on the Ogallala Aquifer, came to a different conclusion. Drawing on the Bemidji studies, Goeke (2011a) argues that "any leak would have minimal impact on the Ogallala Aquifer." The layers of rock would prevent the oil from traveling, and the slow water tendency to move from west to east in the aquifer would also likely prevent such a spill from much drift. In addition to testifying in front of the Nebraska legislature alongside Gates, Goeke wrote op-eds, consulted with TransCanada, and appeared (uncompensated) in one of the pipeline company's television ads. Yet despite their disagreement, each of these scientists claimed that misinformation about the nature of aquifers and pipeline spills—driven by emotion and poor communication rather than science—was overly influential on the pipeline debate (Potter 2011; Gates 2010). A fourth University of Nebraska–Lincoln scientist, James Stansbury, dissented further, writing in a 2011 "worst-case analysis" that portions of the aquifer could still be at risk, largely from benzene. TransCanada denounced this study as "the latest case of opportunistic fear-mongering, dressed up as an academic study" (Duggan 2011).

This shared assumption that an overly emotional public heralds misinformation represents a common analytic position on the relationship between populism and scientific expertise. Skeptical of technocratic and elitist experts and driven by base emotions, populism is taken to have a flexible relationship to "truth." Undoubtedly, we see signs of such activity in right-wing climate skepticism, but surely environmentalism—with its basis in ecological and climate science—would be opposed to such a discourse? Some varieties are, but the previously ascendent "technocratic, expert-oriented, and accommodationist" (Wetts 2020, 1,363) tendency of the last thirty years of environmentalism is now faltering. This is not because populist environmentalisms rest on an assumption that "feelings trump facts" in any simplistic fashion. Instead, I show that populist pipeline opponents were diagnosing that scientific institutions had been overly influenced by the oil industry, a relationship scholars call "regulatory capture." In noting this, pipeline opponents did not shun science tout court but instead attempted to build a more situated political practice of scientific inquiry. In doing so, populist identity coalesced as a reaction to the perceived enmeshing of state and capital. Examining how such populist identities arise in relation to establishment expertise is a significant contribution to a literature that otherwise assumes populists essentially distrust experts, without positing any reason why that would be the case or examining which experts they particularly distrust.

In this chapter, I examine how counter-expertise shaped such populist political identities, with a particular attention to the contestation of knowledge concerning subsurface materials. Aquifers and groundwater, paleontological and archaeological sites, and the character of soil present material and epistemological problems wherein farmers and ranchers, Native Nations, and field paleontologists have place-based knowledge that contradicts that of TransCanada, the state, and scientific contractors such as Cardno ENTRIX and Environmental Resources Management. Goeke (2011b) captures the epistemological quandary of the underground in a *New York Times* discussion post, writing, "Surface water we can see; groundwater is an act of faith: I say that when I talk about aquifers." Similarly, soil science and paleontology alike represent epistemological challenges that make broad claims of certainty impossible.

For environmentalists, landowners, and community organizers fighting KXL and DAPL, populist environmentalism unfolded precisely through an iterative politics of scientific counter-expertise experienced in regulatory hearings. These hearings demonstrated to pipeline opponents that fossil fuel industries had affected third-party contractors performing these studies and the state agencies who review them. When pipeline opponents reached this conclusion, they often consolidated their opposition to what they now understood to be corrupt, elite institutions. But they did not stop engaging in the process; the experience gave them a jaded confidence in their own counter-expertise. They were confident that objective review of the science would support their claims, but they were jaded insofar as experience had taught that such objective review was unlikely. Pipeline opponents learned two further things from these encounters. First, despite pessimism about winning in the court of science, organizers told me that performing the proof that "the people know best" can help gain allies and thus expand the subject of "the people." Second, and relatedly, the jaded confidence of counter-expertise served as important affect for broadening the political engagement of newly political subjects outside official channels. Passing through the scientific process of environmental review developed their sense of an identity as "the people."

Knowing the Land—and What Lies Beneath

In chapter 2, I described how individuals engaged with official forums for public comment on pipeline review. From 2011 onward, more and more people discovered that their skepticism had turned into opposition as the regulatory process shifted from the open-ended "public comment" described earlier to "evidentiary hearings." Nonexperts embraced the opportunity to be heard and enthusiastically built their case that the pipeline would result in negative impacts to tribal and public land and water, farm and ranchland, and sensitive ecological areas. Concerns were especially focused on the effects an oil spill would have on water resources. Here, I turn my frame of analysis to the character of evidence presented by pipeline opponents. This testimony initially served to ground opposition in experience, local knowledge, and long-term heritage. But as one might expect, such a knowledge system frequently ran up against the expert-driven analyses of land and water described in thousands of pages of the EIS and state-level reviews.

In addition to gathering commentary, public input and scoping meetings served as information sessions to transmit knowledge about pipeline projects to landowners and the public. These meetings were frequently the first time that those whose land was not crossed were able to gather important details about potential pipeline impacts. At these meetings, landowners frequently raised complex and sometimes hyper-specific concerns about the character of the land they inhabit. TransCanada agents and contractors would respond with technical specifics about the project, attempting to quell concerns about pipeline spills and the interruptions of everyday life that construction promised. An exchange from a public meeting in Winner, South Dakota, in 2009 demonstrates this process (South Dakota PUC 2009d, 79–80). A landowner raises a concern that in "the low areas" of their property "the soils are highly erodible . . . because it's pretty sandy." They locate this area precisely where the pipeline would cross. In particular, they express a worry that "when you start getting, say, up to [a] 100 foot wide strip in blow sand and it starts moving, there's nothing that you're going to be able to do about that because Mother Nature's going to take care of that. And then you've got to come back and try to reclaim land to where it will at least hold grass." Such erosion would result in uneven reclamation, especially if cattle also pass through the area.

At this hearing, a KXL regulatory and permitting manager was responsible for responding to such queries in a rather generic fashion. To the landowner, the project manager simply replied, "There is a brochure out front that talks about the whole Sand Hills reclamation process and we started dialogue with university extension services that work with the Department of Agriculture and NRCS [National Resources Conservation Service]. Department of Transportation, they deal with this issue all the time as well. And in there you'll see there's a series of steps we'll go through to identify where those locations are." Finally, the manager concludes that such offices will try to route the pipeline around such areas that might provide reclamation difficulties. The landowner's raising of a matter of potential concern was seemingly easily quelled by reference to already-settled facts.

But several months later, the same landowner again raised questions about reclamation (South Dakota PUC 2009c, 25). Again, they described the territory in question as "highly erodible blow sand" for which "reclamation is a key issue." They plead for some recognition of the problem: "I don't see how it can be pastured until it is completely sodded back in. I estimate myself that this will take a minimum of a two- to five-year timeline. And that's because if you run the cattle on the area where the pipeline's been dug in, it's going to break the grass down and cause it to start blowing." The landowner raises a legitimate concern that rooted grass takes some time to establish in sandy soil. If cattle are allowed into this area too soon, then they will disrupt the process of grass coming back to root. The project managers' abstract response about the general characteristics of reclamation in the region, along with a generic pamphlet, was not convincing to the landowner because the question arises from more direct knowledge of the material qualities and relations between land, water, and cattle.

As for the landowner's concerns, these were brought by the PUC chair to evidentiary hearings later that day. Chairman Johnson called a staff witness, a private consultant with a doctorate in soil science and a background in academia. The consultant explains their review of TransCanada's reporting, noting some flaws in their initial assessment of the distribution of soil types in South Dakota. TransCanada had responded to these queries, developing a more comprehensive map of soil types (see Figure 7) and a plan in which "reclamation units" can be identified and "basically mapped on the ground to identify areas where there may be specific—site-specific problems that they can basically adapt their construction procedures to on a site-specific basis" (South Dakota PUC 2009a, 273). Soil units can be identified by land-use patterns or at a finer-grained level, via probes used during surveys and connected to GIS units. Chairman Johnson posed the question: "We've heard from a number of landowners that their particular area, their particular spot of range ground, is highly and perhaps even uniquely erodible. . . . I mean, given your 25 years in this arena, I mean, is it likely that there are areas that are uniquely erodible for which the [erosion] management techniques you described will be insufficient?" The soil scientist responded that though there are "some areas that are going to be like that," the mitigation plan should account for such situations (306).

Interestingly, the cross-examination by lawyers with Dakota Rural Action (DRA) asked the consultant about the process of hiring experts, which the consultant deemed "a process that works in my opinion" (285). However, even then, they were forced to admit that landowners "probably know their land better than anyone else" (285). Despite this admission, the testimony concluded with the PUC commissioners again emphasizing knowledge. Commissioner Hanson remarked that the consultant's résumé "reminded [them] of William Shakespeare." Despite the consultant's joke ("Much ado about nothing?"), Commissioner Hanson continued that "a lot of people say they can't believe that he wrote as much as he did, that he was as prolific of a writer and accomplished as much as he did, and when I look at your résumé I can't believe that one person has written and participated and done as much as you. . . . And obviously we should take note of your expertise" (293).

The more that farmers and ranchers engaged with hearings, the more resolute their beliefs grew in the face of such "noted expertise."

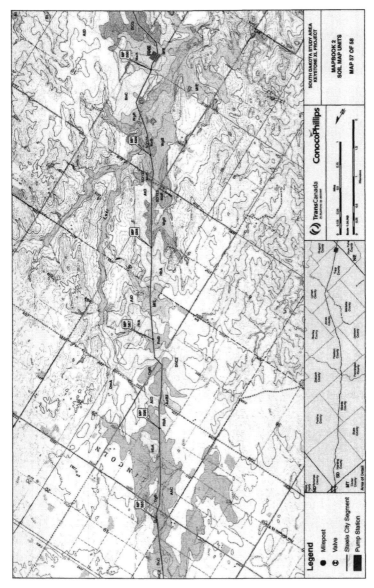

Figure 7. A representative map showing the variety of soil units crossed by the KXL pipeline in south-central South Dakota submitted by TransCanada to the South Dakota PUC. This particular map documents over 250 soil types crossed by the pipeline in this state. The pipeline route is marked by milepost numbers ("MP") and each of the smaller insignia represent a soil type. "WgB," for example, represents "Wewela fine sandy loam, 3 to 6 percent slopes."

For example, the landowner concerned about erosion in the prior 2009 testimony would be active in KXL opposition through 2015. Central to such transformations were community organizing and educational activities undertaken by DRA. In 2009, DRA members began organizing information about landowner rights in relation to KXL due to concern and uncertainty about the pipeline. Although the group was not entirely opposed to the pipeline at this point, DRA did begin distributing legal and scientific information to landowners. They also began developing messaging that would take place at evidentiary hearings later that year. As one landowner put it in a public meeting in 2009, "Dakota Rural Action has been a Godsend help for us to keep us focused with information and direction. And I would like to be here every day to visit with people and help you out and get you information, but we've got ranching duties" (South Dakota PUC 2009b, 31–32). Though information was "made available" during scoping meetings, some landowners felt that information was incomplete or biased. Conducting independent, unpaid research in order to understand the pipeline's effects had to be a matter of collective organization as much as information sharing. Through this organization, dozens of landowners who had not known each other prior to the pipeline's appearance began to work—and learn—together.

After the public scoping meetings, the State of South Dakota held evidentiary hearings covering the necessary environmental permits, from which the above exchanges were drawn. These meetings effectively put expertise on trial, while lawyers hired by DRA and (later) tribal governments assisted in attempting to contest or discredit the evidence submitted by consultants and TransCanada. In these hearings, differences in performance, professionalism, dress, knowledge of the law, and argumentation among paid experts, nonprofit and legal staff, and unpaid people augmented the perception of knowledge and expertise. Parties to the case and PUC commissioners each called witnesses to the stand to attest to the infrastructure project's various safety measures (or lack thereof). These witnesses could then be cross-examined by each of the parties involved, including intervenors, who could choose to be represented by lawyers or to represent themselves. In 2009 already, despite only marginally organized opposition, the parade of expert witnesses called by TransCanada took on a near-absurdist quality. One commenter captured the frustration at such an information overload, re-marking that "TransCanada cannot even get their lies straight between their own expert witnesses. They have to bring in an expert witness to refute what other expert witnesses say when it does not fit their agenda" (South Dakota PUC 2009b, 27).

Another dispute concerning paleontological resources highlights the stakes of this disagreement and the frustration felt in attempting to challenge TransCanada's evidence. Paleontologist and founder of the Black Hills Institute of Geological Research Peter Larson testified that KXL construction could harm fossils in the rich Hell Creek Formation in northwestern South Dakota. This region has been the source of iconic *Tyrannosaurus rex* fossils, alongside numerous other charismatic megafauna that populated the late Cretaceous period. Larson argued in public testimony that fossil resources could be put at risk if professional paleontologists did not accompany construction crews. In written testimony, Larson (2009) further argued that "the fossil record across the boundary preserves not only the record of the extinction of 70% of the life forms then present on the earth, but also the record of the climate changes that followed the asteroid impact. This record provides a chance to study climate change and extinction as it applies to the effects humans are having on our planet." He reiterated this point in public, arguing that "we're still learning a tremendous amount about what effect that had on life forms here on earth, which is very important in our understanding as to what damage we can be doing to the planet today and not even—not even realizing when you pass thresholds what happens to life" (South Dakota PUC 2009b, 65). Larson described that the construction of the pipeline threatened not only to accelerate climate change today but also to destroy scientific capacities to better understand the effects of climate destabilization in the past, a key tool to conceptualizing the incredible complexity of the global climate system.

The PUC commissioners found the testimony compelling and made reference to it several times in later meetings. Yet Larson's testimony was disputed by another PUC witness, who suggested that while they were "not an expert" in paleontology, they did not expect paleontological resources to be overly harmed. As they explained, "if you go to any museum that has fossils, you'll see them in pieces" (South Dakota

PUC 2009c, 259). The presence of the charismatic species overshadowed what was a more complicated process of scientific inquiry, the suggestion being that large animal fossils are generally discovered broken or through processes that might break them. It was even suggested that the construction of the pipeline might increase fossil discovery. In contradistinction to the above testimony concerning soil science, here the witness performs an appeal to common sense, somewhat cordoning off and discrediting the actual expert testimony provided by Larson. Instances such as these reinforced the sentiment that even when the differential in expertise seemed to favor pipeline opponents, actual disagreement about the stakes of scientific inquiry was not sufficiently counted by the PUC commissioners. Disputes were rendered technical rather than political.

Disagreement concerning aquifers and water resources were, of course, important not only to the experts in question but also to pipeline opponents. Citing their long-term life and labor on the land in question, several ranchers testified that the high water table in south-central South Dakota and northern Nebraska was not adequately considered. Increasingly, many argued that a pipeline leak in this area could result in contamination of the Ogallala Aquifer. In another instance of contested expertise, lay opponents and scientists both testified that the "boundaries" of the Sandhills bioregion mapped by the Nebraska Department of Environmental Quality and addressed in the EIS did not correspond to the real extent of the bioregion. These concerns would eventually contribute to a suggested federal corrective of the project and its EIS in 2011, resulting in a rerouting of KXL around the Sandhills region. This could be taken as an example of the meaningful importance of public testimony from the perspective of the environmental review process. Yet of course, a simple rerouting of the pipeline was deeply unsatisfying to increasingly organized pipeline opponents, who still argued that a portion of the Sandhills would be crossed anyway. In order to demonstrate that, they began conducting their own research, taking soil samples, and remapping the region based on this evidence. Again, the mobilization of expert evidence and the development of counter-expertise strengthened the resolve of pipeline opponents in Nebraska.

Environmental Populism and Skepticism of Expertise

The above examples from 2009 highlight the political and scientific terrain that conditioned pipeline opposition organizing in the early 2010s. The scene was one in which scientific evidence was adjudicated by experts, while individual and group opposition were framed as incapable of providing knowledge or evidence adequate to challenging the evidence brought by consultants, TransCanada, and the state. This situation produced a certain kind of affect that I call the jaded confidence of counter-expertise, in which the supposedly unequal balance of knowledge, expertise, and financial resources shored up a certainty in one's own collective position. Much like the examples in previous chapters, this affective infrastructure spatially structured in common a collective, engendering a feeling of coherence or identity as "the people." The confidence that "the people know best" was not given at the outset of a populist movement but was part of its very construction. That construction occurred through processes of counter-expertise: research, data gathering, testimony, and witness. Below, I contend that it is clarifying to understand these practices as a "minor science." But in doing so, I want to resist easily lauding or deriding these practices. I examine the genesis of counter-expertise because I see in it the relations that produced jaded confidence. Pipeline impacts were transformed from a risk about which one hopes one is correct into a situation in which one no longer doubts and is thus confident. But such confidence was jaded because it was attenuated or dulled by the repetitive experience of engaging the state in adjudication. This section theorizes populist counter-expertise before turning to jaded confidence.

Conservative populist leaders analyzed by political scientists and popular media frequently espouse a stance that is explicitly opposed to (certain) experts and expertise. Right-populist leaders claim access to a "common sense" or everyday knowledge that "the people" have, from which other politicians and technocrats are estranged (Moffitt 2016). Sciences are distrusted—especially environmental and climate science, though epidemiology and other health and medical sciences may be as well (Lockwood 2018). Climate scientists are taken to be elites who are simply inventing data so that they can get research grants or remain in power. Appealing to the common sense of personal experience has a greater truth value, especially when such sense bucks the out-of-touch evidence gathered by the ivory tower. Left-populists are purportedly riven by a similar distrust of experts—though their targets are different. Here, it is instead the "depoliticized" technocratic expertise of mainstream political science and economics, punditry and pollsters, and consolidated or jargony academic knowledges that are to blame. The epistemologies of populists—or "epistemological populism"—are thus understood to cohere around or through distrust of experts.[1] Such a position is reinforced by a range of academic theories, including standpoint Marxism, Gramscian cultural studies, affect theory, postphenomenology, and feminist science studies. "Understanding recent history as a showdown between peer-reviewed expertise and mass ignorance is at the core of the anti-populist tradition," Thomas Frank argues (2020, 48).

Such orientations among critical social scientists led Vayda and Walters (1999, 170) to claim that "some political ecologists have put their practice into the service of a populist political agenda." More recently, Swyngedouw decries the manner in which climate change has become simply an accepted fact rather than a political struggle. In this argument, the sense that "the people know best" rests on an uncritical acceptance of a "scientific technocracy assumed to be neutral" (Swyngedouw 2010, 223). Though these could be taken as somewhat disingenuous claims, one problem is that, as Neimark et al. (2019, 614) put it, "both political ecology and post-truth politics take issue with certain hegemonic types of truth making." Critical and sympathetic analyses of left populism alike thus tend to see the role of scientific expertise and knowledge to be instrumental and thus secondary to groups' political agendas or social standpoints (e.g., class, race, gender).[2] Both would then suggest that populism does not actually hinge on practices and processes of scientific knowledge production but only claims-making based on contesting given scientific results. For its critics, environmental populism would suspiciously subordinate ecological expertise to the conspiracy theories of the people. More sympathetic readings suggest environmental populism mobilizes the common sense of lived experiences and thus needs no supplementary scientific expertise or pedagogy.

Why, then, would pipeline populisms engage in critical yet scientific forms of counter-expertise? Are these practices really subordinate to identity, class, or social position? Scholarship on expertise in environmental politics has tended to avoid this question when populism is involved. Fischer, however, argues it is possible that reactions against constituted scientific expertise can engender "both right- and left-wing populisms, [which] hold out a return to grassroots democracy as the key to revitalizing American society" (2000, 28). Meyer suggests that progressive environmental populism can be distinguished from technocratic orientations through an emphasis on "local knowledge rooted in the particularities of place and community" (2008, 225). But is a focus on local knowledge and common sense really the main feature of the epistemological politics of environmental populism? How, then, are we to interpret such populisms' engagements with scientific epistemologies and expert subject positions? Though I do not deny that hopes for grassroots democracy and local knowledge are crucial to environmental populism, this emphasis leaves us without a clear grasp on how populisms construct both their own knowledge and their own emotion not only in a reactive opposition to more technocratic, apolitical forms of expertise but also by confirming their feeling of confidence through the scenes of minor science.

The concept of minor science can help us account for the construction of "the people" as a collective performance that occurs through rather than only against expertise. Attempts to mobilize expert knowledge to contest the parameters of infrastructure projects congeal environmental populisms through practices that appropriate the tools or language of normative science subjected instead to partisan ends. By *minor science,* I wish to indicate the practices involved in the never-finished, always-processual construction of an oppositional genre that composes "a people" through alliance or affinity (Katz 1996). Four features make the concept of minor science particularly helpful for understanding the construction of an oppositional populism. First, a minor science takes part in "the organization of the social field" that is also immanently "a part of that science itself" (Deleuze and Guattari 1987, 368–69). The minor emerges not in outright opposition to the major but from within the major forms of language or scientific fields (Deleuze and Guattari 1986, 19; 1987, 367). Thus, counter-expertise as minor science does not so much elaborate an alternative epistemology based in common sense, popular culture, lay knowledge, or Indigenous epistemology but instead is constructed by learning to speak through science. In the process, the meaning and results of scientific epistemologies can be tweaked or transformed.

Second, minor sciences emerge in "cramped spaces," where they are liable to effectuate a people who otherwise is missing (Thoburn 2003, 2016). A cramped space is neither abstract and smooth nor easily located in a sense of belonging to place. Instead, it is the kind of space where one bumps up against *the specific material conditions of necessity, rather than mere possibility, of becoming active under constraint* (Ruddick 2010, 40). Though these limits are socially mediated, underground spaces can function as such a "cramped space" for thought, insofar as their opacity and obduracy challenges conventional scientific analysis and engenders new modes of thinking (Bosworth 2017, 2021a). This iterative process of scientific contestation and bricolage involves a "taking up of whatever is at hand" (Secor and Linz 2017, 568) that develops new, quasi-scientific and decidedly collective skills that in turn form a loose identity as "the people." A minor science is thus a kind of "situated knowledge" in which the partiality of knowledge also indicates a partisan knowledge (Nightingale 2003; Dean 2016b). The upshot of linking these practices can be seen in the "strong syncretic impulse" (Di Chiro 1997, 209) or "united front politics" (Haraway 1990, 151) highlighted by feminist socialists and environmental justice activists at the epistemological edges of standard scientific practices.[3] As I conclude later in this chapter, "the people" is invented in spaces where "the public" was intended to be gathered.

Third, a minor science functions by way of its affective infrastructure rather than disavowing emotion for rationality. A post-Spinozist account of affective infrastructure helps us see how a felt affect such as the jaded confidence of counter-expertise becomes part and parcel of expertise. Circulating affects such as the felt confidence of conducting counter-expertise compose collective subjects. Yet as much as these subjects were confident that their knowledge about pipeline impacts was correct, they were afflicted by the weakness of their own power to act within the sphere where such knowledge could be adjudicated. Thus, a certain sadness I associate with jadedness—the feeling of oversaturation—accompanied such confidence. Fourth and subsequently, a minor science works on a political edge. It is decidedly not a depoliticized practice of exalting the given of a consensus scientific technocracy but instead a practice of scrambling that technocracy's authority by producing a "science for the people." However, the politics of counter-expertise are not necessarily revolutionary or radical by virtue of being antiestablishment. Experiments with the field of matter at hand can easily fail to transform that field by going unnoticed, being unreliable, or being too specific. As the account of pipeline counter-expertise below will show, a failure of minor sciences can also lead to their own overcoming, leading toward other kinds of political practice. Unlike some uses of the concept, I seek not to valorize minor sciences as such but instead to show them at work in the genre and transitions that populism performs, in all their ambivalence.

Using the lens of minor science to examine counter-expertise provides a more complex portrait than the conventional division between an elite with expert science pitted against a people with overly emotional lay knowledge. Expert and lay knowledges are each capable of engendering or being captured by either paternalistic or populist genre conventions; both expertise and counter-expertise are constituted by emotional circuits within spatial political economies "with the same necessity" (Spinoza 1985, 473 [EIIP36]), though very different ones. Thus, a situation in which counter-expertise congeals a collective subject of "the people" can teach us much about contemporary populism—including, perhaps, the rise of science denialism, which I return to in this chapter's conclusion. Because environmental populism decomposes and recomposes scientific knowledge precisely as if it were not neutral, it can point toward a distinctly political (rather than depoliticizing) ecology. Central to the politicization of expertise for pipeline populists was the increasing recognition that expertise was performed, and that such performance was more readily available to those with more money.

Who Can Buy an Expert?

Finding, paying, and calling upon credible and convincing expert witnesses was incredibly frustrating for community organizing groups in sparse western South Dakota. This reflects a long-standing trend that Sheila Jasanoff notes as "the commodification of the expert" (1995, 45) in her now-classic book on science on trial. Environmental contracting is a massive and global industry that has found its role "grooming" pipeline projects for public acceptance, as one U.K. activist group put it during their tongue-in-cheek "impact assessment" of international consulting firm Environmental Resources Management (ERM), to whom we will return in a moment (Marriott and Minio-Paluello 2013, 203; Barry 2013, 53). Independent (that is, private) consultant agencies have close ties to both the industries for whom they prepare environmental assessments and the government agencies to whom they submit these assessments, such as the EPA, the BLM, the State Department, and state public utilities commissions and departments of natural resources. This is not altogether surprising, for the genre of research and writing environmental assessments is so esoteric that industries, agencies, contractors, and environmental lawyers are frequently the only people literate in its exegesis. The overlapping and circulating goals, members, and money among these institutions subsequently result in frequent conflicts of interest and calls of corruption.

TransCanada made an initial recommendation to the State Department of three consultancy firms to prepare the environmental impact statement and other environmental permits, finally selecting Cardno ENTRIX after discussing with other agencies. But because Cardno ENTRIX counted TransCanada as a prior "major client," the firm maintained conflict of interest in the project, which resulted in a *New York Times* exposé (Rosenthal and Frosch 2011). A federal Office of Inspector General investigation, called for by Senator Bernie Sanders, revealed that in fact the State Department had "limited technical resources, expertise, and experience" to decide among consultants (Hersh 2012). An anonymous federal official described the situation as such: "The people I worked with at State were good, honest people, and they were very inexperienced and naive about environmental laws. . . . They did not have a senior expert on their environmental impact study, and I've never seen that before" (quoted in Hersh 2011). Essentially, the State Department was relying on what looked and sounded like expert knowledge with little reference to actual accuracy. Other agencies were highly critical of this EIS process and its resulting product. The Environmental Protection Agency called the study "insufficient" in 2011 and 2013, and the Department of the Interior labeled it "inaccurate" (McVeigh 2013). Commenting on the review process, legal professor

Oliver A. Houck notes that because Cardno ENTRIX had a "financial interest in the outcome of the project . . . their primary loyalty is getting this project through, in the way the client wants" (quoted in Rosenthal and Frosch 2011).

These worries, among others, eventually led the State Department to reject the first EIS. But although the inspector general found some fault with the initial selection process that led to Cardno ENTRIX, the State Department engaged in the same process for its selection of a new agency, ERM. This international consultant had also previously come under heavy criticism for numerous aspects of their assessment of the Baku-Tbilisi-Ceyhan pipeline in the late 1990s and early 2000s. Upon their announcement as KXL consultant, ERM also came under scrutiny for their failure to disclose previous ties to TransCanada. However, these ties led to no significant changes in environmental assessment.

Populist charges of corruption in the financial relationships between state agencies and firms continued throughout the federal- and state-level review processes, a very frequent theme in public comments from the 2013 EIS. Though some commenters reiterated that the State Department needed to listen to experts like climate scientists, many more argued that the EIS demonstrated an assumption that "the people" were uninformed. One commenter distilled this sentiment: "It shocks me to think that those people who work in government (on the dime of We the People) seem to believe that we, out here in the rest of the country, are morons" (U.S. Department of State 2013a, 13). In drawing evidence of financial ties among private companies and the state, pipeline opponents claimed not only that scientific and technical expertise was possibly incorrect but also that the conditions of the creation of that knowledge were subject to the market rather than the truth.

> The people have said, "NO" to the Keystone XL pipeline. We know the products are intended for export, and we know how dirty the Bitumen is with the blood of Canadian Natives. We know we don't need the money, and we know we will not prosper from it. If BP, Halliburton, and Transcanada can say YES, we can say NO. We have sent a clear message to President Barack Obama, Transcanada, and the US Congress. They need to listen to us, because We Are The People. (U.S. Department of State 2013a, 84)

As this commenter demonstrates, both the constituted knowledge within the EIS and its gaps could be ameliorated if state agencies would simply listen to "the people." However, examining further public comments reveal two limits to which such a sentiment could become effective. First, written public comments surrounding the EIS were addressed to a decisionmaker that is outside of the people. Such comments suggest that government officials need to listen to the people, a mode that, as I discussed in chapter 3, has its own set of shortcomings insofar as it shores up a certain form of state authority. Second, though rhetorically potent, the knowledge-constituting process is opaque in such public comments. How did "the people" come "to know" these things? Examining how individuals and organizations actually interfaced with decision-making structures is more revealing. That said, what I want to emphasize, which I will return to below, is that the comment shows how important the confidence of knowing about the pipeline was to the process of drawing a subject position of "the people" against it.

Charges of corruption in expert processes also played a role in PUC evidentiary hearings in South Dakota. PUC Commissioner Johnson responded to one landowner's charges that the commission was "crawling in bed with big money oil companies" in a dismissive fashion, claiming that the landowner was "insulting" them by "saying people are rich and greedy" (South Dakota PUC 2009c, 27, 28). Another farmer echoed the critique later that day: "I read [TransCanada's] pamphlets. I guess, first of all, all the testimony you hear from them is [from] their experts. They own them. I mean, they're paying them. It makes me a little bit nervous. . . . They kind of sidestep the issues, and they don't really tell the truth. They tell you what they think you want to hear" (60). Commissioner Johnson responded with more clarifying statements, explaining that "Commission staff has called a number of expert witnesses from across the country to testify on this. Those witnesses are paid for by TransCanada . . . but those experts don't correspond with TransCanada except through the normal legal channels. They are working for staff to really vet and question" (64). However, the difference between communication and finance did not matter to pipeline opponents, for it became a sign that experts were already expected to be against the critiques that farmers, ranchers, advocates, and tribal members had brought to these hearings.

To the less well-funded opposition, this difference in financial resources clearly affected the perception of independence or objectivity at stake in the project. DRA frequently acknowledged in testimony that they did not have the financial resources to hire expert witnesses. As Paul Blackburn of DRA wistfully said, "You know, I wish I was an expert in geology pipeline corrosion, and, you know, social economic impacts of pipelines" (South Dakota PUC 2009b, 571). Clearly annoyed by the repeated argument about the lack of financial resources, Chairman Johnson replied, referencing the previously mentioned testimony of Peter Larson: "There was an expert in paleontology—maybe the foremost expert in paleontology in this state—who on his own dime drove here last night to provide public comment. I would have thought that calling him as a witness wouldn't have cost DRA a whole lot of money. It's not my job to put together the case for you all. . . . It just seems to me—I mean, ultimately staff witnesses have determined the things—they don't believe some of the things you're raising are concerns worthy of a far greater fleshing out" (572). In this manner, the onus to finance witnesses is placed back on nonstate individuals and collectives, in the process cementing distrust in public institutions.

The South Dakota PUC granted the right of way permit in 2010, but four years later, the pipeline had still not been built and the permit had expired. This set the stage for another round of public comments and evidentiary hearings in July 2015. New grievances against the proposed pipeline had developed over the prior years, and several more individuals and groups filed as intervenors in the case alongside DRA, including the Rosebud and Lower Brule tribal governments. The opponents also sought to dispute whether TransCanada had been adhering to the conditions placed on the initial permit. Charges of malpractice by TransCanada had piled up, especially under the testimony of Evan Vokes, a former engineer at TransCanada who had become a whistleblower. Called before the Canadian senate, Vokes argued that "the mix of political and commercial interests allows industry to claim they exceed federal requirements when they are building substandard pipelines with no enforcement or accountability in the process" (quoted in Dermansky 2013). In submitted testimony to the South Dakota PUC, Vokes ended by writing that "TransCanada's 'experts' will tell the Commission that my opinion has no relevance. However, this does not change the fact that TransCanada is a corporation with no responsible direction" (Vokes 2015, 5). The presence of Vokes's testimony demonstrated that there were internal cracks to the testimony of experts and, consequently, that the dividing line between pipeline supporters and opponents could not simply be "the people" versus "the experts."

The first five days of testimony at the 2015 evidentiary hearing were marked by considerable controversy, including the contestation of the perceived expertise of Vokes and other witnesses. Of particular contention was the revelation of internal TransCanada documents that showed alarming corrosion rates of the underground piping of the first Keystone pipeline, which had been operational since 2008. This included a dig site analysis, wherein a firm dug into the ground, reexamined pipe "anomalies," and tried to determine the "root cause" of the corrosion in question (see Figure 8). This analysis was particularly important evidence obtained during the hearing, for it demonstrated inconsistent practice from the firm through underground and internal evidence that would not usually be accessible to interveners. TransCanada unsuccessfully tried to prevent this evidence from being admitted to the hearing. Vokes described the section of the pipeline shown in the document: it looked like "it had been gnawed at by rats" (quoted in Dermansky 2015a).

The protracted debates about credibility and expertise resulted in the hearing being extended for another four days. Echoing comments made in 2009, one individual involved in the evidentiary hearings described to me that they felt TransCanada "continually called people as experts—senior company people who knew virtually nothing about any of the things that were going on ostensibly under their direction." When these candidates were less than convincing, TransCanada simply "tried to distance themselves as far as possible from anything that could have given them a fault." In another example, an expert witness called by TransCanada frustrated intervenors by repeatedly stating, "That isn't my area of expertise," when asked what interlocutors had deemed rather general questions (Dermansky 2015b). Intervenors also told me that it was particularly galling to experience what they felt was a clear double standard in how expertise and evidence were being judged by the commissioners. It seemed to them that the granting of intervenor status and admission of evidence was selective, perhaps designed to put the inter-

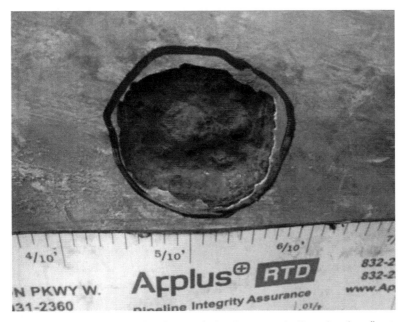

Figure 8. An image of a small pit in the existing Keystone pipeline taken for a "root cause" report submitted as part of testimony concerning the KXL permit renewal at the South Dakota Public Utilities Commission. This testimony became particularly important as it seemed to demonstrate that expert assurances had not accounted for the behavior of the materials themselves. TransCanada, "Study of Root Cause and Contributing Factors, Keystone Pipeline Corrosion Anomaly Investigation Final Report" (2013), https://www.desmog.com.

venors at a disadvantage. Notably, climate change was not allowed to be discussed in the state-level review process in South Dakota. Efforts to call outspoken climate scientist James Hansen to testify were nixed by the PUC. Ultimately, the performance of truth at the hearing was felt to be a matter of buying competing experts.

Craig, who was involved in the hearing, explained to me the problems of expertise and apparent collusion in the hearing in some detail. Consider the following example of TransCanada's diagram outlining horizontal directional drilling underneath the Missouri River. Craig explains a diagram similar to Figure 9, which a commissioner brought up:

> They had this idea that . . . under the major rivers, where they're
> going to do what they call horizontal directional drilling, where they

go at an angle underneath and they come up on the other side. Well, according to their diagram, these slightly bendable pipes would have to bend at an angle over forty-five degrees just to get in the ground. And it was unclear how when they got to the bottom of this thing, they were going to bend again and go up, all the while not corroding any of the surface of the pipe. Because if you put scratches at all in that coating, what's natural in the ground will corrode the iron pipes. And so, you know, this is under your rivers, our rivers.

River crossings like this were of major concern to interlocutors, not least because the corroded part of the existing Keystone pipeline entered as evidence earlier was a mere two hundred feet from the Mississippi River. Opponents were confident that the risk of a pipeline spill to the river, like aquifers, was too great—no matter what number or percentage risk the experts had put on it. The use of seemingly simplistic models as purported evidence gave pipeline opponents more confidence that the risk of a spill in these locations was greater than they were being led to believe.

These are just schematic diagrams, after all. What bothered Craig more was the sense that even in questioning the diagram, the PUC had already made up their mind that it was not a big deal. With a wry and characteristic sarcasm, he described the scene to me: "So, first of all, the

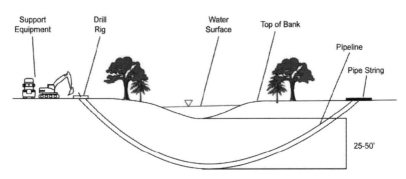

Figure 9. Originally captioned "Cross section of horizontal directional drilling method," this overly simplistic model in the Keystone XL draft supplemental EIS portrays subterranean river crossings. A diagram like this garnered controversy at the South Dakota PUC in 2015. U.S. Department of State, "Keystone XL Draft Supplemental Environmental Impact Statement—Executive Summary" (2013), ES-9.

Commissioner just laughed: [*mocking voice*] 'Ho, ho, ho! I'm sure you'll figure out a way to do this.' [TransCanada replying:] 'Oh, yeah, yeah, we will.' So, so, you know, it was, it was absolutely ludicrous. It was like, these [TransCanada] guys should come back when they're ready. And we kept on trying to say that: 'come back when you're ready.' You know, you've done all these studies, when you're really ready to construct, come back and show our PUC what all your plans are." Summarizing this line, he told me the commission's position was "'Well, the science is nice, but if the company promises us it'll be ok, it will be.' They say, 'Don't worry about the science, we have it under control—and if they prove to be wrong, well, you know we learn from every one of our mistakes.'" Craig's mocking tone here reiterates his complete lack of faith in the adjudication of science by the PUC commissioners. How can the people contest expert knowledge when the conclusion is already foregone?

As an advocate and organizer, Craig interestingly situated the difficult place that pipeline opponents found themselves within the landscape of U.S. environmentalism that I described in the introduction:

> One of the great problems we had is that grassroots groups usually do not have a lot of financial resources. . . . You know TransCanada didn't have any problem paying for its so-called experts, and [similarly] the PUC with our money. And we had people who we could not call [to testify] or it was very difficult to call, because you know just trying to raise resources to do that. And what's pointed out to me is that the so-called "Big Greens" are so caught up with their multimillion dollar budgets and, and, just trying to play nice, um, and they had no time—let alone any willingness—to invest resources. Even a fraction of what they're using on their full page ads in the *Washington Post* or whatever to help us with experts or anything like that.

The problem of buying experts was not simply a matter of regulatory capture and corporate–state alliances. It also extended to the technocratic game of 1990s-style environmentalism, which relied on donor-driven strategies for litigation. Craig's more grassroots orientation was thus built on a critique of the extant system surrounding environmental knowledge production. Later in our conversation, Craig returned to this point with even more disdain. He described how "if we could get

350.org [to] give us one percent of their public relations budget we could downright pay the lawyers and pay the experts. . . . 350.org intervened [in the case against KXL], and we said 'Great, you intervened! Why don't you pay for experts?' [*mocking voice replying to the question:*] 'Ah ah uh duh . . . well we just intervened because we wanted to take a position.' And we said 'No, you intervened 'cause then you want to put it on your fundraising stuff, [but] you're not doing shit.' And so did the Sierra Club." For this reason, Craig suggested that he had "gotten less patient with some of those [groups]." Craig's analysis highlights the split within environmentalism concerning the role of grassroots mobilization, money, and environmental expertise.

As the above accounts demonstrate, it did not seem like a differential in expertise between the intervenors and the defense caused the permit to ultimately be approved. Just like the various kinds of experiential, lay, and local knowledge laid out against the pipeline, scientific counter-expertise was subsumed by the environmental review process that ultimately gave the power of adjudication to the PUC commissioners. In states like Iowa, the utilities board is appointed by the governor, reinforcing the populist sense that democracy was being trampled upon. But in South Dakota, PUC commissioners are elected, and thus criticism took different lines. Furthermore, as in so many scientific cases like this, PUC decisionmakers effectively required interveners to marshal financial resources to build their cases through expertise rather than, say, admit this was a political decision and thus deserved political debate. The forms of expertise to confirm what populists already knew simply were not easy for grassroots groups in far-flung South Dakota to accumulate.

This is not to deny the material results of legal intervention—including the PUC's decision to place over fifty specific conditions on pipeline construction and monitoring upon their granting of the permit in December 2015. But when scientific evidence was disputed by expert witnesses brought by the intervenors, it was often unclear how it was being judged. Native and non-Native activists marched and rode on horses into Pierre, South Dakota, for the hearings and many sat in the crowd to listen to the hearing. This put added pressure on the arguments and affects of the hearing that circulated in the space to go beyond anything like dispassionate rational debate. However, as the July

2015 evidentiary hearing wore on to nine days and the arguments got increasingly technical, it became more difficult to stay engaged. For many people in the audience, the hearing appeared to be a charade.

Was there any point in engaging in this kind of counter-expert activity if it was doomed to failure from the start? What lessons did pipeline opponents take from such experiences, and how did they construct the confidence of counter-expertise alongside and through cynicism and jadedness that also partially composed pipeline populism? The next section examines forms of counter-expertise developed in the field rather than the courtroom.

Extending the Confidence of Pipeline Counter-Expertise

Outside of evidentiary hearings and relationships with formal state institutions, oppositional groups took investigative matters into their own hands. Realizing that experts were inaccessible and increasingly confident in their own accumulated expertise, pipeline opposition groups began trying to research and collect data with which they could possibly better contest KXL and, months later, DAPL. Different expert practices became a central part of nonsanctioned confrontations with pipeline construction and security forces, including learning everything from security culture to protection from tear gas and LRAD sound cannons (even if these are rarely recognized by our current definitions of expertise). The populist portion of opposition to KXL and DAPL encouraged and benefited from the sustained development of some of these minor sciences, which emerged from the cramped space of oppositional politics.

By 2015, and in the following months with the advent of DAPL, many of the individual opponents I talked with were starting to feel a real fatigue at the environmental review hearings. "Nothing we say will ever be good enough," one landowner told me. Another described how he had attempted to engage with the EIS: "I have a laptop, and I figured, 'Well, I'll download it.'" The file took up most of his remaining hard drive and he decided to delete it out of fear it would crash his computer. Most of the KXL landowners had signed their easements. With increasing press coverage and attention, pipeline opponents languished in what another described to me as "information overload." Hearings got more boring as the level of discourse got more detached from the real concerns felt about the pipeline.

We might initially hypothesize that the failure of initial acts of counter-expertise to adequately contest pipeline construction provides a classic example of the depoliticizing effect of technocratic politics. But I was surprised to find that many pipeline opponents, reflecting on their participation in practices of counter-expertise, disagreed with this sentiment. There were two primary reasons. First, the belief that "the people know best" grounded their opposition well beyond whatever form of expertise the state recognized. As I described above, opponents frequently complained that they lacked not knowledge but comparable financial resources as TransCanada to hire experts to testify in evidentiary review. Second, opponents also found that repetitive performance of their expertise and the lack of legitimation by permitting agencies reinforced the grounds of their opposition. The disheartening experience of going through the environmental review process and losing despite the obvious truth of their position reinforced the identities of resistance that they found important in the composition of populist politics, while creating a jadedness toward the possibility of transformation via institutional routes.

Craig attested to both of these sentiments. The environmental review process was "a little bit disconcerting, but it's all educational. . . . We know that ultimately any protection of our water resources is gonna come from the people here and that's the only place it'll come from." He reinforced this position later in our conversation, highlighting his role in trying to guide that pedagogical process: "We're encouraged to work through the system to find remedies. If the system fails to provide the remedies that it claims to do, then it's important that we understand that so that we know it's necessary to think outside the box." This strategy is not without its pitfalls, either, which are as endemic to the affective infrastructure of opposition. Sometimes, when people realize that "the system" does not work, Craig noted it causes "severe depression and anxiety amongst a good percentage of people who truly believed [that we would win in the evidentiary hearing]." Importantly, Craig—a non-Native settler—drew a connection between this feeling and "the result of colonialism. . . . We've just been propagandized." Settler colonialism entails a belief in functional democratic institutions that is something of a fantasy. The hearings provided a limit or bifurcation point. In Craig's analysis, either people are going to be "depressed and demoralized" or they might say, in his words, "Wow, I didn't realize it was going to be this hard, and we've got to work harder." This might be expected, as in Spinoza's terms the passive affect of fear is turned into despair when doubt is removed, just as the active affect of hope is turned into confidence with the same removal of doubt (1985, 534 [EIII DXIV]). But by adding the role of the social in augmenting fear or confidence, Craig highlights that the hearings could become an instructive moment for settler pipeline opponents, who had perhaps entered them with naivety. Finally, Craig noted there are some people (who he most identified with) who say, "I didn't expect it to work, but I'll sure try to make it work." This mirrors the sentiment that Sheila expressed to me concerning participation that I described in chapter 2: "I don't think we have a rat's chance in hell that they'll say, 'No,' but we're gonna fight as hard as we can."

While the position of pipeline opponents was increasingly cynical about the potential role of counter-expertise in environmental review, opponents did believe that the process of engaging and self-educating each other was crucial. Through such acts, they come to exhaust the political potential of contesting the pipeline in the official institutional channels. When Craig notes that "it's all educational," he is suggesting that the people are learning how to contest through expertise and how to do politics beyond that very venue. The failure of counter-expertise to meaningfully contest pipeline review was mirrored by its success in evoking confidence. The demonstration of evidence removed doubt within pipeline opponents, turning their hope into confidence. Confidence played a crucial role in calling forth fortitude, courage, and conviction in political subjects increasingly capable of moving beyond that institutional sphere to do "something else"—organize, blockade, or sabotage. Jaded confidence was thus a sad affect in the sphere of the courtroom, but it grounded active affects that increased capacities outside it.

Such actions were mobilized as the battleground shifted from KXL to DAPL. Just as KXL permitting struggles were waning in 2015, pipeline opponents in Iowa and South Dakota were finding the strategies of public testimony and counter-expertise were failing to prevent the permitting of DAPL. Consequently, many felt compelled to go beyond the established political process. Organized in part through the Science and Environmental Health Network, Indigenous Environmental Network, and DRA, one example of this was the Bakken pipeline watchdogs network. This began monitoring the DAPL construction process, using the law to pester and delay construction while legal cases and blockades elsewhere along the pipeline's route escalated struggle. It is worth reflecting on the manner in which this brief movement activated a different kind of counter-expertise.

The Bakken pipeline watchdogs network was established in the summer of 2016 as the DAPL construction had begun, and I participated from afar in watchdog activities on the section of the pipeline near Brookings, South Dakota. Fast-tracked through state review processes, DAPL was initially deemed to not need a federal environmental impact statement (though this decision was legally challenged and ultimately reversed, albeit after the pipeline had been mostly completed). So, early in June, organizers from DRA, the Indigenous Environmental Network, and the Science and Environmental Health Network held a conference call to discuss the legal recourse we had to delaying the pipeline. Construction of the pipeline was contracted, and like much contracting in capitalism, regulatory corners were tending to be cut. Holding contractors accountable meant observing construction on a daily basis, photographing activity that was breaking regulations, calling state regulatory agencies to report violations, and (hopefully) ensuring a work stoppage. Many watchdogs would post pictures and a narrative of the construction on a Facebook group. As Carolyn Raffensperger of the Science and Environmental Health Network wrote in a pocket guide for watchdogs, "It is an experiment! As far as we know, nobody has ever created a pipeline watchdog team. So we are relying on your creativity and observation skills."

This strategy required not only that opponents understood environmental regulation but also that they cultivated "observation skills" to recognize improper construction. Two regulations we found could be particularly effective. First, construction crews were not supposed to operate after rainfall when any standing water was present nearby. Requiring little skill, finding construction that was occurring after rain was incredibly easy. The construction of Keystone I had produced several instances of improper construction, a major grievance that reappeared in South Dakota's PUC hearings for KXL and DAPL. Second, we learned how to recognize improper erosion into nearby waterways (especially important at river crossings) and improper separation of soil horizons (topsoil from ground soil). The pipeline watchdogs held trainings that helped attune themselves to violations of the law, as well as basic surveillance skills and the fortitude to drive around watching construction crews. Countermapping was also a crucial aspect of monitoring, as pipeline watchdogs frequently updated a public map that displayed active work sites and completed portions of the pipeline. For around a month, the construction watchdogs shared images of legal violations and the general destruction involved in digging a 1,200-mile-long trench in the ground.

It would be easy to dismiss the Bakken pipeline watchdogs as an appeal to state power, a passive intervention if an intervention at all. We were rather ineffective. Roxanne, an Iowan organizer, felt that the pipeline watchdogs were "pretty much fake" and that these activities sanctioned the construction of the pipeline rather than directly opposing it. I do think that there is a bit more going on than perhaps such an assessment would suggest. First, many of the participants were rural and small-town women surveilling the activity of largely nonlocal male construction crews. The watchdog group thus provided a new avenue of explicitly feminist political intervention into the pipeline's construction. It is important to note, as Ahna Kruzic and Angie Carter point out, such a feminist praxis was not without its own internal contradictions. These especially concerned coloniality, capitalism, property, and the role of industrial agriculture in polluting local waters (Kruzic and Carter 2016; Carter and Kruzic 2017, 2020). Second, the knowledge produced by this activity might have been crucial for a whole host of other political activities. These included legal cases against pipeline construction, scouting for possible sites for direct actions, blockades, and sabotage, and publicizing information of code violations. Finally, watchdog activity activated political resistance at the scale of the pipeline's entire length rather than only at points of intervention. As a political activity, then, countersurveillance built power and identity among new activists who were intervening in the conditions of possibility for other political actions at a scale not yet activated in pipeline resistance.

Frustratingly, the utility of this group and tactic was not long lived. As the blockade at Standing Rock escalated, construction crews were rerouted and instructed to finish other sections of the pipeline as quickly as possible. It takes an astonishingly short amount of time to lay a pipeline if a firm is motivated to do so. The prominence of the blockade also led to the end of the internet as a useful medium of exchange, as every Facebook group founded with a limited scope was flooded with postings and repostings of news stories and opinion pieces about DAPL, frequently from internet sleuths following along from afar rather than on the ground in the region. When everyone styled themselves an expert, we became oversaturated with information gathering and posting rather than filtering information through a concerted strategy.

Given the watchdogs' inability to delay or halt pipeline construction, other activists began to cultivate their knowledge of how to sabotage construction equipment. In 2017, Ruby Montoya and Jessica Reznicek, associated with the Des Moines Catholic Worker and an Iowa blockade called Mississippi Stand, stepped forward to claim responsibility for the actions. In many of their accounts of what compelled them to sabotage, Montoya and Reznicek cited their frustration at the inability to stop the pipeline via the sanctioned institutional routes. Furthermore, crucial to their sabotage were also range of scientific and technical knowledges, but in a departure from the populist genre, a necessary aspect of these skills was precisely that they could not circulate in public.

This chapter has traced how practices of counter-expertise led some pipeline opponents to engage in scientific review processes. The latter demonstrated severe limitations, in the minds of many opponents, to adjudicate the potential risks of pipeline spills. Principle to this limitation was a recognition of the enmeshing of expert knowledges in networks of power and wealth. By contrast, pipeline populists developed grassroots forms of counter-expertise first in an attempt to contest the pipeline in courts and later as pathways to go beyond them. This leads me, in the following section, to reflect on the broader social significance of the gathering of pipeline opponents adjacent to arenas of expert knowledge production as a surpassing of the form of "public" toward a politicized social formation.

Jaded Confidence: From Publics to "the People"

The interdisciplinary field of science and technology studies has, following John Dewey, drawn attention to the "publics" as heterogeneous political actors gathered by technological and environmental uncertainty and controversy.[4] Publics are ephemeral political gatherings; they emerge as the consequence of a (material) problem. To give a pertinent example, in *Material Politics: Disputes along the Pipelines,* Andrew Barry examines how controversy surrounding the Baku-Tbilisi-Ceyhan pipeline involved selectively raising certain materials and the boundaries of the "political situation" to the level of political controversy. To make knowledge controversies actionable, these publics rendered them emblematic of the oil industry as such through a "logic of abduction" (Barry 2013, 81) in which a specific or singular example inductively or metonymically stands in for a more general or abstract lesson. For example: hiring expert witnesses who attempt to dispel public concern stands in for the broader corruption of financial interests and the oil industry. Yet Barry shows that "experts as well as non-experts can be viewed as minor political irritants, disrupting the certainties of what is conventionally understood to be the terrain of public debate by making visible problems and reanimating controversies that might otherwise be ignored or lie dormant" (2013, 8). This is a crucial point, which we can see above in the examples of "expert irritants" such as the paleontologist Peter Larson or the whistleblower engineer Evan Vokes.

But scholars less frequently highlight situations in which an interested, heterogeneous public is transformed into a political subject with a felt identity or collectivity, which the realm of populism and other political genres points toward. Indeed, the concept of "publics" has been explicitly contrasted to that of "the people" (e.g., Warner 2005, 67). Publics, or "the public," are named (by commentators, state officials, and academics) rather than collectivities, which invent a name for themselves. Yet the minor science of pipeline opposition above shows that "the people" can be invented as a political subject in the place where we might otherwise expect a public. Or rather, the pipeline public's negative experience of institutional review transforms their identities from a public into "the people." Without a conception of political subjectivity beyond the ephemeral public, we are left with a story of "irritation" without transformation. It is further helpful here to recall the four parts of a minor science. First, populist engagement took part in the "major" technoscientific field itself, rather than remaining outside. Second, it emerged in relation to a cramped space, here including thinking through underground materials. Third, it was organized through its affective infrastructure, in this case a jaded confidence of counter-expertise. Fourth and consequently, it became a political process, knowledge as a kind of praxis. In a nonteleological manner, I wonder whether these might help us understand how other sorts of material publics might become political actors rather than—in my opinion—depoliticized publics.

While material uncertainty gathers publics, attention to affective infrastructures can transform a gathered public into a self-constituting "people." In this chapter, I have highlighted how engagement with thinking the cramped spaces of material undergrounds produces minor sciences of collective pipeline opposition. The latter practices produce and reproduce confidence in counter-expertise and the confidence that these epistemological practices, spaces, and scenes reinforce a populist genre of opposition to consolidated elite expertise. Edging around within this genre, oppositional subjectivities are produced. But there are no guarantees that these will coalesce into a social movement—just as easily, the jadedness of such confidence can lead to dropping out of political struggle. Nor will such a social movement necessarily be populist, as environmental justice coalitions or other forms of radical opposition are further possible. While this politics without guarantees could appear as a form of hedging, my point is that technoscientific epistemologies can help consolidate "the people" beyond simply gathering ephemeral publics.

As liberal notions of the public, the citizen, and civil society have gradually replaced national, cultural, or class-based identities in collective decision-making processes, scientific and technical disputes can seem transitory rather than historical or political. If these disputes are to emerge as durable sites through which people can connect grievances through a logic of abduction, self-constituting identities must reemerge too. If, as Stengers (2005, 160) argues, "the Deweyan public is not as such part of a creation process [because] it asks the state to answer, to provide the solution," then "the people" is one attempt toward a transition to a collective subject that affirms itself and its knowledges. Like the public, this "people" emerges in relation to the state—but here, through state failures. In such moments, "the people" finds that the state is only the exteriorization of their very right of sovereignty or constituent power. Yet this impasse perhaps demands other subjects, perhaps those that exceed the capacity of either "the public" or "the people" to solve. Class subjects such as the working class or the proletariat are one option, though a very difficult one to parse, given their potential accomplishments must be accompanied by the abolition of these very subjects. Party identification is a greater possibility in parliamentary situations; yet in the rural United States, overcoming party identification presents greater opportunities (Ashwood 2021). Climate justice struggles have invented other names—such as "the front lines"—but these are accompanied by their own problems in adjudicating the relationship between marginality and popular power (Slocum 2018). It is possible that "the people" repeatedly crops up because it is one of the few names expansive enough to speak to several of these constituencies.

Historic studies of populism have done well to recognize processes of construction, but their stories can sometimes end with a laudatory moment. As in Laclau's analysis (2005), populism either wins by becoming more universal or dissolves as the very people that compose it lose faith. What I have emphasized in this book instead is that populism could also be a transitional genre of oppositional politics built through a dialectic process of reacting to expert power, consolidating counter-expertise, building oppositional identities, and developing increasing self-constitution. Populism gathers from the scenes of heterogeneous, fractured public life and transforms them affectively and pedagogically into a collective subject able to position itself against an enemy. This construction does not have any easy finality. The coherence of the populist subject is undermined by ways in which confidence in counter-expertise can also lead to political actions that might entail less publicity.

Conclusion

It is important to attest to the wide range of expert knowledges that were contested by pipeline opponents. These included controversies surrounding diluent chemical composition, cultural resource surveys, flow rates of heavy crude in water systems, the economic impact of pipeline construction and oil export, and several other micro- to macroantagonisms attached to the supposed national interest in constructing new oil pipelines. Through this engagement with struggles over, within, and against expertise, pipeline opponents came to construct a fundamental split—not between elite technoscientific knowledge and local or lay experience but between a science in the interests of the state and capital and a minor science of and for the people. The confidence engendered by the practices of contesting science led to jadedness with traditional routes of political contestation and, eventually, to a path more open to radical politics.

Since 2015, the state of pipeline review has become even more complicated. Fossil fuel–funded public relations firms attempt to dispel any counter-expertise through transparent fact-checking websites. In response to this proliferation of so-called fake news, some analysts have doubled down on the liberal distrust of the masses. Others on the political left believe that in forming their identities as an alternative to elites, populists are doomed to subordinate proper politics to unprincipled argumentation with experts. These uncharitable views, I have argued, miss the ways in which populism processually constructs itself through minor science and thus contains the conditions of possibility of a break from the status quo. It does so by maintaining practices of scientific counter-expertise that were precisely interested rather than claiming to be apolitical, neutral, or objective. Pipeline opposition further demonstrates that common people are capable and keen at picking up expertise in a wide range of knowledges. Given that few collectives are born with a ready-made critique of the state and capital in hand, working through the political field via counter-expertise offers a glimpse at the careful cultivation of oppositional—perhaps even radical—identities without recourse to a messianic event. In that process, however, the necessity of certain forms of counter-expertise may wane. In the introduction to this chapter, I described the science of assessing the potential impact of a pipeline spill on aquifers in the region. While aquifers continued to be a subject of concern, the philosophy of praxis embedded in the Indigenous-led opposition organizing under the slogan "Water is life" did not engage in the same form of claims-making and contestation. It was enough to describe the ethical and political stakes that the pipeline clearly threatened. And yet on the early days of the front lines of the blockade, a stack of hundreds of printed pages constituting the environmental assessment still sat around the campfire, fodder for potential contradictions. So long as environmental review attempts to enclose the politics of knowledge, collectives will be forced to try to engage with its parameters. After all, if DAPL is eventually shut down, it will be because of legal challenges to its environmental review—not least those enabled by attention-drawing practices of blockading.

In addressing populist assessments of the politics of expertise, I have focused on how the sentiment that "the people know best" was not automatic but constructed. One final consequence of this argument concerns the parameters of another main division between left and right populisms: climate denial. The postpolitical and technocratic response to denialism—to simply "trust the science"—is nearing a dead end, as distrust of liberal institutions like universities and state departments rises. My reading of pipeline opposition suggests that denialism might be more effectively challenged not by pleading for a simple return to science or rejection of those institutions' antipolitics. Instead, if we take the perspective that scientific and expert practices are not objective modes of depoliticization built in opposition to local experience, then perhaps they can be leveraged to split the hold of the fossil fuel industry on the scientific field by proliferating constructions of interested, partisan collectives who are aware of the constant shaping of science toward political ends (Not an Alternative 2016). This strategy offered by pipeline populism still offers no guarantees. The risk of activating nationalism or other reactionary sentiments is very real, and the deeply U.S. American understanding of scientific authority and governance rests on fundamental epistemological principles that actively reinforce Indigenous erasure or attenuation. In choosing not to examine the differences between Indigenous and Western epistemologies and politics in environmental review as some might expect, I do not wish to suggest that these differences did not matter. Rather, I want to show a field fractured along several more lines, in which scientific expertise as a fundamentally depoliticizing movement runs counter to the experiences and testimony of the struggle against pipelines in North America. If a mass mobilization of some kind is indeed necessary for any chance at climate justice, we will have to learn from activists and organizers that perhaps belief in the political plasticity of expertise could lead to a partisan activation of the people and thus a form of institutional liberation.

CONCLUSION
THE DESIRE TO BE POPULAR

THE 2010S FEATURED AN EXPANSION and renewal of climate justice activism after the defeats of the prior decade. This period has been
defined less by simple urgency than an uptick in antiestablishment political rhetoric opposed to the elitist environmentalisms of the recent
past. With the concurrent failure of the 2009 Waxman-Markey bill and
increasing signs that the Obama administration did not represent the
progressive break many had hoped, climate justice activists began to
reconsider how they might build a mass base. We gave up on policy advocacy, instead attempting to build better relationships with and among
grassroots communities on the front lines of extraction and climate
chaos. These movements were led by Native Nations, migrant farm-
workers, Black liberationists, coastal fisherpeople, farmers and ranchers,
and teaching and nursing unions. They sometimes included environmental justice nonprofits, though the movements overflowed any simplistic direction from them. While climate change might be a component of populist environmentalism's analyses of coal-fired power plants,
hydrofracking fields, and tar sands pipelines, just as often these movements emerged from everyday struggles for land, water, air, and dignity.
These movements differed from their predecessors in the prior decades
of environmental justice struggles in their coordination of strategies
across difference and distance in order to build, in the oft-used phrase
of the Climate Justice Alliance, "the bigger we." Drawing on the afterlives of the U.S. agrarian populist tradition, the easy-to-access rhetoric
of U.S. American democracy, the language of the global justice

movements, and a multiracial populism, the frequent name for that collective has been "the people."

Yet despite the rise in a populist genre of political rhetoric and mobilization, is it possible that we are no closer to producing radical, transformative climate action in 2021 than we were ten or fifteen years prior? Assessments of the progress (or lack thereof) in attenuating global ecological catastrophe likely shape one's optimism or pessimism. The Obama administration signed the United States on to the international Paris Agreement, but the Trump administration withdrew ratification. Many countries are not meeting even these weakened Paris Agreement targets—current pledges would still result in a catastrophic 2 degrees Celsius warming, and current policies have us closer to 3 degrees. The school strikes for the climate laid bare the insufficiency of current (in)action, yet they were also quickly ingested by a global political leadership eager to use these children to fortify appearances of action. If one takes a more radical position suggesting we need worldwide class revolution to halt capitalist exploitation of workers and nonhuman ecologies alike, far more events come into the field of vision, especially (though not only) in the Global South. These could include the leadership and resilience of the Bolivian Movimiento al Socialismo Party, the 2020 social strikes of perhaps hundreds of millions in India led by farmers, and several waves of uprisings in the United States against murderous police violence wielded especially pointedly against Black people. Yet these too have been insufficient, internally complicated, fractured by the difficult external conditions they face. The blip of economic slowdown caused by the Covid-19 pandemic affected carbon emissions, but not in a manner consistent with the prerogatives of climate justice. By 2021, emissions are set to return to prepandemic levels. The warm air feels saturated with the old Gramscian assessment of life in such a holding moment: "The old is dying and the new cannot be born; in this interregnum a great variety of morbid symptoms appear" (Gramsci 1971, 276).

Yet any tally sheet of the last decade of climate politics would include the rise of struggles against the pipelines in the win column. This birthed a movement that—though sparked and often led by Indigenous North Americans—is heterogeneous in its social composition, political commitments, and orientations. In this conclusion, I tie together two remaining questions. First, how do the analytics of affective infrastructure and populism as genre and transition help us reflect on and evaluate populist environmentalism and left populism more generally? Second, how would the affective infrastructures of populism contrast with an expansive, revolutionary socialist climate politics? While the chapters in this book show some of these limitations in action, here I want to be as explicit as possible in outlining why I think the left-populist orientation that underlines aspects of this movement represents an insufficient path for radical social transformation.

Viewing populism as a genre can help us disaggregate and de-essentialize it, while still allowing us to account for its transhistorical and formal elements. Recall that genre is "an institution or formation that absorbs all kinds of small variations or modifications while promising that the persons transacting with it will experience the pleasure of encountering what they expected, with details varying the theme" (Berlant 2008, 4). The populist genre sets expectations, augments desires, and attenuates variation. Contemporary pipeline struggles in North America formed a crucial element in the rise of populist environmentalism. Genre conventions emerged through collective gatherings like public participation meetings, social media forums, and protest marches. Populist environmentalism also worked by renarrating these events back to an audience, through works by movement figures like Naomi Klein and Bill McKibben, local figureheads like Bold Nebraska leader Jane Kleeb, and activist and social media. Any politics works from and within the historical and material elements that precede it (famously not the conditions of our choosing), rearranging and accentuating that which can be changed. Pipeline populism as I have described it emerged within and against past forms of climate justice activism, left politics in the Great Plains, and the broad political-economic and world-historical shifts in sites where capital accumulation occurs (especially extraction and transportation of raw materials). Organizers shape their writings and strategies to meet their intended audience where they are at while also shifting them a few more steps in a certain direction. Populist events gather people who have diverse individual and political backgrounds, providing a common space and language that might prevent those differences from rendering the collective inoperable. The urgency and variegation of global ecological crisis, Chantal

Mouffe surmises (2018, 6, 35, 51–52), is all the more reason why left populism—rather than revolutionary socialism—is necessary.

Although both mainstream liberal and right-wing media sources continue to paint everything from pipeline struggles to the Green New Deal in a "jobs versus the environment" frame, climate politics has moved beyond such reductions toward a complex, if not always coherent, foregrounding of coalitional politics, "real democracy," and political-economic transformation. Although not always explicit, these groups stage a fundamental political problem raised by the climate crisis: Who is the subject that ought to decide the planet's future? Implicitly or explicitly, they reply, "the people." They sometimes even reference the histories of populism, as in Patel and Goodman's suggestion that historic populist struggles ought to be understood as "a counter-hegemonic force" important for "contemporary lessons that it offers organizers for the Green New Deal" (2020, 437). However performative, aspirational, and incomplete, such references shape the politics of the movement. On the one hand, allusions to "the people" render visible and contestable democratic decision-making at a time when technocratic and depoliticizing expertise has been the norm in capitalist liberal democracies. On the other, recognizing that "the people" is under duress and must be actively constructed, the horizon of left populism becomes oriented around (and subsequently constrained by) an imagined political subject who must be "met where they are" in order to not be scared away from transformative politics. The account in this book suggests that the contemporary lessons of actually existing populist politics are more bitter than some might suggest.

The affective infrastructures I have described are channeled into a politics that conditions subjects to think that a recognition of the elites is sufficient to unite "the people." Property, democratic participation, nationhood, and scientific expertise are not only pillars of liberalism, they are also taken to be components of the terrain of popular struggles. Territorial resentment, resigned pragmatism, heartland melodrama, and jaded confidence are affects that emerge in certain sorts of historical-material spaces and operate to open doors to political action while constraining the forms that action might take. But if the injunction to meet people where they are becomes a grounding politics, it can serve as a justification for the left-populist injunction against revolutionaries who, in Mouffe's estimation, "do not engage with *how people are in reality* but with how they should be according to their theories" (2018, 50, emphasis added).

Such a problematic terrain orients desires in left politics for a "mass movement," especially when evaluating the relationship between racism and class domination. Polling and voting data shapes who is imagined to be the constituency of Bernie Sanders, whether the slogan "defund the police" is viable or not, or whether nationalism or border enforcement ought to be criticized or accommodated into left political visions. Some of these debates can be explained in the difference between minimalist and maximalist demands, wherein the latter are seen to potentially frighten regular people. Undoubtedly, problems of timing are crucial to advancing any political demands. Yet many of these arguments take as a baseline assumption that the affective infrastructures that undergird, say, nationalism, are immutable. For example, Mouffe suggests affects and desires need only be "*recognized*" as they are in "reality" in order to be "mobilized" and consequently lead to the design of "a successful left populist strategy" (2018, 76). Hence her capitulation that "left populist strategy cannot ignore the strong libidinal investment at work in national—or regional—forms of identification" and thus must entail "mobilizing [these nationalist investments] around a *patriotic identification* with the best and more egalitarian aspects of the *national tradition*" (71). A U.S. variant of the argument is made by some social democrats, for whom the populist language of the people provides class unity, while any discussion of, say, anticolonialism or degrowth is merely a particularist, divisive, or not-popular-enough set of demands. The problem is that, quite clearly, the imagination of the desires of "the people" is as much at work in left-populist theorists as it is in those "regular people" they claim to understand.

To dispel the myth that populist strategies have some unencumbered or exclusive access to popular desires, I have sought to show in each of the chapters above that populism is a transitional genre, waxing and waning as one among many genre conventions for performing pipeline opposition. Populism both emerged from and provided the retroactive understandings of inchoate emotions, channeling them into political formation. It eventually reached limits—failures—that forced either attenuations or transformations in political approach. Property and defense of territory emerged as a way of stitching together coalitions of landowners and Indigenous activists against pipelines. But by 2017, land defense increasingly meant decolonization, not property rights. Democratic participation was a demand that made sense within the Great Plains political history, drawing on familiar ideals of U.S. liberal democracy. By 2017, pipeline opponents were disaffected with public participation, and many of them began to drop out of the circuit of democratic struggle. Calls for a renewed form of liberal civic nationalism, with the affective structure of heartland melodrama, made more sense when assessing a pipeline as a project of national interest. By 2017, these were headed off in two ways: from the right by Donald Trump's own Sinophobic regime and from the left by the increase of internationalist and anti-imperialist politics that oppose recovering the myth of liberal civic nationalism. Finally, though some organizations continued to push at the utility of scientific counter-expertise—especially in legal challenges to DAPL—this approach met serious problems with the Trump administration's more outright flaunting of even the appearance of environmental review, as well as the amount of time, work, and money required for pipeline opponents to challenge scientific evidence.

Understanding populism as a transitional genre is clarifying to scholars and political movements alike. Rather than hypostasizing or substantializing populism, we can see it as having a limited utility in bringing together formerly depoliticized individuals and transforming them through a collective political project. Yet left populism promises both utopian redemption and pragmatic coalition building, but only infrequently can it tie the two together. First-term elections in which resentment toward other options is immediate—as in early 2010s Greece and Spain—are successful examples. But the political parties Syriza and Podemos respectively faced constraints of international capital and an electoral base with only thin support (Jäger 2019). As tantalizing as the U.S. rise in popularity of Medicare for All and the Green New Deal seem, structural political and economic constraints prevent them from being realized—among these the absence of the mass movement they claim to enroll. A more robust reconstruction of "libidinal attachments" is required, or the pull of disaffection or political nihilism will result in either political disengagement or turns toward the right.

As Balibar exhaustively demonstrates (e.g., 1994, 30–31), a Spinozist analysis of affects not only helps provide a lay of the land after which one makes a rational decision. Becoming more adequately aware of how we are collectively determined to act by affective relationships also shows how we can be determined otherwise—even under conditions not of our own choosing (Balibar 2020, 180). The best of such analyses of populism (see especially Marino 2018), placing performance at the center, provides us with an understanding of political affect that can help explain such failures.

To political movements, critical reflection on the desire to be popular shows the limits of a populist politics that assumes desires are shaped before rather than within organizing. Such limits continued to be operative after the blockade at Standing Rock. In the summer of 2017, Bold Nebraska organized a March to Give Keystone XL the Boot! to coincide with further Nebraska permitting meetings after President Trump had revived KXL. In response, an anonymous call was posted on the website It's Going Down for an "anti-colonial, anti-capitalist, anti-fascist bloc" to participate in the march. This document persuasively suggested it was "time to embrace a deeper critique and sharper tactics to stop [KXL] once and for all." The authors argue that "in this moment it should be clear that this fight is not over one pipeline, but against a complex web of systems. While we wish to see this pipeline project stopped, confronting a broader history of colonialism and genocide cannot be shoved under the rug" (It's Going Down 2017). The call suggests that individuals and groups wear masks and generally anonymize themselves but make their presence known at the march.

The potential attendance of a radical bloc at the march was completely intolerable to organizers, who posted that they "do not support or welcome anarchists or others wearing masks to the march." Anonymity and confrontation were against the supposedly celebratory spirit, and for whatever reason, the organizers imagined that the call was produced by "instigators or disruptors" seeking some violent action that would frighten families, children, and Native allies (presupposing that families, children, or Native people were not among the anticolonial, anticapitalist, or antifascist). The argument that masks, in particular, threatened the popularity of the march contradicted the ubiquity of this attire on the frontlines of the blockade at Standing Rock, where tear gas was constantly being used by police and security forces against water protectors. In ensuing debate, one critic suggested in a since-deleted 2016 Facebook post that such manufactured outrage was a play by "white activist culture" to take ownership of a movement that was not theirs to own. The organization had thus "situated itself with every other peace-policing liberal organization that refuses to resist and instead sits comfortably within its almost entirely white-led, privileged, petition-signing, police-sanctioned/celebratory march status-quo."

This episode demonstrates that the orientation toward popularity can serve as a throttle by the imagined desires of its audience or constituency—"the people." That is not to say that popularity is completely fictional, ephemeral, or ineffective. We should want to be popular. But the desires of "the people" are neither given nor immutable but are assembled or produced. In situations where socialist politics is not familiar or readily accepted, fear of appearing too radical could make some amount of sense. South Dakota is ruled by a reactionary Republican coalition, which is frequently reauthorized by a voting constituency. But in orienting itself to "the popular" against the radical, left populism disavows that people—through the emotions that collectively emerge in space—can actually be assembled or that the left can play any part in such construction. This is an odd cynicism that stands behind left populism of all kinds, a limited imaginary refuted by the blockade at Standing Rock. When people saw images or heard from friends about the blockade, they expressed a desire to join. Though it was place-based, the movement against the pipelines led by the Oceti Sakowin was able to quickly jump scales, drawing transnational allies into the fold and solidarity actions around the world. Though it ought not to be conceived as merely a place of settler self-discovery or, even worse, vacation, the space of the blockade actively constructed a people—a constituency who could semicoherently act in relation to a broader politicized infrastructure. The blockade also increased the popularity and circulation of anticapitalist, anti-imperialist, and revolutionary socialist politics as a new kind of "common sense" (Grossman 2017, 275; LeQuesne 2019, 191) that oriented and reformed the relations among its constituency of Native Nations allied with a diverse constituency of, anecdotally, largely working-class young people. Reflecting on that common sense is how one can strive toward common notions—orienting guides for future actions that can continue to grow the constituency.

However complex, the afterlives of the blockade channeled everything from vengeance and trauma to humor and solidarity. "The people," too, continued to circulate among water protectors, as did numerous expansive understandings of and responsibilities to water, to each other, and to ending colonialism and capitalism here and around the world. I was surprised when I saw some of the farmers and ranchers I knew from KXL meetings at the more radical DAPL blockade, but upon reflecting this is evidence of precisely the transitional element of populism. This is not to say that the affective infrastructure of the blockade had resolved the problems of coalition building with settlers, which Indigenous scholars like Dina Gilio-Whitaker (2019) and Kristen Simmons (2017) show. The enduring legacies of settler colonialism and racial capitalism inscribe themselves in space, forming the situational outlines that produce certain kinds of subjects. Neither common sense nor common notions are entirely adequate because power (as collective capacity) also stems from the various relationships between place, political economy, and institutionality. But history is not destiny, and we have the power to actively foster a variety of kinds of event spaces that exceed those that engender left populism. To me, spaces that can politicize against the status quo are crucial, but especially when they politicize in a certain way.

I am surprised when ideology critique like this is seen as a destructive project. Demonstrating the power of people to collectively transform them/ourselves by strategically rearranging bodies, concepts, and spaces not always of their/our choosing ought to be read as encouraging. Becoming aware of our potential and its limits gives us more resilience and potentially more power to consciously transform ourselves and others into the kind of collective subject(s) with the courage, humor, concepts, spatial strategy, intuition, and self-sufficiency to both weather the oncoming storms and creatively take this terrain as the site through which social revolution must be built. The ongoing movement against the pipelines showed us what we can do, while also demonstrating, indeed, that limits exist to what we accomplished given suboptimal conditions and our own internal strategies. Interregna offer the chance to critically reflect, self-educate, and communicate in order that we might act differently during future events. This is not to suggest a linear or teleologically progressive outlook on struggle. There will be failures and disasters with both internal and external causes. If we want to be able to effectuate transformation, it is crucial to become ever more conscious—as many as possible, thinking as much as possible—of the historical, material, and affective elements that compose us.

To what degree, then, are populism's affective infrastructures implicated in its political strategies? Throughout this book, I have emphasized that specific affective infrastructures condition—but do not necessarily determine—the performative emergence of populism. This is a tough argument to make, but I want to suggest it is crucial. The material, the affective, and the political concatenate to produce fractures, contradictions, and recursive actions that can potentially shape the direction of a political movement. It is easy to fall into a trap of thinking linearly that an affective infrastructure determines a given politics. Somewhat ironically, such an immutability of affect feeds into the reformist left-populist politics described above. Instead, the conclusion I wish to be drawn here is the inverse: numerous pressure points exist through which other sorts of affective infrastructures can be created, developing collective political subjects with the desire necessary to sustain and grow revolutionary socialism. That some settler farmers and ranchers saw themselves in and through the radical blockade shows that an affective infrastructure is not immutable but rather one among many of the complex determinations at play. The problem is we have yet to connect our inchoate affective infrastructures of joy, repair, and sustenance emergent in spaces with a strategy that both weakens the power of capital and folds more of our working-class comrades into the struggle. Strategic blockades and strikes, especially in the logistics sectors, are one example that can do some of this work. What others can we construct? And how might we do so in a way that activates ourselves and others as collective class subjects and agents of global transformation rather than through the modes of liberal recognition and multicultural allyship that presume immutable racial difference?

By opening such questions, *Pipeline Populism* hopes to make a contribution to the project of social revolution for a more robust climate politics. We must consider more than simply the rational economic interests through which subjects might exist. We need to measure the desires of "the bigger we" through a better method than polling and election data. We cannot let an imaginary "regular person" in our head orient our politics. We certainly ought to meet people where they are at, but this is in order to transform all of us into an "us." Our desires are structured by material landscapes and political economies; these are difficult to extract. Territorial resentment and heartland melodramas, for example, flow from property relations and durable nationalism, thus easily flowing into reactionary politics. The pragmatic resentment toward institutions can feed into exhaustion, nihilism, and burnout, or a kind of disaffected maximalism that sees no struggle within or in relation to existing institutions. A maximally cynical confidence of counterexpertise runs the risk of flowing into outright denialism, recently seen in fringe antivaccination movements. Considering the lack of guarantees and "rich totality of many determinations and relations" (Marx 1973, 100) at work means study and struggle alike.

As one element of this rich totality, our emotions are capable of both more flexibility and more resilience than the most cynical argue. The point of ideology critique, as Spinozist-Marxists describe it, is to show that people are not in fact easily duped but only appear to be so as participants and products of the various infrastructures that compose us. We can and should transform these infrastructures, doing so with frequent collectively conscious self-reflection on the process of organization. We need not seek to resolve or negate the affective component of politics but understand it as one variable among many in the active construction of a collective that might avoid some of the eddies, missteps, and traps of "the people" and the desire to be popular. In doing so, we can see that what the movement against KXL and DAPL reveals is not a progressive series of victories for left populism but instead a wider desire for the class project of social revolution through and with Indigenous anticolonialism and internationalism and against the forces of capital. Growing such a movement will require constructing new common sense and new common notions in order to achieve a socialist politics of equality and emancipation on and for this planet.

NOTES

Introduction

1. The historiography of populism is quite rich, and though scholars have recently diversified our understanding of populism, nationalism, and race, settler colonialism remains an understudied element of its agrarian history (though see Rana 2011). On populism and democracy, see most famously Goodwyn (1978). On populism in the Upper Midwest, see among others Pollack (1976), Ostler (1993), Lindell (1982), Pratt (1992, 2011), and Lee (2011). Postel's (2009) wide-ranging history complicates standard portrayals of the 1890s movement further, especially on questions of science and economics. Postel (2009) and Ali (2010) also challenge the racial-nationalist portrayal of populists through examining Black engagement with populism in the South. Though historians have approached populism with more generosity and attention to detail than the abstract schemas of political theorists (as Postel 2019 argues), the transposition from the 1890s to the 2010s sometimes can occur haphazardly, missing crucial political-economic shifts that have occurred since. Most important among these is a shift in economic composition away from agriculture, due to twentieth-century trends in mechanization, the Green Revolution, the globalization of agriculture, and consolidation of farm size (see chapter 3).

2. At the height of populist fervor, the daily *Dakota Ruralist* would praise the Omaha Platform as espousing "the demands of socialism," even saying that "South Dakota populists have followed the socialists beyond the Omaha platform" (quoted in Tweton 1993, 340). Socialist enthusiasm can be especially seen in Father Robert E. Haire, a heretical Catholic priest, and the *Dakota Ruralist* publisher Walter E. Kidd. The latter would take every opportunity to espouse socialist ideas in populist meetings; one instance included hanging a banner that read "Down with Capitalism; Up with the Industrial Republic" at

a populist meeting (Lee 2011, 122). After the demise of the Populist Party, many of the major populist leaders in the state would join the Socialist Party of America in the early 1900s (and often referred to themselves explicitly as socialists much earlier). Though there are risks of overextending the extent of socialism in the Great Plains during this period (Pratt 1988, 1992), these facts seem to run counter to claims that populism was merely an extension of the regional agrarian republicanism of a frontier religious settler community, as argued by conservatives like Lauck (2010).

3. For example, Mudde and Kaltwasser argue that a "defining feature of populism is its reliance on strong leaders who are able to mobilize the masses and/or conduct their parties with the aim of enacting radical reforms" (2017, 62). Müller argues that populism is "always" characterized by a constitutive antipluralism because it is "always a form of identity politics" (2016, 3). Urbinati claims populism is "deeply inimical to political liberty insofar as it . . . revokes the mediation of political institutions and maintains an organic notion of the body politic" (1998, 110). Mounk begrudgingly admits that while there is "a genuinely democratic element to populism," its primary effect is "to undermine liberal institutions [that are], in the long run, needed for democracy to survive" (2018, 35). Most offensive to liberal thinkers is the categorical division drawn between the elites and the "real people," a division which is seen to be anti-institutional and homogenizing in a moral and possibly ethnic, racial, or nationalist sense. For critiques of such antipopulism, see Riofrancos (2017), D'Eramo (2017), Postel (2019), and T. Frank (2020).

4. I do not consider Laclau's and Mouffe's works on populism to retain many insights from Marxism. Hart (2014) does argue Laclau's earlier (1979) work displays a more grounded Marxist character than his—and Mouffe's— later turn to discourse and the symbolic. Contemporary Gramscians tend to critique Laclau's "post-Marxist" moment for delinking political economy from politics (e.g., Andreucci 2019; Ekers, Kipfer, and Loftus 2020). There is good evidence Hall deserves to be distanced from Laclau and Mouffe, as argued by Kipfer (2016), Featherstone and Karaliotas (2019), Hart (2019), and Bosworth (2020). I understand the broader Latin Americanist perspective on populism to be slightly different than Laclau's work, emphasizing that *el pueblo* is not just a heterogeneous vanguard but one that actively multiplies difference (Marino 2018; Ciccariello-Maher 2020).

5. Curley translates one version of the passage as "that they will fight for slavery as they would for their survival" (Spinoza 2016, 68 [TPT P10]), though Spinoza readers like Deleuze and Guattari (1983, 38) and Montag (1999, 26) interpret the political problematic to be why one would "fight for one's servitude as bravely as they would for one's freedom or salvation." See also Stolze (2020, 166–67).

6. Compellingly analogous to Du Bois's theorization, Spinozist naturalism also pushes against the rationalization that would center a given part of humanity as if it were a "dominion within a dominion" (Spinoza 1985, 491 [EIII preface]). Though working in a different theoretical tradition, I see my line of thinking consistent with Sexton's account of libidinal economy, as described by Wilderson: "the economy, or distribution and arrangement, of desire and identification (their condensation and displacement), and the complex relationship between sexuality and the unconscious." He continues (again referencing Sexton) that it is "'the whole structure of psychic and emotional life,' something more than, but inclusive of or traversed by, what Antonio Gramsci and other Marxists call a 'structure of feeling'; it is 'a dispensation of energies, concerns, points of attention, anxieties, pleasures, appetites, revulsions, and phobias capable of both great mobility and tenacious fixation'" (2010, 7).

7. Many theorists argue, correctly in my mind, that emotion differs from affect, for the former is our more or less conscious and more or less individualized reflection on excessive "virtual" affects that insist in between and prior to human and nonhuman bodies in space (e.g., Massumi 2002). Contemporary affect theory is right to suggest that affect is "visceral forces beneath, alongside, or generally *other than* conscious knowing, vital forces insisting beyond emotion" (Gregg and Seigworth 2010, 1). But pointing out the ephemerality and formlessness of affect sometimes serves as a retreat from understanding how it serves as a condition for those formal emotions that can be named (Anderson 2014, 161).

8. While Massumi quips that affect should be understood as "beyond infrastructural" (2002, 45), Marxist and feminist scholarship occasionally use a concept of affective infrastructure to show the role of affect in political economy rather than suggesting that desire offers a simplistic escape from capture. Two different genealogies of affective infrastructure exist. The first examines the affect of infrastructure, examining how material infrastructure systems such as roads and dams generate and mobilize intimacies, enchantments, and political imaginations (Harvey and Knox 2012; Knox 2017; Larkin 2013; Wilson 2016). This is a crucial insight and contribution to both infrastructure studies and the politics of affect. A second genealogy of affective infrastructure appears in Marxist accounts of the "structures of feeling" that course through both the extant political economy and the forms of organization that might resist it (Anderson 2014; Dean 2016a; Gilmore 2017). A working out of the precise but divergent genealogies of these two accounts is a productive exercise I engage elsewhere; for the purposes of this book, I simply shortcut to suggest that my understanding of affective infrastructure hews closer to the latter tradition.

9. Ideology is an overdetermined unity, which is to say a "structured

unity" (Gidwani 2008, 4). This means that any given ideological system is a site of struggle and leakage of desires and a consolidation of capital reproduction. The concept of structure and the long-running structure-agency debates in the social sciences posit structure as spatial and temporal homogeneity. In Deleuze's understanding, "structuralism is not at all a form of thought that suppresses the subject, but one that breaks it up and distributes it systematically, that contests the identity of the subject, that dissipates it and makes it shift from place to place" (2004, 190). Instead, it is a kind of "virtual, unconscious structure that is realized only in practice" (Gidwani 2008, 7; see also Saldanha 2017, 190). Rather than abandon the concept of structure, I find it essential to understanding social reproduction and its possible leakages.

10. Without this argument, Spinoza's understanding of adequate and inadequate ideas could lead to a kind of baseless relativism. Kordela (2012) develops the counter in a psychoanalytic vein following: "As the light makes both itself and the darkness plain, so truth is the standard both of itself and of the false" (Spinoza 1985, 479 [EIIP43Schol]).

11. In some ways, the relationship between genre and style—like those of theory and practice, signifier and signified, extension and thought, and space and time—is reflective of lengthy debates concerning the relationship between form and content. The postphenomenological interpretation of affect theory eschews the abstractions of symbolic form, instead relying on supposedly "more real" matter. Gramscians frequently highlight the necessity of historicism against the detached formalism of theory (Bosworth 2020). Both Berlant and Silva argue against the historicist impulse when it fails to disclose the formal characteristics of historicity; Berlant goes so far as to state that "affect is formalism *avant la lettre*" (2008, 268).

1. "This Land Is Our Land"

1. Woody Guthrie's anthem contained a stanza that implicitly critiques the concept of private property but that has largely fallen out of popular usage (M. A. Jackson 2002). In rerecording a version of the song for his 2012 album *Americana,* Young made an explicit point of resuscitating the "No Trespassing" stanza. Nonetheless, even this original, more radical version promotes a settler colonial understanding of land—collectivized and universalized rather than privatized (V. Deloria 1973, 63; Ross 2016). References to Guthrie's song were common among anti–eminent domain media—as in headlines such as "This Land Was Your Land, Now It's Our Land: Keystone XL and Eminent Domain" (Henry 2012) and "This Land is (Still) Their Land: Meet the Nebraskan Farmers Fighting Keystone XL" (Pierre-Louis 2017). Derek Moscato analyzes the

rhetoric of the Harvest the Hope event and suggests that Young's lyrics articulate "a populism that incorporates both empowered citizens and a special contempt for elites responsible for environmental woes" (2019, 33). Young and Nelson have frequently performed "This Land Is Your Land" at Farm Aid events since the mid-1980s, sometimes paying respects to Indigenous activists invited to share the stage with them. At this event, both were presented by Indigenous leaders with gifts for their antipipeline activism.

2. See, among others, V. Deloria (1973), L. B. Simpson (2017), Coulthard (2014), Estes (2013, 2019), Karuka (2019), Dunbar-Ortiz (2014, 2016), Tuck and Yang (2012), and Moreton-Robinson (2015). I unpack this literature in a forthcoming book chapter entitled "Land Alienation as Inclusive Disjunction: Settler Pipeline Struggles in the Context of Indigenous Resistance in the U.S. Great Plains."

3. "Private property no longer expresses the bond of personal dependence but the independence of a Subject that now constitutes the sole bond" (Deleuze and Guattari 1987, 453). Through an examination of social contract theory, Mitropoulos (2012) demonstrates that the familial/sexual/religious moral economy of property (in and since Locke) is not merely superstructural, and certainly not opposed to capitalist organizations of property that some assume, but inherent in its administration and governance. This normative *oikonomic* element of property further demonstrates the heteropatriarchal and white supremacist principles lodged directly in the heart of property's material and historical relations.

4. As Guenther (2019, 201) argues, it is not about "phenotypic race" expressed in property so much as "an enforced collective investment in personhood as property: a historico-racial schema that owes its existence primarily to the intellectual and material legacies of European colonization and the transatlantic slave trade."

5. The production of transparency is codependent upon comparison with racialized others that are taken to be determined (and thus nonsovereign) by their "affectability"—their interior historical development or their exterior material/spatial relationships (Silva 2007). To be affectable is to be dependent, whether upon an affective infrastructure or upon relations with a natural or social environment. From Indigenous perspectives, as Coulthard (2014) and Karuka (2019) describe, sovereignty is in fact understood through that dependency or affectability constituted by modes of relationship with the land and nonhuman entities—and the obligations such dependency produces. Much like the settler state's attempts to constitute itself by disavowing Indigenous sovereignty, the supposed self-mastery of the transparent subject of whiteness is a countersovereignty (see Bosworth and Chua 2021).

6. Insufficient attention has been paid to the messy politics of eminent domain resistance in literatures following David Harvey's expansive understanding of accumulation by dispossession. This is a crucial oversight that this chapter seeks to redress, in part because Harvey uncritically presents eminent domain as if it were "the contemporary version of [Locke's] doctrine" of res nullius, using examples of colonialism to evidence the latter (D. Harvey 2014, 40). If eminent domain is about more than value, as Locke's theory clearly shows, then it is not so easy to denounce its use as solely in the service of capital—or, certainly, to presume a metaphoric urban colonialism, as Harvey does.

7. The phrase became the title of Wagoner's thin book. But Wagoner takes the statement "They're treating us like Indians" at face value in a quite reductive anthropological manner. The ethnographic exploration of race relations, land, and "blood" presented is one where regional and ultralocal identity means the crude social categories of "fullbloods, mixedbloods, and whites" (which, it is argued, somehow have "nonracial connotations") are all "contingent upon their social, legal, and historical contexts" (Wagoner 2002, 57). This explanation allows the conclusion that "it's not pretty, but sometimes people just 'settle' [their differences]. And that is how it is in West River South Dakota, whether or not it offends some outsiders' sensibilities" (93). This anthropological relativism simply accepts the order of everyday disagreements without any reference to differentials of power, while uncritically reinforcing a colonial understanding of race via blood and blood quantum.

8. Here, I am guided by Jodi Melamed's discussion of how "neoliberal multiculturalism" displaces attention on racial capitalism (2006, 2015). For a more detailed discussion of problems with a solely "cultural" approach to understanding race, nation, and private property, see the slightly different framing in Bosworth (2021b).

2. "Keystone XL Hearing Nearly Irrelevant"

1. The etymological roots of "the people" are not in the demos that is invoked by democracy (or in the ethnonationalist sense of the *volk*). "The people"—*populus*—instead seems to initially connote a human collectivity structured by constructed agreements and interests to live together (through law) (see Laugier 2014; Crépon, Cassin, and Moatti 2014). Though the roots are notoriously complex, in everyday parlance (especially in the English language) the meaning of "the people" functionally blurs several scenes together, while also adding subsequent connotations associated with the multitude, plebs, common people, the mob, the nation, and the crowd.

2. I&R, as it was widely known, was a proposal for a more direct form of

democracy, allowing citizens the right to propose legislation and sending all citizen-proposed legislation to a statewide vote. Father Haire was a champion of I&R in the state and had a unique claim to innovation on the idea (other Populist parties from around the United States would import it from the Swiss). So too was Walter E. Kidd, a state representative and publisher of the *Dakota Ruralist,* a major I&R supporter. Both avid socialists ensured that I&R was on the legislative ballot throughout the 1890s, eventually passing in 1898. Haire described the political situation in South Dakota as a "plutocracy, given over to fleecing the values that labor produces." Yet the government was "afraid of the people," and I&R would recognize that "the people are capable of feeling for, giving form to, and finally decreeing their own laws" (quoted in Gallagher 2009, n.p.). South Dakota was the first state to pass an I&R law. Although it was not used much in the early twentieth century, it reemerged as an important part of the state's political culture in the 1980s.

3. Mitchell argues that "fossil fuels helped create both the possibility of modern democracy and its limits" (2013, 1). By this, he means both the internal affluence of the United States and its economic and political introjection and projection into the world order. However, he also maintains a sometimes crudely materialist perspective that emphasizes carbon democracy is the redirection of material flows when it is the economic value at stake in such flows that affords power.

4. Though the constituent/constituted power dyad exceeds his province by now, it is odd that its Spinozist resonances (whether via readings of Schmitt or not) are not mentioned much in contemporary usage. Negri (1999) is the major exception, but beyond his work the dual conception of power in Spinoza as *potential/postestas* (which exists in Latin, Italian, and French, but not English) elucidates a difference in kind rather than degree.

5. Intimate publics mobilize "*the political* as that which magnetizes a desire for intimacy, sociality, affective solidarity, and happiness" (Berlant 2011, 252). They try to escape "*politics* as a scene of antagonism" (252); the partial subjects of cruel optimism, and the possibility of exceeding it, emerge precisely "*not* by taking up a position in the intimate zones of political immediacy that orient the body politic to the belief that world-building at a historic scale requires the drama of inflated sovereignty, or politics" (258). They inhabit "domains *proximate* to contemporary politics" (259).

6. Numerous methods could test support. By my personal experience, the simple polling, and more complicated measures (e.g., Gravelle and Lachapelle 2015), support for KXL was widespread in the state.

7. The 2016 campaign of Lakota renewable energy advocate Henry Red Cloud for a PUC board membership was unsuccessful.

8. A vast literature in Indigenous studies theorizes the broader dynamics of Native sovereignty as nested, counter-, or alter-sovereignty (Barker 2005; Bruyneel 2007; Coulthard 2014; Deloria and Lytle 1984; Deloria and Wilkins 1999; A. Simpson 2014).

3. Canadian Invasion for Chinese Consumption

1. On the veracity of these claims, see Kessler (2014).

2. Both Lye (2005) and Day (2016) draw on Postone's "Anti-Semitism and National Socialism: Notes on the German Reaction to 'Holocaust'" (1980) in thinking through how Asian Americans and Asian immigrants to North America, through finance, stand in for the abstracting power of capital alongside supposed Jewish financial power.

3. An exception to this assessment is Louisiana populist governor Huey Long's critique of Standard Oil, which continued into the 1930s and included a critique of the corporation's imperialist aspirations (Woods 2017, 114–15; Kazin 1998, 227).

4. The ultimate causes and perceptions of the 1973 crisis were complex and linked to Nixon's lifting of the import quota system, the formal end of the Gold Standard, and the unavailability of excess production in the United States rather than to the OAPEC embargo, which lasted only six months (Mitchell 2013; Vitalis 2020).

5. As Hamilton compellingly writes, "Like the agrarian revolts of the late nineteenth century, the independent truckers who struck in the 1970s expressed an angry dissatisfaction with the broad contours of industrial capitalism, the distant powers-that-be that applauded the self-made man while simultaneously constraining his opportunities to be that man. Also like the agrarian protests, the shutdowns were characterized by the difficulties of organizing a political movement composed of fiercely independent individuals, making the truckers as unsuccessful as the Populists at achieving their direct demands for reform" (2008, 216).

6. Public comment sets from the 2014 final supplemental EIS, for example, only include excerpts rather than complete comments.

7. "Regional studies" in geography and history have fallen out of fashion due to appropriate criticism of the supposed "naturalness" of region (Entrikin 1996; Marston 2000). Nonetheless, like other scalar distinctions, constructivist accounts of region that attend to the dissonant relations of culture, identity, economy, and power are still possible and clarifying (Massey 1994; Woods 1998).

8. Higbie gives an example of a 1979 *Chicago Tribune* review of the film

Breaking Away. This review is instructive, in part for hitching the heartland melodrama to a broader cultural (geo)politics that narrates woundedness and redemption. To this film, we might add other heartland melodramas of the period such as *The Last Picture Show* (Bogdanovich 1971), *Days of Heaven* (Malick 1978), and *Field of Dreams* (Robinson 1989).

4. The People Know Best

1. In their study of conservative talk radio in Canada, Saurette and Gunster (2011, 210) summarize what they call "epistemological populism": "the assertion that individual opinions based upon first-hand experience are much more reliable as a form of knowledge than those generated by theories and academic studies; the valorization of specific types of experience as particularly reliable sources of legitimate knowledge and the extension of this knowledge authority to unrelated issues; the privileging of emotional intensity as an indicator of the reliability of opinions; the use of populist-inflected discourse to dismiss other types of knowledge as elitist and therefore illegitimate; and finally, the appeal to 'common sense' as a discussion-ending trump card." Though this definition appears in an entirely different context, transposing it to pipeline opposition helps us see that the confluence of epistemology and identity in populist movements is more difficult to dismiss if its political ends are different.

2. A similar bifurcation has structured historians' assessments of the Farmers' Alliance and the People's Party, which has shaped my approach in this chapter. As Postel writes, "historians have tended to cast academic experts in the role of modernizers battling to overcome the inertia of 'reluctant farmers,' who were mired in tradition and unconvinced of the value of education" (2009, 47). Postel challenges this thesis through portraying populism as a campaign that mobilized forms of scientific and economic counter-expertise not against the modernizing ideals but against the method and ends to which they were used.

3. A vast range of studies examine how sciences and expert knowledges are produced and contested by environmental justice movements (for relevant reviews, see Pellow and Brulle 2005; Ottinger, Barandiarán, and Kimura 2017). Though critical environmental justice scholars and movements contest the epistemological hegemony of a disinterested science, they often engage in appropriating some scientific practices as well—though frequently contesting the terms of such practices (Wylie, Shapiro, and Liboiron 2017). This chapter does not examine environmental justice contestation of KXL and DAPL, as I have been most interested in the populist element. Readers might also expect

"citizen science" to be discussed (Irwin 1995; Irwin and Wynne 2003; Davies and Mah 2020), though this term can encompass a rather wide range of political and scientific activities (e.g., bird-watching or river monitoring) and can entail a somewhat passive public directed by scientific experts. For these reasons, it does not capture the relationship quite like counter-expertise.

4. As Dewey defines it, the public is the name for "all those who are affected by the indirect consequences of [private] transactions to such an extent that it is deemed necessary to have those consequences systematically cared for" (1927, 15–16). At several points, Dewey mentions the infrastructure and transportation of materials and energy as emblematic of the kinds of problems that gather publics into being (e.g., 30, 107, 126); for these reasons, concern with "material publics" has become common in infrastructure studies. Consequently, Dewey argues that our understanding of democracy must change to take into account the fact that the public has a stake in decision-making about infrastructure projects. Scholars like Bennett (2010) and Marres (2012) argue that a Deweyian focus on the ability of materials to gather heterogenous publics offers a new sort of environmental politics or ethics. However, this argument fails to examine the self-reflective moment of politics that must occur if a public is to be transformed into a political collective, such as a people.

BIBLIOGRAPHY

Ahmed, Sara. 2004. "Affective Economies." *Social Text* 22 (2): 117–39.

Ali, Omar H. 2010. *In the Lion's Mouth: Black Populism in the New South, 1886–1900.* Jackson: University Press of Mississippi.

Althusser, Louis. 1969. *For Marx.* London: Verso Books.

Althusser, Louis. 1997. "The Only Materialist Tradition, Part I: Spinoza." In *The New Spinoza,* edited by Warren Montag and Ted Stolze, 3–19. Minneapolis: University of Minnesota Press.

Anderson, Ben. 2014. *Encountering Affect: Capacities, Apparatuses, Conditions.* Surrey, U.K.: Ashgate Publishing.

Andreucci, Diego. 2019. "Populism, Emancipation, and Environmental Governance: Insights from Bolivia." *Annals of the American Association of Geographers* 109 (2): 624–33.

Anker, Elisabeth Robin. 2014. *Orgies of Feeling: Melodrama and the Politics of Freedom.* Durham, N.C.: Duke University Press.

Arnstein, Sherry R. 1969. "A Ladder of Citizen Participation." *Journal of the American Institute of Planners* 35 (4): 216–24.

Aronoff, Kate, Alyssa Battistoni, Daniel Aldana Cohen, and Thea Riofrancos. 2019. *A Planet to Win: Why We Need a Green New Deal.* London: Verso Books.

Ashwood, Loka. 2021. "'No Matter If You're a Democrat or a Republican or Neither': Pragmatic Politics in Opposition to Industrial Animal Production." *Journal of Rural Studies* 82:586–94.

Associated Press. 2015. "Hearing on Keystone Pipeline Plan Nearly Irrelevant." *Rapid City Journal,* July 7, 2015. http://rapidcityjournal.com/news/local/hearing-on-keystone-pipeline-plan-nearly-irrelevant/article_7071ca1c-be32-53c3-890d-a51714d50077.html.

Badiou, Alain. 2005. *Metapolitics.* London: Verso Books.

Balibar, Étienne. 1994. *Masses, Classes, Ideas: Studies on Politics and Philosophy before and after Marx.* New York: Routledge.

Balibar, Étienne. 1998. *Spinoza and Politics.* London: Verso Books.

Balibar, Étienne. 2014. *Equaliberty: Political Essays.* Translated by James Ingram. Durham, N.C.: Duke University Press.

Balibar, Étienne. 2020. *Spinoza, the Transindividual.* Translated by Mark G. E. Kelly. Edinburgh: Edinburgh University Press.

Barca, Stefania. 2020. *Forces of Reproduction: Notes for a Counter-Hegemonic Anthropocene.* Cambridge: Cambridge University Press.

Barker, Joanne, ed. 2005. *Sovereignty Matters: Locations of Contestation and Possibility in Indigenous Struggles for Self-Determination.* Lincoln: University of Nebraska Press.

Barry, Andrew. 2013. *Material Politics: Disputes along the Pipeline.* Oxford: Wiley-Blackwell.

Bennett, Jane. 2010. *Vibrant Matter: A Political Ecology of Things.* Durham, N.C.: Duke University Press.

Benton-Connell, Kylie, and D. T. Cochrane. 2020. "'Canada Has a Pipeline Problem': Valuation and Vulnerability of Extractive Infrastructure." *South Atlantic Quarterly* 119 (2): 325–52.

Berlant, Lauren. 2008. *The Female Complaint: The Unfinished Business of Sentimentality in American Culture.* Durham, N.C.: Duke University Press.

Berlant, Lauren. 2011. *Cruel Optimism.* Durham, N.C.: Duke University Press.

Bevington, Douglas. 2009. *The Rebirth of Environmentalism: Grassroots Activism from the Spotted Owl to the Polar Bear.* Washington, D.C.: Island Press.

Bhandar, Brenna. 2018. "Possessive Nationalism: Race, Class, and the Lifeworlds of Property." *Viewpoint Magazine.* https://www.viewpointmag.com/2018/02/01/possessive-nationalism-race-class-lifeworlds-property/.

Biolsi, Thomas. 2005. "Imagined Geographies: Sovereignty, Indigenous Space, and American Indian Struggle." *American Ethnologist* 32 (2): 239–59.

Bird, David. 1970. "U.S. and Canada in Conflict on Drilling in Lake Erie." *New York Times,* January 25, 1970. https://www.nytimes.com/1970/01/25/archives/us-and-canada-in-conflict-on-drilling-in-lake-erie.html.

Bledsoe, Adam, and Willie Jamaal Wright. 2019. "The Anti-Blackness of Global Capital." *Environment and Planning D: Society and Space* 37 (1): 8–26.

Bleifuss, Joel. 2017. "The Political Revolution Is Alive and Well in Nebraska." *In These Times,* June 14, 2017. http://inthesetimes.com/article/20214/lighting-a-fire-on-the-prairie-kleeb-nebraska-mello-keystone-xl.

Blomley, Nicholas. 2011. "Cuts, Flows, and the Geographies of Property." *Law, Culture, and the Humanities* 7 (2): 203–16.

Blomley, Nicholas. 2013. "Performing Property: Making the World." *Canadian Journal of Law & Jurisprudence* 26 (1): 23–48.

Bogdanovich, Peter, dir. 1971. *The Last Picture Show*. Columbia Pictures.

Borrows, John. 2002. *Recovering Canada: The Resurgence of Indigenous Law*. Toronto: University of Toronto Press.

Bosworth, Kai. 2017. "Thinking Permeable Matter through Feminist Geophilosophy: Environmental Knowledge Controversy and the Materiality of Hydrogeologic Processes." *Environment and Planning D: Society and Space* 35 (1): 21–37.

Bosworth, Kai. 2020. "The People's Climate March: Environmental Populism as Political Genre." *Political Geography* 83:1–12.

Bosworth, Kai. 2021a. "The Crack in the Earth: Environmentalism after Speleology." In *A Place More Void*, edited by Anna Secor and Paul Kingsbury, 48–65. Lincoln: University of Nebraska Press.

Bosworth, Kai. 2021b. "'They're Treating Us like Indians!': Political Ecologies of Property and Race in North American Pipeline Populism." *Antipode* 53 (3): 665–85.

Bosworth, Kai. Forthcoming. "The Dakota Access Pipeline Struggle: Vulnerability, Security, and Settler Colonialism in the Oil Assemblage." In *Settling the Bakken Boom*, edited by Bruce Braun and Mary Thomas, chap. 7. Minneapolis: University of Minnesota Press.

Bosworth, Kai, and Charmaine Chua. 2021. "The Countersovereignty of Critical Infrastructure Security: Settler-State Anxiety versus the Pipeline Blockade." *Antipode*. https://www.doi.org/10.1111/anti.12794.

Boyte, Harry C. 1986. *Citizen Action and the New American Populism*. Philadelphia: Temple University Press.

Braun, Bruce. 2015. "Rethinking Political Ecology for the Anthropocene." In *The Routledge Handbook of Political Ecology*, edited by Tom Perreault, Gavin Bridge, and James McCarthy, 102–14. London: Routledge.

Bridge, Gavin, and Tom Perreault. 2015. "Environmental Governance." In *The Routledge Handbook of Political Ecology*, edited by Tom Perreault, Gavin Bridge, and James McCarthy, 475–97. Abingdon, U.K.: Routledge.

Brown, Elizabeth M. 2012. "The Rights to Public Participation and Access to Information: The Keystone XL Oil Sands Pipeline and Global Climate Change under the National Environmental Policy Act." *Journal of Environmental Law and Litigation* 27:499–538.

Brown, Gavin, and Jenny Pickerill. 2009. "Space for Emotion in the Spaces of Activism." *Emotion, Space, and Society* 2 (1): 24–35.

Brown, Nicholas A. 2014. "The Logic of Settler Accumulation in a Landscape of Perpetual Vanishing." *Settler Colonial Studies* 4 (1): 1–26.

Bruyneel, Kevin. 2007. *The Third Space of Sovereignty: The Postcolonial Politics of U.S.–Indigenous Relations.* Minneapolis: University of Minnesota Press.

Bureau of Indian Affairs. 2016. "Federal Consultation with Tribes Regarding Infrastructure Decision-Making—Framing Paper." https://www.bia.gov/sites/bia.gov/files/assets/as-ia/raca/pdf/idc2-049011.pdf.

Cadieux, Kirsten Valentine, Stephen Carpenter, Alex Liebman, Renata Blumberg, and Bhaskar Upadhyay. 2019. "Reparation Ecologies: Regimes of Repair in Populist Agroecology." *Annals of the American Association of Geographers* 109 (2): 644–60.

Caffentzis, George. 2017. *No Blood for Oil: Essays on Energy, Class Struggle, and War, 1998–2017.* New York: Autonomedia.

Campbell, Anneke, and Thomas Linzey. 2016. *We the People: Stories from the Community Rights Movement in the United States.* Oakland, Calif.: PM Press.

Canetti, Elias. 1962. *Crowds and Power.* New York: Seabury.

Canovan, Margaret. 1999. "Trust the People! Populism and the Two Faces of Democracy." *Political Studies* 47 (1): 2–16.

Carse, Ashley. 2016. "Keyword: Infrastructure: How a Humble French Engineering Term Shaped the Modern World." In *Infrastructures and Social Complexity: A Companion,* edited by Penelope Harvey, Casper Bruun Jensen, and Atsuro Morita, 45–57. London: Routledge.

Carter, Angela L. 2014. "Petrocapitalism and the Tar Sands." In *A Line in the Tar Sands: Struggles for Environmental Justice,* edited by Toban Black, Stephen D'Arcy, Tony Weis, and Joshua Kahn Russell, 23–35. Oakland, Calif.: PM Press.

Carter, Angie, and Ahna Kruzic. 2017. "Centering the Commons, Creating Space for the Collective: Ecofeminist #NoDAPL Praxis in Iowa." *Journal of Social Justice* 7:1–22.

Carter, Angie, and Ahna Kruzic. 2020. "'No Oil in Our Soil!': Shifting Narratives from Commodities to the Commons in Iowa, USA." In *Social Movements Contesting Natural Resource Development,* edited by John F. Devlin, 112–32. London: Earthscan.

Casarino, Cesare. 2019. "Farewell to the University (without Nostalgia); or, Thoughts on the Relation between the University and the Common." *Minnesota Review* 2019 (93): 141–49.

Chakravartty, Paula, and Denise Ferreira da Silva. 2012. "Accumulation, Dispossession, and Debt: The Racial Logic of Global Capitalism—An Introduction." *American Quarterly* 64 (3): 361–85.

Chan, Sunny. 2018. "A Brief History of Asian American Activism and Why It Matters for Environmental Justice." In *Racial Ecologies,* edited by Leilani

Nishime and Kim D. Hester Williams, 170–84. Seattle: University of Washington Press.

Chen, Mel Y. 2012. *Animacies: Biopolitics, Racial Mattering, and Queer Affect.* Durham, N.C.: Duke University Press.

Ciccariello-Maher, George. 2020. "Cutting the Populist Knot." *Latin American Research Review* 55 (2): 368–78.

Ciplet, David, Mizanur Rahman Khan, and J. Timmons Roberts. 2015. *Power in a Warming World: The New Global Politics of Climate Change and the Remaking of Environmental Inequality.* Cambridge, Mass.: MIT Press.

Clough, Nathan L. 2012. "Emotion at the Center of Radical Politics: On the Affective Structures of Rebellion and Control." *Antipode* 44 (5): 1667–86.

Connolly, William E. 2013. *The Fragility of Things: Self-Organizing Processes, Neoliberal Fantasies, and Democratic Activism.* Durham, N.C.: Duke University Press.

Cooke, Bill, and Uma Kothari, eds. 2001. *Participation: The New Tyranny?* London: Zed Books.

Cooke, Jason. 2015. "Statement from the Yankton Sioux Tribe to the South Dakota Public Utilities Commission Regarding the Proposed Keystone XL Pipeline." South Dakota Public Utilities Commission docket HP14–001. https://puc.sd.gov/commission/dockets/HydrocarbonPipeline/2014/HP14-001/ystcomments.pdf.

Coulthard, Glen, and Andrew Bard Epstein. 2015. "The Colonialism of the Present." *Jacobin,* January 13, 2015. https://jacobinmag.com/2015/01/indigenous-left-glen-coulthard-interview/.

Coulthard, Glen Sean. 2014. *Red Skin, White Masks: Rejecting the Colonial Politics of Recognition.* Minneapolis: University of Minnesota Press.

Cramer, Kevin. 2016. "What the Dakota Access Pipeline Is Really About." *Wall Street Journal,* December 7, 2016. http://www.wsj.com/articles/what-the-dakota-access-pipeline-is-really-about-1481071218.

Crang, Mike, and Divya P. Tolia-Kelly. 2010. "Nation, Race, and Affect: Senses and Sensibilities at National Heritage Sites." *Environment and Planning A* 42 (10): 2315–31.

Crehan, Kate. 2016. *Gramsci's Common Sense: Inequality and Its Narratives.* Durham, N.C.: Duke University Press.

Crépon, Marc, Barbara Cassin, and Claudia Moatti. 2014. "People/Race/Nation." In *Dictionary of Untranslatables: A Philosophical Lexicon,* edited by Barbara Cassin, Emily Apter, Jacques Lezra, and Michael Wood, 751–63. Princeton, N.J.: Princeton University Press.

Curley, Andrew. 2019. "Beyond Environmentalism: #NoDAPL as Assertion of

Tribal Sovereignty." In *Standing with Standing Rock: Voices from the #NoDAPL Movement,* edited by Nick Estes and Jaskiran Dhillon, 158–68. Minneapolis: University of Minnesota Press.

Curnow, Joe, and Anjali Helferty. 2018. "Contradictions of Solidarity: Whiteness, Settler Coloniality, and the Mainstream Environmental Movement." *Environment and Society* 9 (1): 145–63.

Dalrymple, Jack. 2016. "Dakota Access Pipeline: Mob Rule Triumphed over Law and Common Sense." *Star Tribune,* December 15, 2016. http://www .startribune.com/dakota-access-pipeline-mob-rule-triumphed-over-law -and-common-sense/406939436/.

Davies, Thom, and Alice Mah, eds. 2020. *Toxic Truths: Environmental Justice and Citizen Science in a Post-Truth Age.* Manchester, U.K.: Manchester University Press.

Day, Iyko. 2016. *Alien Capital: Asian Racialization and the Logic of Settler Colonial Capitalism.* Durham, N.C.: Duke University Press.

Dean, Jodi. 2009. *Democracy and Other Neoliberal Fantasies: Communicative Capitalism and Left Politics.* Durham, N.C.: Duke University Press.

Dean, Jodi. 2010. *Blog Theory: Feedback and Capture in the Circuits of Drive.* Cambridge, U.K.: Polity.

Dean, Jodi. 2016a. *Crowds and Party.* London: Verso Books.

Dean, Jodi. 2016b. "A View from the Side: The Natural History Museum." *Cultural Critique* 94:74–101.

Dean, Jodi. 2017. "Not Him, Us (and We Aren't Populists)." *Theory & Event* 20 (S1): S38–44.

Deleuze, Gilles. 1983. *Nietzsche and Philosophy.* Translated by Hugh Tomlinson. New York: Columbia University Press.

Deleuze, Gilles. 1989. *Cinema 2: The Time Image.* Translated by Hugh Tomlinson and Robert Galeta. Minneapolis: University of Minnesota Press.

Deleuze, Gilles. 1994. *Difference and Repetition.* Translated by Paul Patton. New York: Columbia University Press.

Deleuze, Gilles. 1997. *Essays Critical and Clinical.* Translated by Daniel W. Smith. Minneapolis: University of Minnesota Press.

Deleuze, Gilles. 2004. "How Do We Recognize Structuralism?" In *Desert Islands and Other Texts, 1953–1974,* translated by David Lapoujade and Michael Taormina, 170–92. Los Angeles: Semiotext(e).

Deleuze, Gilles, and Félix Guattari. 1983. *Anti-Oedipus: Capitalism and Schizophrenia.* Translated by Robert Hurley, Mark Seem, and Helen Lane. Minneapolis: University of Minnesota Press.

Deleuze, Gilles, and Félix Guattari. 1986. *Kafka: Toward a Minor Literature.* Translated by Dana Polan. Minneapolis: University of Minnesota Press.

Deleuze, Gilles, and Félix Guattari. 1987. *A Thousand Plateaus: Capitalism and Schizophrenia.* Translated by Brian Massumi. Minneapolis: University of Minnesota Press.

Deloria, Philip Joseph. 1998. *Playing Indian.* New Haven, Conn.: Yale University Press.

Deloria, Vine. 1973. *God Is Red: A Native View of Religion.* New York: Grosset and Dunlap.

Deloria, Vine, and Clifford M Lytle. 1984. *The Nations Within: The Past and Future of American Indian Sovereignty.* New York: Pantheon Books.

Deloria, Vine, and David E Wilkins. 1999. *Tribes, Treaties, and Constitutional Tribulations.* Austin: University of Texas Press.

Denvir, Daniel. 2020. *All-American Nativism: How the Bipartisan War on Immigrants Explains Politics As We Know It.* London: Verso Books.

D'Eramo, Marco. 2017. "They, The People." *New Left Review* 103 (January): 129–38.

Dermansky, Julie. 2013. "Keystone Whistleblower: Catastrophe Ahead." *Progressive,* October 8, 2013. https://progressive.org/%3Fq%3Dnews/2013/10/184778/keystone-whistleblower-catastrophe-ahead/.

Dermansky, Julie. 2015a. "Evidence Released at TransCanada's Keystone XL Permit Renewal Hearing Sheds Light On Serious Pipeline Risks." *DeSmog* (blog), July 28, 2015. https://www.desmogblog.com/2015/07/28/evidence-released-transcanada-s-keystone-xl-permit-renewal-hearing-sheds-light-serious-pipeline-risks.

Dermansky, Julie. 2015b. "Permits Required to Build TransCanada's Keystone XL Pipeline in Jeopardy as Hearings Reveal Missteps." *DeSmog* (blog). August 3, 2015. https://www.desmogblog.com/2015/08/03/permits-required-build-transcanada-s-keystone-xl-pipeline-jeopardy-hearings-reveal-missteps.

Derrida, Jacques. 2002. "Declarations of Independence." In *Negotiations: Interventions and Interviews, 1971–2001,* edited by Elizabeth Rottenberg, 46–54. Stanford, Calif.: Stanford University Press.

Dewey, John. 1927. *The Public and Its Problems.* Athens: Swallow Press.

Di Chiro, Giovanna. 1997. "Local Actions, Global Visions: Remaking Environmental Expertise." *Frontiers: A Journal of Women Studies* 18 (2): 203–31.

Dittmer, Jason, and Nicholas Gray. 2010. "Popular Geopolitics 2.0: Towards New Methodologies of the Everyday." *Geography Compass* 4 (11): 1664–77.

Dowie, Mark. 1995. *Losing Ground: American Environmentalism at the Close of the Twentieth Century.* Cambridge, Mass.: MIT Press.

Dowler, Lorraine, and Joanne Sharp. 2001. "A Feminist Geopolitics?" *Space and Polity* 5 (3): 165–76.

Dryzek, John S., David Downes, Christian Hunold, David Schlosberg, and Hans-Kristian Hernes. 2003. *Green States and Social Movements: Environmentalism in the United States, United Kingdom, Germany, and Norway.* Oxford: Oxford University Press.

Du Bois, W. E. B. (1920) 1999. *Darkwater: Voices from Within the Veil.* New York: Dover.

Du Bois, W. E. B. 1935. *Black Reconstruction in America.* New York: Free Press.

Duggan, Joe. 2011. "Dismissal of Pipeline Warning Draws Ire." *Scottsbluff Star Herald,* October 15, 2011. https://starherald.com/news/state-and-regional /dismissal-of-pipeline-warning-draws-ire/article_3619da42-e470-5d8a -a18d-4d9abcf18b90.html.

Dunbar-Ortiz, Roxanne. 2014. *An Indigenous Peoples' History of the United States.* Boston: Beacon Press.

Dunbar-Ortiz, Roxanne. 2016. "The Relationship between Marxism and Indigenous Struggles and Implications of the Theoretical Framework for International Indigenous Struggles." *Historical Materialism* 24 (3): 76–91.

Ekers, Michael, Stefan Kipfer, and Alex Loftus. 2020. "On Articulation, Translation, and Populism: Gillian Hart's Postcolonial Marxism." *Annals of the American Association of Geographers* 110 (5): 1–17.

Entrikin, J. Nicholas. 1996. "Place and Region 2." *Progress in Human Geography* 20 (2): 215–21.

Estes, Nick. 2013. "Wounded Knee: Settler Colonial Property Regimes and Indigenous Liberation." *Capitalism Nature Socialism* 24 (3): 190–202.

Estes, Nick. 2019. *Our History Is the Future: Standing Rock versus the Dakota Access Pipeline, and the Long Tradition of Indigenous Resistance.* London: Verso Books.

Estes, Nick, and Jaskiran Dhillon, eds. 2019. *Standing with Standing Rock: Voices from the #NoDAPL Movement.* Minneapolis: University of Minnesota Press.

Ewen, Stuart. 1996. *PR!: A Social History of Spin.* New York: Basic Books.

Featherstone, David. 2012. *Solidarity: Hidden Histories and Geographies of Internationalism.* London: Zed Books.

Featherstone, David, and Lazaros Karaliotas. 2019. "Populism." *Soundings* 72:31–47.

Ferguson, Cody. 2015. *This Is Our Land: Grassroots Environmentalism in the Late Twentieth Century.* New Brunswick, N.J.: Rutgers University Press.

Ferorelli, Josephine. 2014. "No More Red Scares: Fighting Fair against Keystone XL and Fossil Fuel Expansion." Occupy.com, February 7, 2014.

http://www.occupy.com/article/no-more-red-scares-fighting-fair-against
-keystone-xl-and-fossil-fuel-expansion.

Fischer, Frank. 2000. *Citizens, Experts, and the Environment: The Politics of Local Knowledge.* Durham, N.C.: Duke University Press.

Fite, Gilbert C. 1985. "'The Only Thing Worth Working For': Land and Its Meaning for Pioneer Dakotans." *South Dakota History* 15 (1): 2–25.

Foreman, Christopher H. 1998. *The Promise and Peril of Environmental Justice.* Washington, D.C.: Brookings Institution Press.

Foucault, Michel. 1980. *Power/Knowledge: Selected Interviews and Other Writings, 1972–1977.* Edited by Colin Gordon. Translated by Colin Gordon, Leo Marshall, John Mepham, and Kate Soper. New York: Pantheon Books.

Frank, Jason. 2009. *Constituent Moments: Enacting the People in Postrevolutionary America.* Durham, N.C.: Duke University Press.

Frank, Jason. 2017. "Populism and Praxis." In *The Oxford Handbook of Populism,* edited by Cristóbal Rovira Kaltwasser, Paul Taggart, Paulina Ochoa Espejo, and Pierre Ostiguy, 629–43. Oxford: Oxford University Press.

Frank, Thomas. 2018. "Forget Trump—Populism Is the Cure, Not the Disease." *Guardian,* May 23, 2018. https://www.theguardian.com/books/2018/may/23/thomas-frank-trump-populism-books.

Frank, Thomas. 2020. *The People, No: A Brief History of Anti-Populism.* New York: Metropolitan Books.

Frankel, Boris. 1997. "Confronting Neoliberal Regimes: The Post-Marxist Embrace of Populism and Realpolitik." *New Left Review* 226:57–92.

Fraser, Nancy. 1990. "Rethinking the Public Sphere: A Contribution to the Critique of Actually Existing Democracy." *Social Text* 25/26:56–80.

Gallagher, Patrick. 2009. "Faith in the Voters." *South Dakota Magazine,* 2009. http://www.southdakotamagazine.com/faith-in-the-voters.

Gates, John B. 2010. "Ease Public Concern over Oil Pipeline." *Nature* 468 (7325): 765.

Gates, John, and Wayne Woldt. 2011. "UNL Professors Gates and Woldt Comments on Keystone XL." https://www.scribd.com/document/203587067/UNL-Professors-Gates-and-Woldt-Comments-on-Keystone-XL.

Gerbaudo, Paolo. 2017. *The Mask and the Flag: Populism, Citizenism, and Global Protest.* Oxford: Oxford University Press.

Gidwani, Vinay. 2008. *Capital, Interrupted: Agrarian Development and the Politics of Work in India.* Minneapolis: University of Minnesota Press.

Gilio-Whitaker, Dina. 2019. *As Long as Grass Grows: The Indigenous Fight for Environmental Justice, from Colonization to Standing Rock.* Boston: Beacon Press.

Gilmore, Ruth Wilson. 2007. *Golden Gulag: Prisons, Surplus, Crisis, and Opposition in Globalizing California.* Berkeley: University of California Press.

Gilmore, Ruth Wilson. 2017. "Abolition Geography and the Problem of Innocence." In *Futures of Black Radicalism,* edited by Gaye Theresa Johnson and Alex Lubin, 225–40. London: Verso Books.

Glassman, Jim. 2006. "Primitive Accumulation, Accumulation by Dispossession, Accumulation by 'Extra-Economic' Means." *Progress in Human Geography* 30 (5): 608–25.

Goeke, James. 2011a. "Local View: A Science-Based Approach to the Ogallala Aquifer." *Lincoln Journal-Star,* September 24, 2011. https://journalstar .com/news/opinion/editorial/columnists/local-view-a-science-based-ap proach-to-the-ogallala-aquifer/article_40586032-0597-5375-815a -8f91284a5fbf.html.

Goeke, James. 2011b. "The Pipeline Poses Minimal Risk to the Ogallala Aquifer." *New York Times,* October 4, 2011. https://www.nytimes.com/room fordebate/2011/10/03/what-are-the-risks-of-the-keystone-xl-pipeline -project/the-pipeline-poses-minimal-risk-to-the-ogallala-aquifer.

Goodrich, Matthew Miles. 2019. "The Climate Movement's Path to the Green New Deal." *Dissent Magazine,* February 15, 2019. https://www.dissent magazine.org/online_articles/sunrise-movement-green-new-deal.

Goodwyn, Lawrence. 1978. *The Populist Moment: A Short History of the Agrarian Revolt in America.* Oxford: Oxford University Press.

Gottlieb, Robert. 2005. *Forcing the Spring: The Transformation of the American Environmental Movement.* Rev. ed. Washington, D.C.: Island Press.

Gould, Deborah B. 2009. *Moving Politics: Emotion and ACT UP's Fight against AIDS.* Chicago: University of Chicago Press.

Gould, Deborah B. 2010. "On Affect and Protest." In *Political Emotions,* edited by Janet Staiger, Ann Cvetkovich, and Ann Reynolds, 32–58. London: Routledge.

Gramsci, Antonio. 1971. *Selections from the Prison Notebooks.* New York: International Publishers.

Grant, Sonia. 2014. "Securing Tar Sands Circulation: Risk, Affect, and Anticipating the Line 9 Reversal." *Environment and Planning D: Society and Space* 32 (6): 1019–35. https://doi.org/10.1068/d13144p.

Grattan, Laura. 2016. *Populism's Power: Radical Grassroots Democracy in America.* Oxford: Oxford University Press.

Grattan, Laura. 2021. "Populism, Race, and Radical Imagination: #FeelingTheBern in the Age of #BlackLivesMatter." In *Populism in Global Perspective: A Performative and Discursive Approach,* edited by Pierre Ostiguy, Francisco Panizza, and Benjamin Moffitt, 136–54. New York: Routledge.

Gravelle, Timothy B. 2014. "Love Thy Neighbo(u)r? Political Attitudes, Proximity, and the Mutual Perceptions of the Canadian and American Publics."
Canadian Journal of Political Science/Revue Canadienne de Science Politique
47 (1): 135–57.

Gravelle, Timothy B., and Erick Lachapelle. 2015. "Politics, Proximity, and
the Pipeline: Mapping Public Attitudes toward Keystone XL." *Energy Policy* 83 (August): 99–108.

Gregg, Melissa, and Gregory J. Seigworth, eds. 2010. *The Affect Theory Reader.*
Durham, N.C.: Duke University Press.

Grossman, Zoltán. 2002. "Unlikely Alliances: Treaty Conflicts and Environmental Cooperation between Native American and Rural White Communities." PhD diss., University of Wisconsin–Madison.

Grossman, Zoltán. 2017. *Unlikely Alliances: Native Nations and White Communities Join to Defend Rural Lands.* Seattle: University of Washington Press.

Grueskin, Caroline. 2016. "Protesters Move Camp to Dakota Access Property,
Claiming It as Treaty Land." *Bismarck Tribune,* October 23, 2016. http://
bismarcktribune.com/news/state-and-regional/protesters-move-camp-to
-dakota-access-property-claiming-it-as/article_bc3a5f6a-b2fe-5e77-8d49
-cbcee49c5878.html.

Guenther, Lisa. 2019. "Seeing Like a Cop: A Critical Phenomenology of
Whiteness as Property." In *Race as Phenomena: Between Phenomenology and
Philosophy of Race,* edited by Emily Lee, 189–206. Lanham, Md.: Rowman
and Littlefield.

Guha, Ramachandra, and Juan Martinez-Alier. 1997. *Varieties of Environmentalism.* London: Earthscan Publications.

Habermas, Jürgen. 1997. "Popular Sovereignty as Procedure." In *Deliberative
Democracy: Essays on Reason and Politics,* edited by James Bohman and William Rehg, 35–65. Cambridge, Mass.: MIT Press.

Hall, Stuart. 1980. "Popular Democratic vs. Authoritarian Populism: Two
Ways of Taking Democracy Seriously." In *Marxism and Democracy,* edited
by Alan Hunt, 157–85. London: Lawrence and Wishart.

Hall, Stuart. (1983) 2021a. "The Problem of Ideology: Marxism without
Guarantees." In *Selected Writings on Marxism,* edited by Gregor McLellan,
134–57. Durham, N.C.: Duke University Press.

Hall, Stuart. (1985) 2021b. "Authoritarian Populism: A Reply to Jessop et. al."
In *Selected Writings on Marxism,* edited by Gregor McLellan, 282–92.
Durham, N.C.: Duke University Press.

Hall, Stuart. (1990) 2017. "The 'First' New Left: Life and Times." In *Selected
Political Writings: The Great Moving Right Show and Other Essays,* 117–41.
Durham, N.C.: Duke University Press.

Hall, Stuart. 1997. "The Local and the Global: Globalization and Ethnicity." In *Culture, Globalization, and the World-System: Contemporary Conditions for the Representation of Identity,* edited by Anthony D. King, 19–40. Minneapolis: University of Minnesota Press.

Hall, Stuart. 2016. *Cultural Studies 1983: A Theoretical History.* Durham, N.C.: Duke University Press.

Hamilton, Shane. 2008. *Trucking Country: The Road to America's Wal-Mart Economy.* Princeton, N.J.: Princeton University Press.

Hansen, James. 2012. "Game Over for the Climate." *New York Times,* May 9, 2012. http://www.nytimes.com/2012/05/10/opinion/game-over-for-the -climate.html.

Haraway, Donna. 1990. *Simians, Cyborgs, and Women: The Reinvention of Nature.* New York: Routledge.

Hardin, Garrett. 1974. "Lifeboat Ethics: The Case against Helping the Poor." *Psychology Today* 8:38–43.

Harkin, Michael Eugene, and David Rich Lewis. 2007. *Native Americans and the Environment: Perspectives on the Ecological Indian.* Lincoln: University of Nebraska Press.

Harrison, Trevor. 2007. "Anti-Canadianism: Explaining the Deep Roots of a Shallow Phenomenon." *International Journal of Canadian Studies/Revue Internationale d'études Canadiennes* 35:217–39.

Hart, Gillian. 2014. *Rethinking the South African Crisis: Nationalism, Populism, Hegemony.* Athens: University of Georgia Press.

Hart, Gillian. 2019. "From Authoritarian to Left Populism?: Reframing Debates." *South Atlantic Quarterly* 118 (2): 307–23.

Hartmann, Betsy. 1999. *Reproductive Rights and Wrongs.* Boston: South End Press.

Harvey, David. 2005. *The New Imperialism.* Oxford: Oxford University Press.

Harvey, David. 2014. *Seventeen Contradictions and the End of Capitalism.* London: Profile Books.

Harvey, Penelope. 2012. "The Topological Quality of Infrastructural Relation: An Ethnographic Approach." *Theory, Culture & Society* 29 (4–5): 76–92.

Harvey, Penny, and Hannah Knox. 2012. "The Enchantments of Infrastructure." *Mobilities* 7 (4): 521–36.

Healy, Jack. 2016. "Neighbors Say North Dakota Pipeline Protests Disrupt Lives and Livelihoods." *New York Times,* September 13, 2016, sec. U.S. https://www.nytimes.com/2016/09/14/us/north-dakota-pipeline-protests .html.

Hébert, Karen. 2016. "Chronicle of a Disaster Foretold: Scientific Risk Assessment, Public Participation, and the Politics of Imperilment in Bristol Bay, Alaska." *Journal of the Royal Anthropological Institute* 22 (S1): 108–26.

Hébert, Karen, and Samara Brock. 2017. "Counting and Counter-Mapping: Contests over the Making of a Mining District in Bristol Bay, Alaska." *Science as Culture* 26 (1): 56–87.

Heefner, Gretchen. 2012. *The Missile Next Door: The Minuteman in the American Heartland.* Cambridge, Mass.: Harvard University Press.

Henry, Terrence. 2012. "This Land Was Your Land, Now It's Our Land: Keystone XL and Eminent Domain." StateImpact Texas, National Public Radio. February 14, 2012. https://stateimpact.npr.org/texas/2012/02/14/this-land-was-your-land-now-its-our-land-keystone-xl-and-eminent-domain/.

Herbstreuth, Sebastian. 2016. *Oil and American Identity: A Culture of Dependency and US Foreign Policy.* London: I. B. Tauris.

Herreria, Carla. 2019. "White Nationalists Storm Bookstore Reading: 'This Land Is Our Land!'" *Huffington Post,* April 27, 2019. https://www.huffpost.com/entry/white-nationalists-protest-washington-bookstore_n_5cc4de01e4b04eb7ff96aa50.

Hersh, Joshua. 2011. "Keystone XL: Haste and Inexperience Hampered State Department's Environmental Review." *Huffington Post,* November 3, 2011, sec. Green. https://www.huffingtonpost.com/2011/11/03/keystone-xl-haste-and-ine_n_1074010.html.

Hersh, Joshua. 2012. "Keystone XL Pipeline Review Lacked 'Expertise and Experience,' State Department IG Finds." *Huffington Post,* February 9, 2012, sec. Green. https://www.huffingtonpost.com/2012/02/09/keystone-xl-state-dept-ig_n_1266041.html.

Higbie, Frank Tobias. 2014. "Heartland: The Politics of a Regional Signifier." *Middle West Review* 1 (1): 81–90.

Hofstadter, Richard. 1960. *The Age of Reform.* New York: Vintage.

Hoganson, Kristin L. 2019. *The Heartland: An American History.* New York: Penguin Press.

Holifield, Ryan. 2004. "Neoliberalism and Environmental Justice in the United States Environmental Protection Agency: Translating Policy into Managerial Practice in Hazardous Waste Remediation." *Geoforum* 35 (3): 285–97.

Holmes, Brian. 2017. "What Can Art Do about Pipeline Politics?" *South Atlantic Quarterly* 116 (2): 426–31.

Honig, Bonnie. 2009. *Democracy and the Foreigner.* Princeton, N.J.: Princeton University Press.

Huber, Matthew T. 2013. *Lifeblood: Oil, Freedom, and the Forces of Capital.* Minneapolis: University of Minnesota Press.

Hultgren, John. 2015. *Border Walls Gone Green: Nature and Anti-immigrant Politics in America.* Minneapolis: University of Minnesota Press.

Husmann, John. 2011. "Environmentalism in South Dakota: A Grassroots Approach." In *The Plains Political Tradition: Essays on South Dakota Political Culture,* edited by Jon K. Lauck, John E. Miller, and Donald C. Simmons, 239–66. Pierre: South Dakota State Historical Society.

Hyndman, Jennifer. 2001. "Towards a Feminist Geopolitics." *Canadian Geographer/Le Géographe Canadien* 45 (2): 210–22.

Iowa Utilities Board. 2015. "State of Iowa Department of Commerce Utilities Division Docket No. HLP-2014–0001 Consumer Comments, Community Room, Boone County Fairgrounds." Iowa Utilities Board Archive.

Irwin, Alan. 1995. *Citizen Science: A Study of People, Expertise, and Sustainable Development.* London: Routledge.

Irwin, Alan, and Brian Wynne. 2003. *Misunderstanding Science?: The Public Reconstruction of Science and Technology.* Cambridge: Cambridge University Press.

It's Going Down. 2017. "Call for Anti-colonial Bloc against Keystone XL, August 6th in Lincoln, NE." It's Going Down (website). July 17, 2017. https://itsgoingdown.org/call-anti-colonial-bloc-keystone-xl-august-6th-lincoln-ne/.

Jackson, Mark Allan. 2002. "Is This Song Your Song Anymore?: Revisioning Woody Guthrie's 'This Land Is Your Land.'" *American Music* 20 (3): 249–76.

Jackson, Steven J. 2014. "Rethinking Repair." In *Media Technologies: Essays on Communication, Materiality, and Society,* edited by Tarleton Gillespie, Boczkowski Pablo, and Kirsten Foot, 221–39. Cambridge, Mass.: MIT Press.

Jafri, Beenash. 2013. "Desire, Settler Colonialism, and the Racialized Cowboy." *American Indian Culture and Research Journal* 37 (2): 73–86.

Jäger, Anton. 2019. "We Bet the House on Left Populism—and Lost." *Jacobin,* November 25, 2019. https://jacobinmag.com/2019/11/we-bet-the-house-on-left-populism-and-lost.

Jasanoff, Sheila. 1995. *Science at the Bar: Law, Science, and Technology in America.* Cambridge, Mass.: Harvard University Press.

Johnson, Kirk, and Dan Frosch. 2011. "A Pipeline Divides along Old Lines: Jobs versus the Environment." *New York Times,* September 28, 2011, sec. U.S. https://www.nytimes.com/2011/09/29/us/rancor-grows-over-planned-oil-pipeline-from-canada.html.

Kanngieser, AM, and Nicholas Beuret. 2017. "Refusing the World: Silence, Commoning, and the Anthropocene." *South Atlantic Quarterly* 116 (2): 363–80.

Karuka, Manu. 2019. *Empire's Tracks: Indigenous Nations, Chinese Workers, and the Transcontinental Railroad.* Oakland: University of California Press.

Katz, Cindi. 1996. "Towards Minor Theory." *Environment and Planning D: Society and Space* 14 (4): 487–99.

Kay, Kelly. 2016. "Breaking the Bundle of Rights: Conservation Easements and the Legal Geographies of Individuating Nature." *Environment and Planning A: Economy and Space* 48 (3): 504–22.

Kazin, Michael. 1998. *The Populist Persuasion: An American History.* Ithaca, N.Y.: Cornell University Press.

Kearns, Gerry. 2009. *Geopolitics and Empire: The Legacy of Halford Mackinder.* Oxford: Oxford University Press.

Keeler, Jacqueline. 2021. *Standoff: Standing Rock, the Bundy Movement, and the American Story of Sacred Lands.* Salt Lake City: Torrey House Press.

Kessler, Glenn. 2014. "Four Pinocchios for an Over-the-Top Ad Attacking the Keystone XL Pipeline." *Washington Post,* January 31, 2014. https://www.washingtonpost.com/news/fact-checker/wp/2014/01/31/an-over-the-top-ad-attacking-the-keystone-xl-pipeline/.

Kingsnorth, Paul. 2017. "The Lie of the Land: Does Environmentalism Have a Future in the Age of Trump?" *Guardian,* March 18, 2017. http://www.theguardian.com/books/2017/mar/18/the-new-lie-of-the-land-what-future-for-environmentalism-in-the-age-of-trump.

Kipfer, Stefan. 2016. "Populism." In *Keywords for Radicals: The Contested Vocabulary of Late-Capitalist Struggle,* edited by Kelly Fritsch, Clare O'Connor, and A. K. Thompson, 160–63. Oakland, Calif.: AK Press.

Kleeb, Jane Fleming. 2016. "Let's Get Rural: Middle America Wants Less Establishment, More Populism." *Medium* (blog). December 12, 2016. https://medium.com/@janekleeb/lets-get-rural-middle-america-wants-less-establishment-more-populism-c182224adca3.

Klein, Naomi. 2014. *This Changes Everything: Capitalism vs. the Climate.* New York: Simon & Schuster.

Knox, Hannah. 2017. "Affective Infrastructures and the Political Imagination." *Public Culture* 29 (2 [82]): 363–84.

Koenig, Biko, and Lee Scaralia. 2019. "Populism, Identity Work, and Progressive Organizing in Rural America." *New Political Science* 41 (4): 604–21.

Kojola, Erik D. 2017. "(Re)Constructing the Pipeline: Workers, Environmentalists, and Ideology in Media Coverage of the Keystone XL Pipeline." *Critical Sociology* 43 (6): 893–917.

Kordela, A. Kiarina. 2012. *$urplus: Spinoza, Lacan.* Albany: SUNY Press.

Kosek, Jake. 2004. "Purity and Pollution: Racial Degradation and Environmental Anxieties." In *Liberation Ecologies: Environment, Development, Social Movements,* edited by Richard Peet and Michael Watts, 2nd ed., 115–52. London: Routledge.

Krupar, Shiloh R. 2013. *Hot Spotter's Report: Military Fables of Toxic Waste.* Minneapolis: University of Minnesota Press.

Kruzic, Ahna, and Angie Carter. 2016. "A Feminist's Guide to Fighting Pipelines." In *Fracture: Essays, Poems, and Stories on Fracking in America,* edited by Stefanie Brook Trout and Taylor Brorby, 226–30. North Liberty, Iowa: Ice Cube Press.

Kuznick, Peter J. 1987. *Beyond the Laboratory: Scientists as Political Activists in 1930s America.* Chicago: University of Chicago Press.

Labban, Mazen. 2008. *Space, Oil, and Capital.* London: Routledge.

Laclau, Ernesto. 1979. *Politics and Ideology in Marxist Theory: Capitalism, Fascism, Populism.* London: Verso Books.

Laclau, Ernesto. 2005. *On Populist Reason.* London: Verso Books.

LaDuke, Winona. 2020. *To Be a Water Protector: The Rise of the Wiindigoo Slayers.* Halifax: Fernwood Publishing.

LaDuke, Winona, and Ward Churchill. 1985. "Native America: The Political Economy of Radioactive Colonialism." *Journal of Ethnic Studies* 13 (3): 107–32.

LaDuke, Winona, and Sean Aaron Cruz. 2013. *The Militarization of Indian Country.* East Lansing: Michigan State University Press.

Larkin, Brian. 2013. "The Politics and Poetics of Infrastructure." *Annual Review of Anthropology* 42 (1): 327–43.

Larsen, Soren C., and Jay T. Johnson. 2017. *Being Together in Place: Indigenous Coexistence in a More than Human World.* Minneapolis: University of Minnesota Press.

Larson, Peter. 2009. Letter to J. Brian Duggan, April 13, 2009. https://puc.sd.gov/commission/dockets/hydrocarbonpipeline/2009/hp09-001/comments/bhinstitute.pdf.

Latour, Bruno. 2004. "Why Has Critique Run Out of Steam? From Matters of Fact to Matters of Concern." *Critical Inquiry* 30 (2): 225–48.

Lauck, Jon K. 2010. *Prairie Republic: The Political Culture of Dakota Territory, 1879–1889.* Norman: University of Oklahoma Press.

Laugier, Sandra. 2014. "People." In *Dictionary of Untranslatables: A Philosophical Lexicon,* edited by Barbara Cassin, Emily Apter, Jacques Lezra, and Michael Wood, 750–51. Princeton, N.J.: Princeton University Press.

Lee, R. Alton. 2011. *Principle over Party: The Farmers' Alliance and Populism in South Dakota, 1880–1900.* Pierre: South Dakota State Historical Society Press.

Leitner, Helga, Eric Sheppard, and Kristin M. Sziarto. 2008. "The Spatialities of Contentious Politics." *Transactions of the Institute of British Geographers* 33 (2): 157–72.

LeQuesne, Theo. 2019. "Petro-hegemony and the Matrix of Resistance: What Can Standing Rock's Water Protectors Teach Us about Organizing for Climate Justice in the United States?" *Environmental Sociology* 5 (2): 188–206.

Li, Fabiana. 2009. "Documenting Accountability: Environmental Impact Assessment in a Peruvian Mining Project." *PoLAR: Political and Legal Anthropology Review* 32 (2): 218–36.

Li, Tania Murray. 2014. *Land's End: Capitalist Relations on an Indigenous Frontier.* Durham, N.C.: Duke University Press.

Lieberman, Henry R. 1974. "Arctic Gas Pipeline Route the New Issue in Alaska." *New York Times,* May 28, 1974. https://www.nytimes.com/1974 /05/28/archives/arctic-gas-pipeline-route-the-new-issue-in-alaska-arctic -pipeline.html.

Lindell, Terrence J. 1982. "South Dakota Populism." Master's thesis, University of Nebraska–Lincoln.

Lizza, Ryan. 2013. "The President and the Pipeline." *New Yorker,* September 9, 2013. https://www.newyorker.com/magazine/2013/09/16/the-president -and-the-pipeline.

Lockwood, Matthew. 2018. "Right-Wing Populism and the Climate Change Agenda: Exploring the Linkages." *Environmental Politics* 27 (4): 712–32.

Luke, Tim. 1995. "Searching for Alternatives: Postmodern Populism and Ecology." *Telos* 1995 (103): 87–110.

Lye, Colleen. 2005. *America's Asia: Racial Form and American Literature, 1893–1945.* Princeton, N.J.: Princeton University Press.

Macpherson, C. B. 1964. *The Political Theory of Possessive Individualism: Hobbes to Locke.* Oxford: Oxford University Press.

Malick, Terrence. 1978. *Days of Heaven.* Paramount Pictures.

Mancus, Shannon Davies. 2016. "Appealing to Better Natures: Genre and the Politics of Performance in the Modern American Environmental Movement." PhD diss., George Washington University.

Marino, Angela. 2018. *Populism and Performance in the Bolivarian Revolution of Venezuela.* Evanston, Ill.: Northwestern University Press.

Marres, Noortje. 2012. *Material Participation: Technology, the Environment, and Everyday Publics.* New York: Palgrave Macmillan.

Marriott, James, and Mika Minio-Paluello. 2013. *The Oil Road: Journeys from the Caspian Sea to the City of London.* London: Verso Books.

Marston, Sallie A. 2000. "The Social Construction of Scale." *Progress in Human Geography* 24 (2): 219–42.

Marx, Karl. 1973. *Grundrisse.* London: Penguin.

Marx, Karl. 1976. *Capital: A Critique of Political Economy.* Vol. 1. Translated by Ben Fowkes. London: Penguin Classics.

Marx, Karl. 1981. *Capital: A Critique of Political Economy.* Vol. 3. Translated by David Fernbach. London: Penguin Classics.

Masco, Joseph. 2014. *The Theater of Operations: National Security Affect from the Cold War to the War on Terror.* Durham, N.C.: Duke University Press.

Massey, Doreen. 1994. *Space, Place, and Gender.* Minneapolis: University of Minnesota Press.

Massumi, Brian. 2002. *Parables for the Virtual: Movement, Affect, Sensation.* Durham, N.C.: Duke University Press.

Maxwell, Lida. 2017. "Queer/Love/Bird Extinction: Rachel Carson's *Silent Spring* as a Work of Love." *Political Theory* 45 (5): 682–704.

McCreary, Tyler A, and Richard A. Milligan. 2014. "Pipelines, Permits, and Protests: Carrier Sekani Encounters with the Enbridge Northern Gateway Project." *Cultural Geographies* 21 (1): 115–29.

McKibben, Bill. 2013. *Oil and Honey: The Education of an Unlikely Activist.* New York: Times Books.

McKittrick, Katherine. 2013. "Plantation Futures." *Small Axe: A Caribbean Journal of Criticism* 17 (3 [42]): 1–15.

McVeigh, Karen. 2013. "US Department of Interior Criticises State over Keystone XL Impact Report." *Guardian,* August 20, 2013, sec. Environment. http://www.theguardian.com/environment/2013/aug/20/interior-state -keystone-xl-pipeline-impact.

Mehta, Uday Singh. 1999. *Liberalism and Empire: A Study in Nineteenth-Century British Liberal Thought.* Chicago: University of Chicago Press.

Mei-Singh, Laurel. 2016. "Carceral Conservationism: Contested Landscapes and Technologies of Dispossession at Ka'ena Point, Hawai'i." *American Quarterly* 68 (3): 695–721.

Melamed, Jodi. 2006. "The Spirit of Neoliberalism: From Racial Liberalism to Neoliberal Multiculturalism." *Social Text* 24 (4 [89]): 1–24.

Melamed, Jodi. 2015. "Racial Capitalism." *Critical Ethnic Studies* 1 (1): 76–85.

Mercer, Bob. 2013. "Eco-terrorists, Intimidation, and the Keystone Hearing." *Pure Pierre Politics* (blog). June 25, 2013. http://my605.com/pierrereview /?p=8806.

Merriman, Peter, and Rhys Jones. 2017. "Nations, Materialities, and Affects." *Progress in Human Geography* 41 (5): 600–617.

Meyer, John M. 2008. "Populism, Paternalism, and the State of Environmentalism in the US." *Environmental Politics* 17 (2): 219–36.

Meyerhoff, Eli. 2019. *Beyond Education: Radical Studying for Another World.* Minneapolis: University of Minnesota Press.

Mitchell, Timothy. 2013. *Carbon Democracy: Political Power in the Age of Oil.* 2nd ed. London: Verso Books.

Mitropoulos, Angela. 2012. *Contract and Contagion: From Biopolitics to Oikonomia*. Wivenhoe, N.Y.: Minor Compositions.

Moe, Kristin. 2014. "When Cowboys and Indians Unite—Inside the Unlikely Alliance That Is Remaking the Climate Movement." *Waging Nonviolence* (blog). May 2, 2014. http://wagingnonviolence.org/feature/cow boys-indians-unite-inside-unlikely-alliance-foretells-victory-climate -movement/.

Moffitt, Benjamin. 2016. *The Global Rise of Populism: Performance, Political Style, and Representation*. Palo Alto, Calif.: Stanford University Press.

Moffitt, Benjamin. 2020. *Populism*. London: Polity.

Montag, Warren. 1999. *Bodies, Masses, Power: Spinoza and His Contemporaries*. London: Verso Books.

Moore, Donald S. 2005. *Suffering for Territory: Race, Place, and Power in Zimbabwe*. Durham, N.C.: Duke University Press.

Moore, Jason W. 2015. *Capitalism in the Web of Life: Ecology and the Accumulation of Capital*. London: Verso Books.

Moreton-Robinson, Aileen. 2015. *The White Possessive: Property, Power, and Indigenous Sovereignty*. Minneapolis: University of Minnesota Press.

Moscato, Derek. 2019. "The Metanarrative of Rural Environmentalism: Rhetorical Activism in Bold Nebraska's Harvest the Hope." *Public Relations Inquiry* 8 (1): 23–47.

Mott, Carrie. 2016. "The Activist Polis: Topologies of Conflict in Indigenous Solidarity Activism." *Antipode* 48 (1): 193–211.

Mouffe, Chantal. 2000. *The Democratic Paradox*. London: Verso Books.

Mouffe, Chantal. 2018. *For a Left Populism*. London: Verso Books.

Mounk, Yascha. 2018. *The People vs. Democracy: Why Our Freedom Is in Danger and How to Save It*. Cambridge, Mass.: Harvard University Press.

Mudde, Cas, and Cristóbal Rovira Kaltwasser. 2017. *Populism: A Very Short Introduction*. Oxford: Oxford University Press.

Mufson, Steven. 2012. "Keystone XL Pipeline Is Issue of Property Rights for Some Ranchers." *Washington Post,* July 27, 2012. https://www.washington post.com/keystone-xl-pipeline-is-issue-of-property-rights-for-some-ranch ers/2012/07/27/gJQAqlQgDX_story.html.

Müller, Jan-Werner. 2016. *What Is Populism?* Philadelphia: University of Pennsylvania Press.

Murphy, Michelle. 2017. *The Economization of Life*. Durham, N.C.: Duke University Press.

Myers, Ella. 2019. "Beyond the Psychological Wage: Du Bois on White Dominion." *Political Theory* 47 (1): 6–31.

National Science Foundation. 2020. "News from the Human-Environment and Geographical Sciences (HEGS) Program at the National Science

Foundation (NSF)." American Association of Geographers. http://news.aag.org/2020/08/news-from-the-human-environment-and-geographical-sciences-hegs-program-at-the-national-science-foundation-nsf-september-2020/.

Negri, Antonio. 1991. *The Savage Anomaly: The Power of Spinoza's Metaphysics and Politics.* Translated by Michael Hardt. Minneapolis: University of Minnesota Press.

Negri, Antonio. 1999. *Insurgencies: Constituent Power and the Modern State.* Translated by Maurizia Boscagli. Minneapolis: University of Minnesota Press.

Neimark, Benjamin, John Childs, Andrea J. Nightingale, Connor Joseph Cavanagh, Sian Sullivan, Tor A. Benjaminsen, Simon Batterbury, Stasja Koot, and Wendy Harcourt. 2019. "Speaking Power to 'Post-Truth': Critical Political Ecology and the New Authoritarianism." *Annals of the American Association of Geographers* 109 (2): 613–23.

Nichols, Robert. 2020. *Theft Is Property!: Dispossession and Critical Theory.* Durham, N.C.: Duke University Press.

Nightingale, Andrea J. 2003. "A Feminist in the Forest: Situated Knowledges and Mixing Methods in Natural Resource Management." *ACME: An International Journal for Critical Geographies* 2 (1): 77–90.

Nishime, Leilani, and Kim D. Hester Williams, eds. 2018. *Racial Ecologies.* Seattle: University of Washington Press.

Nordhaus, Ted, and Michael Shellenberger. 2007. *Break Through: From the Death of Environmentalism to the Politics of Possibility.* Boston: Houghton Mifflin.

Not an Alternative. 2016. "Institutional Liberation." *e-flux* 77. https://www.e-flux.com/journal/77/76215/institutional-liberation/.

Obama, Barack. 2015. "Statement by the President on the Keystone XL Pipeline." The White House (website). November 6, 2015. https://obamawhitehouse.archives.gov/the-press-office/2015/11/06/statement-president-keystone-xl-pipeline.

O'Hara, Sarah, and Michael Heffernan. 2006. "From Geo-strategy to Geo-economics: The 'Heartland' and British Imperialism before and after MacKinder." *Geopolitics* 11 (1): 54–73.

Ostiguy, Pierre, Francisco Panizza, and Benjamin Moffitt. 2021. *Populism in Global Perspective: A Performative and Discursive Approach.* New York: Routledge.

Ostler, Jeffrey. 1993. *Prairie Populism: The Fate of Agrarian Radicalism in Kansas, Nebraska, and Iowa, 1880–1892.* Lawrence: University Press of Kansas.

Ostler, Jeffrey. 2011. *The Lakotas and the Black Hills: The Struggle for Sacred Ground.* New York: Penguin Books.

Ostler, Jeffrey, and Nick Estes. 2017. "The Supreme Law of the Land." In *Standing with Standing Rock: Voices from the #NoDAPL Movement,* edited by Nick Estes and Jaskiran Dhillon, 96–100. Minneapolis: University of Minnesota Press.

O'Sullivan, Joe. 2014. "State Gets Millions in Homeland Security Grants, but Where Does It Go?" *Rapid City Journal,* June 8, 2014. http://rapidcity journal.com/news/local/state-gets-millions-in-homeland-security-grants -but-where-does/article_1be9acf1-b8e6-5bdb-a01d-5d2e4e2362ca.html.

Ottinger, Gwen, Javiera Barandiarán, and Aya H. Kimura. 2017. "Environmental Justice: Knowledge, Technology, and Expertise." In *The Handbook of Science and Technology Studies,* edited by Ulrike Felt, Rayvon Fouché, Clark A. Miller, and Laurel Smith-Doerr, 4th ed., 1029–58. Cambridge, Mass.: MIT Press.

Pain, Rachel. 2009. "Globalized Fear? Towards an Emotional Geopolitics." *Progress in Human Geography* 33 (4): 466–86.

Park, Lisa Sun-Hee, and David N. Pellow. 2013. *The Slums of Aspen: Immigrants vs. the Environment in America's Eden.* New York: NYU Press.

Pasternak, Shiri, and Tia Dafnos. 2018. "How Does a Settler State Secure the Circuitry of Capital?" *Environment and Planning D: Society and Space* 36 (4): 739–57.

Patel, Raj, and Jim Goodman. 2020. "The Long New Deal." *Journal of Peasant Studies* 47 (3): 431–63.

Pellow, David Naguib. 2017. *What Is Critical Environmental Justice?* Cambridge: Polity.

Pellow, David Naguib, and Robert J. Brulle. 2005. *Power, Justice, and the Environment: A Critical Appraisal of the Environmental Justice Movement.* Cambridge, Mass.: MIT Press.

Phadke, Roopali. 2010. "Steel Forests or Smoke Stacks: The Politics of Visualisation in the Cape Wind Controversy." *Environmental Politics* 19 (1): 1–20.

Phadke, Roopali. 2011. "Resisting and Reconciling Big Wind: Middle Landscape Politics in the New American West." *Antipode* 43 (3): 754–76.

Pierre-Louis, Kendra. 2017. "This Land Is (Still) Their Land. Meet the Nebraskan Farmers Fighting Keystone XL." *Popular Science,* September 15, 2017. https://www.popsci.com/keystone-xl-pipeline-nebraska-farmers/.

Pitt, David. 2016. "Iowa Judge Tosses Flag Desecration Charge in Pipeline Protest." *Des Moines Register,* August 15, 2016. https://www.desmoines register.com/story/news/crime-and-courts/2016/08/15/iowa-judge-tosses -flag-desecration-charge-pipeline-protest/88803254/.

Pollack, Norman. 1976. *The Populist Response to Industrial America: Midwestern Populist Thought.* Cambridge, Mass.: Harvard University Press.

Postel, Charles. 2009. *The Populist Vision.* Oxford: Oxford University Press.

Postel, Charles. 2019. "Populism as a Concept and the Challenge of U.S. History." *IdeAs: Idées d'Amériques* 14. https://doi.org/10.4000/ideas.6472.

Postone, Moishe. 1980. "Anti-Semitism and National Socialism: Notes on the German Reaction to 'Holocaust.'" *New German Critique* 19:97–115.

Potter, Lori. 2011. "Pipeline Debate Battle between Science, Emotion." *Kearney Hub,* November 26, 2011. https://www.kearneyhub.com/news/local/pipeline-debate-battle-between-science-emotion/article_c4428880-1809-11e1-b17a-001cc4c03286.html.

Povinelli, Elizabeth A. 2011. "The Governance of the Prior." *Interventions* 13 (1): 13–30.

Prakash, Varshini. 2020. "People Power and Political Power." In *Winning the Green New Deal: Why We Must, How We Can,* edited by Varshini Prakash and Guido Girgenti, 137–63. New York: Simon & Schuster.

Pratt, William C. 1988. "Socialism on the Northern Plains, 1900–1924." *South Dakota History* 18 (7): 11.

Pratt, William C. 1992. "South Dakota Populism and Its Historians." *South Dakota History* 22 (4): 309–29.

Pratt, William C. 1996. "Using History to Make History? Progressive Farm Organizing during the Farm Revolt of the 1980s." *Annals of Iowa* 55 (1): 24–45.

Pratt, William C. 2011. "Another South Dakota or the Road Not Taken: The Left and the Shaping of South Dakota Political Culture." In *The Plains Political Tradition: Essays on South Dakota Political Culture,* edited by Jon K. Lauck, John E. Miller, and Donald C. Simmons, 105–32. Pierre: South Dakota State Historical Society.

Pulido, Laura. 2017. "Geographies of Race and Ethnicity II: Environmental Racism, Racial Capitalism, and State-Sanctioned Violence." *Progress in Human Geography* 41 (4): 524–33.

Purdy, Jedediah. 2019. *This Land Is Our Land: The Struggle for a New Commonwealth.* Princeton, N.J.: Princeton University Press.

Rana, Aziz. 2011. *The Two Faces of American Freedom.* Cambridge, Mass.: Harvard University Press.

Read, Jason. 2016. *The Politics of Transindividuality.* Chicago: Haymarket Books.

Riofrancos, Thea. 2017. "Democracy without the People." *N+1* (blog). February 6, 2017. https://nplusonemag.com/online-only/online-only/democracy-without-the-people/.

Riofrancos, Thea. 2020. *Resource Radicals: From Petro-nationalism to Post-Extractivism in Ecuador.* Durham, N.C.: Duke University Press.

Robinson, Phil Alden. 1989. *Field of Dreams.* Universal Pictures.

Rodriguez, Rebecca Jane. 2014. "Guest Column: The CIA, the Black Snake, and the Last Man Standing." *Madville Times* (blog). March 15, 2014. https://madvilletimes.com/2014/03/guest-column-the-cia-the-black-snake-and-the-last-man-standing/.

Roman-Alcalá, Antonio, Garrett Graddy-Lovelace, and Marc Edelman. 2021. "Authoritarian Populism and Emancipatory Politics in the Rural United States." *Journal of Rural Studies* 82:500–504.

Rome, Adam. 2013. *The Genius of Earth Day: How a 1970 Teach-In Unexpectedly Made the First Green Generation.* New York: Hill and Wang.

Romm, Joe. 2011. "James Hansen Slams Keystone XL Canada–U.S. Pipeline." *Think Progress* (blog). June 3, 2011. https://thinkprogress.org/james-hansen-slams-keystone-xl-canada-u-s-pipeline-exploitation-of-tar-sands-would-make-it-implausib-bce6d044bb93/.

Rose, Carol M. 1994. *Property and Persuasion: Essays on the History, Theory, and Rhetoric of Ownership.* Boulder, Colo.: Westview Press.

Rosenthal, Elisabeth, and Dan Frosch. 2011. "State Dept. Assigned Keystone XL Review to Company with Ties to TransCanada." *New York Times,* October 7, 2011. https://www.nytimes.com/2011/10/08/science/earth/08pipeline.html.

Ross, Gyasi. 2016. "Crazy White People Are the New Native Americans: Woody Guthrie, Ammon Bundy & Donald Trump." *Indian Country Media Network.* January 8, 2016. https://indiancountrymedianetwork.com/culture/thing-about-skins/crazy-white-people-are-the-new-native-americans-woody-guthrie-ammon-bundy-donald-trump/.

Routledge, Paul. 2017. *Space Invaders: Radical Geographies of Protest.* London: Pluto Press.

Roy, Ananya. 2017. "Dis/Possessive Collectivism: Property and Personhood at City's End." *Geoforum* 80:A1–11.

Ruddick, Susan. 2010. "The Politics of Affect: Spinoza in the Work of Negri and Deleuze." *Theory, Culture & Society* 27 (4): 21–45.

Russell, Joshua Kahn, Linda Capato, Matt Leonard, and Rae Breaux. 2014. "Lessons from Direct Action at the White House to Stop the Keystone XL Pipeline." In *A Line in the Tar Sands: Struggles for Environmental Justice,* edited by Toban Black, Stephen D'Arcy, Tony Weis, and Joshua Kahn Russell, 167–80. Oakland, Calif.: PM Press.

Sabin, Paul. 2012. "Crisis and Continuity in U.S. Oil Politics, 1965–1980." *Journal of American History* 99 (1): 177–86.

Saldanha, Arun. 2017. *Space after Deleuze*. London: Bloomsbury Publishing.

Sale, Kirkpatrick. 1993. *The Green Revolution: The Environmental Movement 1962–1992*. New York: Macmillan.

Sargent, Greg. 2014. "Rick Weiland: Real Populism Can Win in South Dakota." *Washington Post,* October 10, 2014. https://www.washington post.com/blogs/plum-line/wp/2014/10/10/rick-weiland-real-populism -can-win-in-south-dakota/?utm_term=.ce48b9c85cff.

Saurette, Paul, and Shane Gunster. 2011. "Ears Wide Shut: Epistemological Populism, Argutainment, and Canadian Conservative Talk Radio." *Canadian Journal of Political Science/Revue Canadienne de Science Politique* 44 (1): 195–218.

Saxton, Alexander. 1971. *The Indispensable Enemy: Labor and the Anti-Chinese Movement in California*. Berkeley: University of California Press.

Schlosberg, David. 1999. *Environmental Justice and the New Pluralism: The Challenge of Difference for Environmentalism*. Oxford: Oxford University Press.

Schneider-Mayerson, Matthew. 2015. *Peak Oil: Apocalyptic Environmentalism and Libertarian Political Culture*. Chicago: University of Chicago Press.

Schuster, Aaron. 2016. *The Trouble with Pleasure: Deleuze and Psychoanalysis*. Cambridge, Mass.: MIT Press.

Secor, Anna, and Jess Linz. 2017. "Becoming Minor." *Environment and Planning D: Society and Space* 35 (4): 568–73.

Sexton, Jared. 2010. "People-of-Color-Blindness: Notes on the Afterlife of Slavery." *Social Text* 28 (2 [103]): 31–56.

Sexton, Jared. 2016. "The *Vel* of Slavery: Tracking the Figure of the Unsovereign." *Critical Sociology* 42 (4–5): 583–97.

Seymour, Nicole. 2018. *Bad Environmentalism: Irony and Irreverence in the Ecological Age*. Minneapolis: University of Minnesota Press.

Sharp, Hasana. 2011. *Spinoza and the Politics of Renaturalization*. Chicago: University of Chicago Press.

Sibertin-Blanc, Guillaume. 2016. *State and Politics: Deleuze and Guattari on Marx*. Translated by Ames Hodges. South Pasadena, Calif.: Semiotext(e).

Silva, Denise Ferreira da. 2007. *Toward a Global Idea of Race*. Minneapolis: University of Minnesota Press.

Simmons, Kristen. 2017. "Settler Atmospherics." *Cultural Anthropology Fieldsights* (blog). 2017. https://culanth.org/fieldsights/settler-atmospherics.

Simpson, Audra. 2014. *Mohawk Interruptus: Political Life across the Borders of Settler States*. Durham, N.C.: Duke University Press.

Simpson, Leanne Betasamosake. 2017. *As We Have Always Done: Indigenous Freedom through Radical Resistance*. Minneapolis: University of Minnesota Press.

Simpson, Michael, and Philippe Le Billon. 2021. "Reconciling Violence: Policing the Politics of Recognition." *Geoforum* 119:111–21.

Singh, Nikhil Pal. 2016. "On Race, Violence, and So-Called Primitive Accumulation." *Social Text* 34 (3 [128]): 27–50.

Skaria, Ajay. 2016. *Unconditional Equality: Gandhi's Religion of Resistance.* Minneapolis: University of Minnesota Press.

Slocum, Rachel. 2018. "Climate Politics and Race in the Pacific Northwest." *Social Sciences* 7 (10): 192.

Smith, Anna V. 2018. "Why Don't Anti-Indian Groups Count as Hate Groups?" *High Country News,* October 8, 2018. https://www.hcn.org/issues/50.20/tribal-affairs-why-dont-anti-indian-groups-count-as-hate-groups.

Smith, Mitch. 2017. "Risen from the Grave, Keystone XL Pipeline Again Divides Nebraska." *New York Times,* April 27, 2017. https://www.nytimes.com/2017/04/27/us/keystone-pipeline-nebraska.html.

Smith, Neil. 2008. *Uneven Development: Nature, Capital, and the Production of Space.* Athens: University of Georgia Press.

Snelgrove, Corey, Rita Dhamoon, and Jeff Corntassel. 2014. "Unsettling Settler Colonialism: The Discourse and Politics of Settlers, and Solidarity with Indigenous Nations." *Decolonization: Indigeneity, Education & Society* 3 (2): 1–32.

Solnit, Rebecca. 2019. "Standing Rock Inspired Ocasio-Cortez to Run. That's the Power of Protest." *Guardian,* January 14, 2019. http://www.theguardian.com/commentisfree/2019/jan/14/standing-rock-ocasio-cortez-protest-climate-activism.

South Dakota Public Utilities Commission. 2009a. "HP09–001 Transcript of Proceedings, Vol II." South Dakota Public Utilities Commission docket HP14–001. https://puc.sd.gov/commission/minutes/2009/hp09-001/110309vol2.pdf.

South Dakota Public Utilities Commission. 2009b. "HP09–001 Transcript of Proceedings, Vol III." South Dakota Public Utilities Commission docket HP14–001. https://puc.sd.gov/commission/minutes/2009/hp09-001/110409vol3.pdf.

South Dakota Public Utilities Commission. 2009c. "HP09–001 Transcript of Public Input Hearing." South Dakota Public Utilities Commission docket HP14–001. https://puc.sd.gov/commission/minutes/2009/hp09-001/110309public.pdf.

South Dakota Public Utilities Commission. 2009d. "Transcript of Proceedings April 27, 2009 Winner, South Dakota." South Dakota Public Utilities Commission docket HP14–001. https://puc.sd.gov/commission/dockets/hydrocarbonpipeline/2009/hp09-001/transcriptwinner.pdf.

Spice, Anne. 2018. "Fighting Invasive Infrastructures: Indigenous Relations against Pipelines." *Environment and Society* 9 (1): 40–56.

Spinoza, Benedictus de. 1985. *The Collected Works of Spinoza.* Vol. 1. Edited and translated by Edwin Curley. Princeton, N.J.: Princeton University Press.

Spinoza, Benedictus de. 2016. *The Collected Works of Spinoza.* Vol. 2. Edited and translated by Edwin Curley. Princeton, N.J.: Princeton University Press.

Stein, Samuel. 2019. *Capital City: Gentrification and the Real Estate State.* London: Verso Books.

Steinberg, Theodore. 1995. *Slide Mountain: Or, The Folly of Owning Nature.* Oakland: University of California Press.

Stengers, Isabelle. 2005. "Deleuze and Guattari's Last Enigmatic Message." *Angelaki* 10 (2): 151–67.

Stock, Catherine McNicol. 2017. *Rural Radicals: Righteous Rage in the American Grain.* Ithaca, N.Y.: Cornell University Press.

Stolze, Ted. 2020. "An Ethics for Marxism: Spinoza on Fortitude." In *Becoming Marxist: Studies in Philosophy, Struggle, and Endurance,* 153–76. Chicago: Haymarket Books.

Swyngedouw, Erik. 2010. "Apocalypse Forever? Post-Political Populism and the Spectre of Climate Change." *Theory, Culture & Society* 27 (2–3): 213–32.

Szasz, Andrew. 1994. *Ecopopulism: Toxic Waste and the Movement for Environmental Justice.* Minneapolis: University of Minnesota Press.

Sze, Julie. 2015. *Fantasy Islands: Chinese Dreams and Ecological Fears in an Age of Climate Crisis.* Oakland: University of California Press.

Sze, Julie. 2020. *Environmental Justice in a Moment of Danger.* Oakland: University of California Press.

Tarbell, Ida M. (1904) 1963. *The History of the Standard Oil Company.* Gloucester, Mass.: Peter Smith.

Taylor, Astra. 2019. *Democracy May Not Exist, But We'll Miss It When It's Gone.* New York: Metropolitan Books.

Taylor, Dorceta E. 2016. *The Rise of the American Conservation Movement: Power, Privilege, and Environmental Protection.* Durham, N.C.: Duke University Press.

Taylor, Keeanga-Yamahtta. 2019. *Race for Profit: How Banks and the Real Estate Industry Undermined Black Homeownership.* Chapel Hill: University of North Carolina Press.

Tchen, John Kuo Wei, and Dylan Yeats. 2014. *Yellow Peril!: An Archive of Anti-Asian Fear.* London: Verso Books.

Thoburn, Nicholas. 2003. *Deleuze, Marx, and Politics.* London: Routledge.

Thoburn, Nicholas. 2016. "The People Are Missing: Cramped Space, Social Relations, and the Mediators of Politics." *International Journal of Politics, Culture, and Society* 29 (4): 367–81.

Tokar, Brian. 2014. *Toward Climate Justice: Perspectives on the Climate Crisis and Social Change.* Rev. ed. Porsgrunn, Norway: New Compass Press.

Tuan, Yi-Fu. 1977. *Space and Place: The Perspective of Experience.* Minneapolis: University of Minnesota Press.

Tuck, Eve. 2010. "Breaking Up with Deleuze: Desire and Valuing the Irreconcilable." *International Journal of Qualitative Studies in Education* 23 (5): 635–50.

Tuck, Eve, and K. Wayne Yang. 2012. "Decolonization Is Not a Metaphor." *Decolonization: Indigeneity, Education & Society* 1 (1): 1–40.

Tuck, Eve, and K. Wayne Yang. 2014. "Unbecoming Claims: Pedagogies of Refusal in Qualitative Research." *Qualitative Inquiry* 20 (6): 811–18.

Tweton, D. Jerome. 1993. "Considering Why Populism Succeeded in South Dakota and Failed in North Dakota." *South Dakota History* 22:330–44.

Tysiachniouk, Maria S., Leah S. Horowitz, Varvara V. Korkina, and Andrey N. Petrov. 2020. "Indigenous-Led Grassroots Engagements with Oil Pipelines in the US and Russia: The NoDAPL and Komi Movements." *Environmental Politics* 30 (6): 896–917. https://doi.org/10.1080/09644016.2020.185 1534.

Urbinati, Nadia. 1998. "Democracy and Populism." *Constellations* 5 (1): 110–24.

U.S. Department of State. 2013a. "Keystone XL Draft Environmental Impact Statement—Public Comment Unique Submissions, March 21 Part 01."

U.S. Department of State. 2013b. "Keystone XL Draft Environmental Impact Statement—Public Comment Unique Submissions, March 21 Part 02."

U.S. Department of State. 2013c. "Keystone XL Draft Environmental Impact Statement—Public Comment Unique Submissions, March 21 Part 03."

U.S. Department of State. 2013d. "Keystone XL Draft Environmental Impact Statement—Public Comment Unique Submissions, April 08."

U.S. Department of State. 2013e. "Keystone XL Draft Environmental Impact Statement—Public Comment Unique Submissions, April 14."

U.S. Department of State. 2013f. "Keystone XL Draft Environmental Impact Statement—Public Comment Unique Submissions, April 16."

Vasudevan, Pavithra. 2012. "Performance and Proximity: Revisiting Environmental Justice in Warren County, North Carolina." *Performance Research* 17 (4): 18–26.

Vayda, Andrew P., and Bradley B. Walters. 1999. "Against Political Ecology." *Human Ecology* 27 (1): 167–79.

Verhovek, Sam Howe. 1996. "Texas Meeting Seeks a Rebirth of Populism." *New York Times,* November 25, 1996. https://www.nytimes.com/1996/11/25/us/texas-meeting-seeks-a-rebirth-of-populism.html.

Vitalis, Robert. 2020. *Oilcraft: The Myths of Scarcity and Security That Haunt U.S. Energy Policy.* Stanford, Calif.: Stanford University Press.

Vokes, Evan. 2015. "Testimony of Evan Vokes on Behalf of Dakota Rural Action." https://puc.sd.gov/commission/dockets/HydrocarbonPipeline/2014/HP14-001/exhibits/dra/1003a.pdf.

Wagoner, Paula L. 2002. *"They Treated Us Just Like Indians": The Worlds of Bennett County, South Dakota.* Lincoln: Bison Books.

Walia, Harsha. 2021. *Border and Rule: Global Migration, Capitalism, and the Rise of Racist Nationalism.* Chicago: Haymarket Books.

Warner, Michael. 2005. *Publics and Counterpublics.* New York: Zone Books.

Welker, Marina. 2012. "The Green Revolution's Ghost: Unruly Subjects of Participatory Development in Rural Indonesia." *American Ethnologist* 39 (2): 389–406.

Wetts, Rachel. 2020. "Models and Morals: Elite-Oriented and Value-Neutral Discourse Dominates American Organizations' Framings of Climate Change." *Social Forces* 98 (3): 1339–69.

Whatmore, Sarah J. 2009. "Mapping Knowledge Controversies: Science, Democracy, and the Redistribution of Expertise." *Progress in Human Geography* 33 (5): 587–98.

Whyte, Kyle. 2017. "The Dakota Access Pipeline, Environmental Injustice, and US Colonialism." *Red Ink: An International Journal of Indigenous Literature, Arts, & Humanities* 19 (1): 154–69.

Wiederstein, Ed. 2016. "Pipeline Protest Shifts to Anti-development Agenda." *Bismarck Tribune,* August 29, 2016. http://bismarcktribune.com/news/opinion/guest/pipeline-protest-shifts-to-anti-development-agenda/article_3d237a83-0ed8-59fb-aa81-a324b939835b.html.

Wiken, Douglas. 2009. "PUC Meeting in Winner, SD on TransCanada/Phillips XL Pipeline." *Dakota Today* (blog). April 27, 2009. http://dakotatoday.typepad.com/dakotatoday/2009/04/-puc-meeting-in-winner-sd-on-transcanadaphillips-xl-pipeline.html.

Wilderson, Frank, III. 2003. "Gramsci's Black Marx: Whither the Slave in Civil Society?" *Social Identities* 9 (2): 225–40.

Wilderson, Frank, III. 2010. *Red, White & Black: Cinema and the Structure of U.S. Antagonisms.* Durham, N.C.: Duke University Press.

Williams, Kyle. 2020. "Roosevelt's Populism: The Kansas Oil War of 1905 and the Making of Corporate Capitalism." *Journal of the Gilded Age and Progressive Era* 19 (1): 96–121.

Wilson, Ara. 2016. "The Infrastructure of Intimacy." *Signs: Journal of Women in Culture and Society* 41 (2): 247–80.

Wolfe, Patrick. 2006. "Settler Colonialism and the Elimination of the Native." *Journal of Genocide Research* 8 (4): 387–409.

Wood, Ellen Meiksins. 1995. *Democracy against Capitalism: Renewing Historical Materialism.* Cambridge: Cambridge University Press.

Woodhouse, Keith Makoto. 2018. *The Ecocentrists: A History of Radical Environmentalism.* New York: Columbia University Press.

Woods, Clyde. 1998. *Development Arrested: The Blues and Plantation Power in the Mississippi Delta.* London: Verso Books.

Woods, Clyde. 2017. *Development Drowned and Reborn: The Blues and Bourbon Restorations in Post-Katrina New Orleans.* Edited by Laura Pulido and Jordan T. Camp. Athens: University of Georgia Press.

Wooten, Will, Candice Bernd, and Ron Seifert. 2012. "Why We're Putting Ourselves on the (Pipe)Line with the Tea Party." *YES! Magazine,* August 24, 2012. https://www.yesmagazine.org/planet/why-we-put-ourselves-on-the-pipeline-with-the-tea-party-keystone (accessed on January 20, 2020).

Wylie, Sara, Nick Shapiro, and Max Liboiron. 2017. "Making and Doing Politics through Grassroots Scientific Research on the Energy and Petrochemical Industries." *Engaging Science, Technology, and Society* 3:393–425.

Wynne, Brian. 2007. "Public Participation in Science and Technology: Performing and Obscuring a Political–Conceptual Category Mistake." *East Asian Science, Technology, and Society: An International Journal* 1 (1): 99–110.

Young, Iris Marion. 2001. "Activist Challenges to Deliberative Democracy." *Political Theory* 29 (5): 670–90.

Žižek, Slavoj. 2006. "Against the Populist Temptation." *Critical Inquiry* 32 (3): 551–74.

INDEX

Page numbers in italics refer to illustrations.

antiglobalism, 161
antipolitics, 13
antipopulism, 16
anti-Semitism, 130, 218n2
anxiety of property, 69–70
Aronoff, Kate, 1
Asia, settler colonialism and, 48,
    129, 142–44, 147. *See also*
    China
Asian Americans, 142, 143

Badiou, Alain, 44
Bakken field, 19, 20
Bakken pipeline watchdogs network,
    190–92
Baku-Tbilisi-Ceyhan pipeline, 179,
    193
Balibar, Étienne, 8, 69–70, 86, 205
Barry, Andrew, 193
Bemidji, Minnesota, study, 163–64
Bennett, Jane, 220n4
Berlant, Lauren, 7, 37, 42, 98–99,
    214n11, 217n5
Bernd, Candice, 74
Betty (South Dakota landowner), 58,
    68–69, 106, 150
Beuret, Nicholas, 120–21
Bhandar, Brenna, 158
Biden, Joe, 28
"bigger we, the," 199, 209
Big Greens: anti-pipeline protests
    and, 19, 22, 24, *24*; fundraising
    tactics of, 78–79; global warm-
    ing and, 17; money of, 185–86;
    populism feared by, 15
"Big Oil," 134–35, 156. *See also* oil
    companies
bitumen, 19–20
Blackburn, Paul, 181
Black Hills Alliance, 13–14

Black Hills International Survival
    Gathering, 14
Blomley, Nicholas, 69
Bold Iowa, 73
Bold Nebraska, 22, 25, 28, 45,
    72–73; and It's Going Down,
    205–6; tactics of, 83
Borrows, John, 99, 119, 123
Bosworth, Annette, 56
Bosworth, Kai, 44, 106, 176, 212n4,
    214n11
Boyte, Harry C., 15
Braun, Bruce, 40
Breaking Away, 219n8
Bridge, Gavin, 97
Brookings, South Dakota, 45
Brown, Elizabeth, 115
Bryan, William Jennings, 28
Bundy, Ammon, 53
Bundy, Cliven, 53
Bush, George W., 132, 136
Butler, Bobby, 131

Canada: First Nations of, 148,
    153–54, 179; "invasion" by, 150,
    156–57, 159; United States'
    relationship with, 133, 148–53;
    xenophobia towards, 48, 126,
    127, 128–29, 148–54
Canetti, Elias, 112
Canovan, Margaret, 109
capitalism: "Big Oil" as metonym
    for, 156; landed private proper-
    ty in, 59, 60–61; land relations
    threatened by, 71, 76; racial, 30,
    35–37, 44, 76, 85, 122–23, 143,
    158–59, 207, 216n8; romantic
    critiques of, 142–43, 144,
    146–47
Cardno ENTRIX, 165, 178–79

Kai Bosworth is assistant professor of international studies in the School of World Studies at Virginia Commonwealth University.